Women in Political Theory

Women in Political Theory

From Ancient Misogyny to Contemporary Feminism

Diana H. Coole
Lecturer in Politics,
University of Leeds

WHEATSHEAF BOOKS · SUSSEX
LYNNE RIENNER PUBLISHERS · BOULDER

First published in Great Britain in 1988 by
WHEATSHEAF BOOKS LTD
A MEMBER OF THE HARVESTER PRESS PUBLISHING GROUP
Publisher: John Spiers
16 Ship Street, Brighton, Sussex
and in the United States of America by
LYNNE RIENNER PUBLISHERS, INC.
948 North Street, Boulder, Colorado 80302

British Library Cataloguing in Publication Data
Coole, Diana H.
  Women in political theory: from ancient
  misogyny to contemporary feminism.
  1. Philosophy
  I. Title
  100 B72

ISBN 0-7450-0144-0
ISBN 0-7450-0268-4 *Pbk*

Library of Congress Cataloging in Publication Data
Coole, Diana H.
  Women in political theory/by Diana Coole.
    p.   cm.
  Bibliography: p.
  Includes index.
  ISBN 1-55587-075-9. ISBN 1-55587-076-7 (pbk.)
  1. Women in politics—History. 2. Political science—History.
I. Title.
HQ1236.C64 1988
320′.088042—dc19   87-22883
                                                     CIP

Typeset in 11/12 Times by Quality Phototypesetting Ltd, Bristol
Printed in Great Britain by Mackays of Chatham, Kent

For my mother, Shirley Margaret Coole

Contents

Introduction

This book is a history of political thought; its focus is on the way in which women have been treated within the tradition. It is organized chronologically, beginning with the inception of recorded Western culture and ending with contemporary feminist theory. I did not begin the book with any particular themes in mind, apart from the overall focus of the approach. Yet as the chapters unfolded, a thematic thread did unravel itself with increasing clarity, leading me to conclude that there was a definite dialectic to debates about women's relationship to politics which is no less evident in ancient discussions than it is in contemporary thought.

Western thought is fundamentally dualistic. Debates within it suggest that the boundaries between dualities have some fluidity, since they are continually contested. Nevertheless, such debates are possible and resonant only because they accept a series of binary oppositions which structure their horizons: mind–body; subject–object; reason–passion (or appetite); form–content; culture–nature; order–chaos, and so on. In politics they spawn related antitheses, such as state (or community)–individual; public–private; universal–particular. Correlating with them is a further polarity: male–female. Indeed, this is often treated as the primary dualism and used to illustrate, or give meaning to, the rest.

Throughout the series, there is an alignment, or correspondence, between the first-mentioned terms and between the last-mentioned. There is also an equivalent relationship between the two terms in each particular case. For they are further aligned with a set of evaluative terms such as

1

good–bad, superior–inferior. Their relationship is not, then, one of reciprocity. Two consequences ensue. First, and most obviously, the relationship between terms is a hierarchical one: the first-mentioned component is to dominate the second (by force or will or knowledge). And second, it is the first-mentioned term which is posited as a standard, or norm, gaining its identity by distinguishing itself from its antithesis—that which it is not. It is positive, central; its opposite is negative, other. Both consequences have had profound implications for the treatment of women.

In the first case, these are especially obvious: male is to dominate female. A literal domination might be proposed (woman is subjected to her husband) or a more subtle case might be made, making use of the symbolic associations which the sexual opposition invokes. Then the female principle, and all it represents—nature, flesh, appetite—is to be subordinated to that of the male, signifying culture, spirit and reason. The reason that these symbolic associations have been so powerful is that they tend to lead a subterranean existence, structuring Western thought in general and its political tradition in particular. It is the male, and everything which is associated with it, that defines humanity and the highest goals and ideals of the species. And although the symbolism equated with what is female need not necessarily extend to women as such, the evocations have been too close to avoid (in virtually every case) their becoming synonymous.

This basic opposition, it seems to me, underlies all the discussions of actual man–woman relationships, often lending to them a profound but unstated resonance, which helps to account for women's enduring subjection. It is most manifest in the debates about differences and identity and allows almost all the thinkers considered in the following chapters, to be classed according to one of two basic approaches. I shall provisionally designate these *conservative* and *radical,* although it will soon become apparent that the latter is something of a misnomer.

The conservatives include Aristotle, Aquinas, Rousseau and Hegel. They argue that there is a natural and unassailable difference between the sexes, which must be reflected in social place and function. All of them in some sense perceive an organic community in which there is a natural hierarchy.

Within this, women are granted a significant role, perceived as consonant with their nature, which yields them a definite place in the order of things. It is a place associated with reproduction and domesticity, with the organic, the necessary and the emotional. Since this status is natural, it is never presented as oppressive; some exponents of this position even speak of complementarity. But it is accepted that women occupy a lower echelon among the ranks of humanity. They are incapable of the freedom and rationality which define the telos of the race and are therefore excluded from its noblest pursuit: the art of politics.

The alternative position is *prima facie* more radical because it speaks of sexual equality and, indeed, it would be churlish to deny that it has facilitated some real gains here. Socrates, Plato, Augustine, Wollstonecraft, the Utilitarians, Marx and Engels, de Beauvoir and Firestone all to some extent exemplify this approach. Yet on close inspection, its demands for sexual equality, which have looked to identity rather than difference between the sexes, have often rested on a profound rejection of all things female. Women tend to gain equality, for these thinkers, in so far as they are able to subdue their female/feminine characteristics: passion, intuition, emotion, even (in the cases such as Plato and Firestone and to a lesser extent in Marxism and de Beauvoir) their relationship to reproduction. In other words, the primary sexual opposition is not overcome; all that happens is that everyone is to be resolved into one side of the equation.

Emancipated women are consequently those who approximate the male norm; they are rational, repressed, self-disciplined, autonomous, competitive and so on. If they conceive children, it is as the result of a rare and dispassionate act; if they rear them, it is in the cool spirit of civic duty. While the opportunity to adopt such roles might be liberating and exhilerating for some women, it cannot in itself resolve the dilemma of sexual identity. For the female with which woman is associated remains an inferior category and continues to exert its influence beneath the trappings of formal equality. Women as such are still seen by these thinkers as lowly and subversive. They believe in equality only because, unlike the conservatives, they see feminine psychology as malleable; that woman has the potential to transcend her sexual identity and to enter the ethereal world of the human norm which is misleadingly presented as supra-sexual. It is true that sexual difference is to be eradicated, then, but it is resolved into an ideal of enlightened masculinity rather than into any genuine sexual synthesis. Individual women might then be raised up, but not the category of woman as such. This accounts for the élitism of many of the proponents of this position: there is an illusion of freedom and opportunity but underlying it there is the assumption, whether it is Plato or J.S. Mill who speaks, that few can succeed. For the process of transcending one's sexual identity is rightly glimpsed as a precarious and unhappy one. The reason that so many of the ostensibly egalitarian accounts of women seem riddled with inconsistency, is ultimately that they rarely mean what they say (even though they might say it quite sincerely). Few are able to break substantially with the pervasive dualism of Western thought. Finally, there is a more general problem of cultural improverishment in so far as those qualities associated with woman are to be banished.

In this twofold schema a number of thinkers who have been discussed in the book have not been categorized: Hobbes and Locke, the Utopian Socialists and most of the contemporary feminists are missing. Hobbes and Locke, I think, occupy an ambiguous position between the two approaches. They generally speak, with the second, as if women were free to compete as individuals with men. It is also true, as the interpretations in Chapter 4 suggest, that they do not anticipate many women triumphing. Their view of human nature, and this is especially true of Hobbes, simply does not seem to accommodate any perception of typically feminine qualities and so there are none for women to surrender. Despite the problems this raises, these early liberals nevertheless seem to have written at a time when treatment of the sexes could have had a radical resolution, since as far as oppositions were concerned, their traditional forms were crumbling with the decline of religious and naturalistic beliefs, while the public–private split, in which they would take on their modern form, had not yet crystallized. They therefore wrote during an unusually fluid transitional stage. Unfortunately, as we will see, the result was merely a hiatus between radical sexual implications, on the one hand, and their subversion by traditional assumptions, on the other. Certainly, traditional beliefs that reason is to subdue appetite continue to structure these contract theories. For the state itself represents a victory of rationality (via the natural laws which are themselves rational formulas) over those unbridled passions which make the state of nature untenable.

In this sense the Utopians mark a real innovation, since they self-consciously challenge the usual oppositions by looking to the rehabilitation of the flesh, valuing its pleasures and incentives while questioning the imperialism of reason and the sterility it brings. If it is true that the oppositions which structure Western thought have a powerful affinity with sexual polarity and hierarchy, then it follows that sexual equality must involve a challenge to all related antitheses. The Utopians, like Romantics generally, begin to do this. They suggest, too, that if real communities and harmony are to emerge, men must become more feminine. Yet in so far as they glorify the feminine and associate it irremediably with women, their position remains problematic. For any evocation of sexual difference which suggests a natural or definitive foundation for it, must reintroduce those original oppositions on which women's subjugation has been predicated. Merely to reverse the ranking of such polarities seems to be a fragile and precarious basis on which to build sexual equality.

Such debates are today explicitly replayed among contemporary feminists. Ideals of androgynous equality have floundered under accusations that they mean merely women's emulation of men in a male world and according to masculine values. Yet the more recent assertions of difference, of the value of women's traditional roles and qualities (whether natural or contingent), again seem dangerous, given the cultural density which silently and massively sustains their original connotations and ranking. At least, however, the existence of a profound sexual structuration of Western culture is now recognized and can be interrogated. Feminists have tried to rectify women's designation as 'other' while seeking alternatives to the phallocentrism in which all meaning radiates out from the male at its centre.

The question of what woman's liberation might mean in the context of such debates remains a fascinating one. Is there a female counter-culture, which has always endured, connected with motherhood, domesticity and a women's knowledge (magic, healing, caring, etc.) that a patriarchal culture has simply rendered invisible and which might now be recovered? Or have women's lives excluded them from participation in the creation of culture? If this is so, have men merely been privileged actors in an essentially neutral human project in which woman might now join? Or might women's participation, assuming that it can be severed from the tentacles of patriarchal culture, be quite unique and genuinely other to masculine forms? Can we expect, as some feminists assert, to see a new aesthetic, a new logic, a new epistemology, a new writing, in short, a whole new way of being-in-the-world and of expressing it? Unfortunately, there is no space in this book to more than touch upon such questions. I have concluded, however, with a discussion of how women's politics and, more briefly and tentatively, feminine theory, might be distinguished from their traditional forms.

The motivation to write this book arose from my teaching experiences. Involved in both history of political thought courses and an option on women in political theory, I felt that the two should be integrated. The task has been surprisingly difficult; traditional and 'woman-centred' interpretations of the classic texts have been quite different, and this impression is reinforced by secondary texts, which tend to divide neatly into mainstream and feminist readings.

Feminists have of course been acutely aware of the relevance to them of the political tradition. On the one hand, it has provided a vocabulary and conceptual apparatus for their own analyses and visions. This was especially true for 'first wave' feminism, which stretched liberal and socialist frameworks to include women, but without challenging their basic way of organizing the world. On the other hand, however, there is also a realization that political thought has made a massive and privileged ideological contribution to patriarchy: it has provided the arguments and assumptions which have legitimized women's exclusion from public life and their subordination in the private realm. Before women can be truly accepted as men's equals, it seems that the beliefs and mystifications which are buried in the tradition must be disclosed and subjected to critical scrutiny.[1] Accordingly, some excellent analyses of virtually all the major political thinkers, have appeared over recent years.

My aim in this book has been to integrate and make available in one text the sort of arguments and interpretations which such readings have offered. References to more detailed investigations of particular topics are provided in the footnotes at the end of the book, as well as in the bibliography. I have also, as the above discussion suggests, tried to present the classics' treatment of women according to certain themes in order to reveal a continuity and coherence in the historical debates about women. My main concern is that these be incorporated into mainstream interpretations of the history of political thought and political theory. I have therefore tried to show, for each thinker, that the references to women's place were no marginal or optional concern. Although women were generally excluded from political life, they were frequently ascribed an indispensable role in providing its preconditions; their treatment was an integral part of an overall philosophy and is ignored at the price of impoverishing that philosophy. Moreover, discussions of women often provide an excellent illustration of the application of certain approaches to politics, and therefore have great pedagogical value. For all these reasons, I hope that this book will help to convince students and teachers of the political tradition, that relationships between the sexes are a significant element in the more explicit and general discussions between citizens or between individual and state.

I have already suggested that for feminists, a critical reading of political thought represents, as well as an intellectual exercise, a contribution to challenging women's oppression through the questioning of its legitimizing ideas. Any interpretation of the tradition inevitably enters into a hermeneutic circle, whereby the reader approaches historical texts from a perspective of contemporary interests and concerns. This is what allows the tradition still to speak to us in a vibrant and living way. Of course, anachronism must be avoided and I have been wary of those critics who have, for example, designated Plato an early feminist. But while a 'woman-centred' reading is clearly inspired by current concerns about women's oppression, something like a 'good' and self-conscious circularity emerges when texts are criticized from a perspective which they unwittingly helped to incite.

Moreover, much contemporary debate about patriarchy focuses on the relative significance of ideological and material structures to its endurance. Is Western culture itself responsible for women's otherness and exclusion from power, or is this rooted in economic structures which change over time? The transitions between different world-views and between different modes of production are of interest here as test-cases, and so while the discussions in, for example, Chapter 3, of medieval thought and the slippage of feudalism into capitalism, are important in their own right, they are also significant in the light of questions asked by contemporary feminists, discussed in Chapter 10. Similarly, the discussion of cultural oppositions in Chapter 1, has a bearing on recent claims that all of Western culture is massively male-centred. Although the book is organized chronologically, then, I would suggest that there is a certain circularity in the argument which unfolds.

Because the book is intended as a contribution to interpretations of the history of political thought, I have concentrated on the main figures in that tradition. Nevertheless, from the seventeenth century on, two ways of proceeding presented themselves. I could have continued the critique of major writers up to the present, concluding, for example, with a feminist reading of Rawls. This would have been a valuable task and one to which too little attention has been paid.[2] Instead, however, I decided to let feminist theorists speak for themselves and to show how feminist arguments developed within political thought as an integral and critical element of it. Since the perspective from which the book is written is one developed by feminist thinkers, it seemed appropriate to trace its own history and to show how it turned back upon the tradition from which it was born, to criticize and, in its more recent phases, develop it in a radically new direction. If readings of the classic texts must take into account what they said about women, then, any appreciation of contemporary developments in the tradition must equally recognize the very significant contribution of feminist theory.

Because the book is about political theory, it inevitably emphasizes ideas and their history. I do not believe that these mirror economic changes; indeed, they might sometimes inspire or retard developments which would have otherwise turned out differently. But they are circumscribed by their times, and on the whole there appears to be a general correspondence between the ideas and material practices of an age. I have accordingly sketched in socioeconomic developments and referred to political movements, where these have seemed relevant to an understanding of certain debates and tensions.

I would like to thank the following people for their help during the preparation of the book. Janet Coleman and Ian Forbes made helpful and encouraging comments during the early stages. Susan Mendus offered valuable suggestions when the manuscript was nearing completion, and these have undoubtedly improved the final product. I would also like to express gratitude to my colleagues at the University of Leeds, many of whom offered sympathetic advice and support during the two years it took to complete the manuscript. Very special thanks are also due to Christine Sypnowich, Jenny Taylor and Bob West. Finally, and perhaps most importantly, mention must be made of all those students who took my Women in Political Thought option at Leeds, 1984–7. I owe a special debt of gratitude to them for their interest and enthusiasm.

1 The Origin of Western Thought and the Birth of Misogyny

Western political philosophy first flourished in Athens, in the fourth century BC; it is the names of Plato and Aristotle that are most often associated with these origins. Their concern with arrangements for a just and stable state involved more than constitutional organization, however. Questions regarding the nature of virtue and the good life were meshed with broader inquiries regarding the status of knowledge; birth and death; the order of the universe. Such fundamental questions involved speculations about woman's place in the design of Being and her role in the city-state (*polis*). The answers given would exert a strong influence on more than two millennia of subsequent political theory, offering both assumptions and explicit arguments to its expositors. Over and again we will find the debate between Plato and Aristotle regarding women's nature and role, echoing across the centuries. For their pronouncements on the subject have remained influential well beyond the function they actually ascribed to women in the well-ordered state. Powerful associations between the female and certain qualities viewed as antithetical to politics, even to civilization itself, have also been inherited from these early examples of political thought. Yet Plato and Aristotle were by no means the first to make such allusions. They already wrote within a cultural tradition of misogyny and a social context of women's subjugation. In order to understand the premises underlying their references to woman, it is first necessary, therefore, to look back to the origins of Greek civilization itself.

It is tempting to think that such an excursion into the past might answer that ubiquitous question: how and why did women's oppression begin? The earliest records of Greek life cannot, however, resolve this conundrum; at best they yield a glimpse of the late Bronze Age, when a sexual division of labour and a general pattern of male dominance were already well established. What they do offer us are the earliest literary presentations of women in the West and an opportunity to speculate on the reasons for the generally unfavourable nature of these.

Peoples speaking an early form of Greek began to infiltrate the Attic and Peloponnesian region early in the second millennium BC. Here they encountered a Near Eastern culture, some of whose elements became integrated into their own. The Greek-speaking Dorians probably arrived as a second wave around 1200 BC, shortly before the Trojan War. It was about this time that the Mycenean–Minoan civilization that preceded Iron Age Hellenic Greece, mysteriously disappeared. We know very little about this earlier Bronze Age culture apart from the obscure Linear B Tablets. These already record women spinning, weaving, grinding corn, reaping, fetching water and drawing baths.[1] There are great kings who rule yet the priests apparently worship the Great Mother. Subsequently, the art of writing was lost and the first Greek literature appears with the poems of Homer and Hesiod, probably composed around the eighth century BC. These were constructed from myths and histories passed verbally across the generations of the Dark Age and were facilitated by the introduction of the alphabet.

Homer's *Iliad* and *Odyssey* tell of the Trojan War and its aftermath, ostensibly depicting something of the older twelfth-century culture, although scholars now locate the social structures described more in the tenth and ninth centuries.[2] Although most commentators find little trace of misogyny in Homer,[3] some of the images that would later degrade women were already present. A misogynous approach is more readily discernible in the work of Hesiod, who recorded events of daily life in Archaic Greece in his *Works and Days* and offered a mythical account of cosmic evolution in his *Theogony*. Over the next three centuries, a clear picture of woman's lesser status and qualities would emerge via equivalent and interlocking accounts offered in myth, drama, science and philosophy.

Although these early works were not political tracts, then, they did articulate those ideas pertaining to the sexes that later political writers would adopt.

Homer's depiction of women, in an age he associated with the Heroic past, would be of lasting significance since his poems were still read and recited in Plato's day as an authentic narrative of Greek history, as well as a source of moral exhortation. While the chief females of the *Iliad* and *Odyssey* appear as strong characters and avoid the sort of denigration women would receive in subsequent literature, their subordinate role in the household (*oikos*) remains unquestioned. Indeed, it was the arrangement presented here that Engels would later describe as a manifestation of the new relations imposed after the *'world-historical defeat of the female sex'*.[4]

The heroes of the Homeric epics are the kings who went to fight Sparta in the Trojan Wars, among whom attention focuses on Odysseus and Agamemnon. The heroic virtues they display are manly qualities: courage, physical strength, bravery, prowess. For this was an age when status and duty were defined by one's position in the social structure and virtue was manifested by performing with excellence the virtues ascribed to a given station. The role of the hero is defence of homeland and household.[5] There is no role women can perform that will allow them to excel in this manner, and the term 'hero' has no feminine form.[6] Nevertheless, women's social position does allot them a function and thus an opportunity to display excellence of a different kind. The unity of the household depends upon the loyalty of its members and so the key virtue of the women is fidelity.[7] It is Helen's infidelity that starts the Trojan War to begin with, while Agamemnon's faithless wife Clytemnestra brings political chaos when she takes a new lover. In stark contrast, there is the chaste and honourable Penelope, who maintains Odysseus' kingdom for him during his ten years of wandering. While it is true that fidelity is also demanded of men, it does not in their case have a sexual implication: the husbands are hardly monogamous.

Homer's leading women are powerful agents who use intelligence and cunning to further their ends; they are never passive figures in this virile world. If Penelope cannot become queen in her own right but must choose a new husband who will replace the missing Odysseus as king, and if her son Telemachus is able to silence her and bid her depart to engage in womanly tasks during the proceedings, she is nevertheless successful in deflecting her suitors and in sustaining a public presence that would be denied to women of a later age. And although Penelope and Helen are frequently to be found engaged in domestic pursuits like weaving, no denigration is applied by Homer to such activities.

Nevertheless, the tapestry that underlies the main characters of the Homeric epics tells a rather different tale of women: one where they are viewed merely as pieces of movable property, to be allocated as prizes of war like other booty. The first book of the *Iliad* is illustrative here. Agamemnon has been awarded Khryseis, a beautiful captive, by the army. At first he refuses to return her to her father, swearing he will have her back in Argos 'working my loom and visiting my bed'.[8] He rates her higher than his wife in beauty, womanhood, mind and skill. Learning that Apollo has put a curse on the Greek army while the girl is kept captive, however, Agamemnon agrees to send her home provided the army supplies him with an equivalent prize. This provokes a violent quarrel with Achilles, also recipient of a lovely female captive, whom Agamemnon now seizes. Achilles laments that she is 'my prize, given by the army'[9] and persuades his mother to take his case to Zeus. But Zeus is also having woman trouble: he agrees to help but fears the wrath of his wife Hera, who 'will be at me all day long. Even as matters stand she never rests from badgering me before the gods'. We thus find women depicted in unflattering terms and ones with which they already seem to be stereotyped: the beautiful slave/concubine, unwitting cause of rage and jealousy among men; the nagging and scheming wife (Hera, Clytemnestra) versus her pure and patient antithesis (Penelope).

The background against which these roles were performed was one where society and state had not yet clearly emerged from kinship structures. The household was the unit for the satisfaction of material needs but also the locus of ethical norms and values, obligations and responsibilities, personal and religious relations. When crimes were committed, it was the family which pursued retribution. In so far as public life existed, its main concern was with defence, and its authority relations were understood by analogy with those of kinship roles.

The world of which Homer wrote was therefore one where social relations still centred on *oikos* (household) rather than *polis* (city-state) and where the *oikos* was identified with property rather than with affective bonds. The household did not refer simply to the family but included land, goods, slaves, wives, relatives' wives and children all under the patriarchal authority of the male head. Throughout archaic and classical Greece, emotional bonds between husband and wife would remain weak. Women functioned predominantly as bearers of children and servicers of the household, and their performance was evaluated accordingly.[10] When their husbands took female slaves as sexual partners, no jealousy was expected (although Clytemnestra clearly fails to rise to the occasion when she kills Cassandra, whom Agamemnon brings back from the war as his concubine).

Gods and goddesses perform a significant role in the Homeric poems. Indeed, myth figured strongly in Greek culture as a whole and the line between historical and mythic events or actors is not drawn with any clarity. The function of such myths remains controversial: whether they symbolize real historical events or merely justify a status quo whose origins are unknown; whether they are the playing out of oppositions or emotions underlying all cultures or a primitive attempt to understand and systematize the world. Whatever the answer, it is certain that the male–female antithesis provides a central theme for Greek mythology. And when the conflict is played out between gods and goddesses, it drags in its train a whole series of related oppositions, since the notions of male and female already resonate with a powerful symbolism. Reconciliation is required, but in successful resolutions it is invariably the male principle which triumphs and this result is implied to be necessary if progress is to occur. One account of such a process can be found in Hesiod's *Theogony*.

The *Theogony* became the standard Greek account of creation, although it was composed in a tradition of theogonies (of which Genesis is another example) and probably owed much to Near Eastern models.[11] It tells of the evolution of the gods and of a cosmos personified in deities. Thus Hesiod begins with the Earth, who is mother of all and gives birth parthenogenetically to Sea and Sky. She needs no sexual partner; she is the first and supreme matriarch. However, she subsequently mates with Sky, thereby initiating the line of the gods. In the fourth generation the Olympians, headed by the patriarchal Zeus, appear. While early male gods had played only a hazy role compared with the more significant mothers, it is they who come to the fore once Zeus claims ascendency. The divine hierarchy now moves from female to male dominance and also, with the passing of power from Mother Earth to Sky God, it shifts from material to non-material hegemony. [12] Zeus is himself equated with the law as opposed to an original chaos. The poem thus tells how the earth goddesses, associated with fertility cults and nature, were defeated by the Olympian patriarchs, who represent reason, order and wisdom. It is an account that probably bears some relation to the actual replacement of one religion by another.

The *Theogony* is of symbolic interest *vis-à-vis* its attitudes toward the female in two additional ways: the generation of woman and generation *per se*. First, although its subject is divine creation, it also explains how woman appeared. [13] Angry at Prometheus for stealing the secret of fire, Zeus contrives an 'evil' for all men that will destroy their sojourn in peace and plenty: he bids his co-deities create a 'modest' maiden out of clay and proceeds to parade her for all to see:

Immortal gods and mortal men/were amazed when they saw this tempting snare/from which men cannot escape. From her comes the fair sex;/yes, wicked womenfolk are her descendants./They live among mortal men as a nagging burden/and are no good sharers of abject want, but only of wealth./Men are like swarms of bees clinging to cave roofs/to feed drones that contribute only to malicious deeds;/the bees themselves all day long until sundown/are busy carrying and storing the white wax, but the drones stay inside in their roofed hives and cram their bellies full of what others harvest./So, too, Zeus who roars on high made woman/to be an evil for mortal men, helpmates in deed of harshness. [14]

A yet nastier version of this story of Pandora's creation is told by Hesiod in his *Works and Days*. Here the various divinities teach woman her work ('intricate weaving'). They give her 'stinging desire and limb-gnawing passion', 'the mind of a bitch' and a 'thievish nature'. She is made full of 'lies' and 'coaxing words'. She is a 'scourge to toiling men'; with her arrival, 'toilsome hardship' and 'painful illness' appear. For 'the woman with her hands removed the lid of the jar and scattered its contents, bringing grief and cares to men'.[15] It is woman, then, who brings a whole series of misfortunes into the world and whose very existence is but the infliction of punishment. In the *Theogony,* Hesiod says that even he who marries a woman of sound and prudent mind, will spend his life trying to balance the good and bad in her. But he does acknowledge a wife's benefits: she will look after a man in his old age and give him descendants to inherit his property, so her malice must be suffered.[16]

Since the account suggests that men did originally live happily without women, it seems that their birth must have been somehow accomplished without female assistance. Such a possibility is made more explicit in a further passage in the *Theogony,* where Hesiod describes the birth of the goddess Athena. Thus a second level of significance relates to Hesiod's account of generation itself.

Prior to Zeus' rule, there had been a pattern of depositions of male rulers by mothers and sons in alliance. Zeus is warned that the pregnant Metis, goddess of wisdom, will bear him a son and repeat the syndrome. So he swallows her. Eventually, he gives birth, out of his skull, to a fully-armed Athena.[17] A number of benefits accrue to this solution. Zeus ends threats to his sovereignty by giving birth to a female. She has no mother to ally with and is also sufficiently androgynous both to identify with him and to remain impotent. By swallowing Metis he appropriates wisdom, rendering it a male prerogative. And finally, the myth achieves a further erosion of female power by reversing the natural order of generation. It is now the male who gives birth to the female and reproductive capacity is transferred from womb to head, suggesting that the male version is of a superior kind, rooted in reason rather than in the dark recesses of the flesh.

On a more mundane level, Hesiod's *Works and Days,* which gives counsel to tillers of the soil, is sprinkled with misogynous advice. Thus: 'you trust a thief when you trust a woman';[18] 'Five years past puberty makes a woman a suitable bride. Marry a virgin so you can teach her right from wrong';[19]

'Nothing is better for a man than a good wife, and no horror matches a bad one'.[20]

Four major themes pertaining to the female thus appear in Hesiod's poems: the overthrow of the old fertility goddesses by the rational, patriarchal Olympian deities; the explanation of men's woes as a function of woman's creation; the myth of male generation and the more prosaic anecdotes concerning women's generally amoral and unpleasant nature. Such themes reappear in subsequent Greek literature; it is instructive to look at some of the later dramatic presentations of the conflict between male and female principles.

Drama flourished in classical Athens during the fifth century BC. The three major playwrights, Aeschylus, Sophocles and Euripides, all produced plays which enacted conflicts related to the male–female opposition. In the tradition of the *Theogony,* the male order is associated with reason and the *polis;* with political and legal relations, justice, progress and good organization. The female is correspondingly aligned with the old world of kinship bonds and family honour; with a certain madness that threatens the impersonal relations of justice, with chaos and prejudice. Thus in Sophocles' *Antigone,* the heroine opposes the rational laws of Creon's *polis* in favour of the traditional duties owed to blood relatives. The consequences are tragic. In Euripides' *Bacchae,* failure to reconcile male and female elements ends in disequilibrium and disaster when the irrational forces associated with the women are left to run their course.[21] But it is Aeschylus' *Oresteia* which offers the most resonant account of sexual contradiction across a variety of levels.

The *Oresteia* is a trilogy whose component parts— *Agamemnon, The Choephorae* and *The Eumenides*— tell a continuous story. This draws on Homer's *Odyssey* for its narrative, but its theology is taken from Hesiod. When Clytemnestra murders Agamemnon and takes a new lover, a series of tragic consequences ensues. Orestes slays his mother to avenge his father and thereby re-establishes male authority. But he is in turn pursued by the female Erinyes, who seek retribution on his mother's behalf, for the Erinyes are beings from the Underworld who punish murderers of kin. Orestes turns to Apollo for help, and the god purifies him, insisting that Orestes' crime is a justifiable one, whereupon conflict erupts between the female goddesses and the male Apollo. Crucial to its outcome is the question of whether matricide or homicide is the greater crime and therefore whether blood-bond or bed-bond, kinship or legal relations, mother-right or father-right, takes precedence. Eventually, Orestes flees to Athens, where Athena herself agrees to mediate. She refers the conflict to a tribunal over which she presides. The Erinyes prosecute, Apollo is Orestes' advocate; the tribunal votes inconclusively; Athena intervenes in support of Orestes and the latter wins his case.

What does this victory symbolize? It is not insignificant that Apollo is the son of Zeus, who is identified with law and order. Nor is it incidental that it is a human court that is engaged in judicial procedures and judges the crime, for it represents the *polis* and impersonal justice. The outcome means that marital relations take precedence over those of kinship, and this suggests both control over women's sexuality by the male and the dominance of legal over familial bonds. Furthermore, it is appropriate that the androgynous Athena should be the one to tip the tied vote in Orestes' favour: she argues that she is unable to sympathize with a mother's position, lacking one herself. But most important of all, the outcome is a victory for the new order over the old, since the defeated Erinyes belonged to the ancient pre-Olympian divinities and were regarded as defenders of the natural order of things. Daughters of the Night, they represent primitive incarnations of the female, bloodsucking and oozing poison from every orifice. Thus Clytemnestra exhorts them: 'waft your bloody breath upon him! Dry him up with its vapour, your womb's fire!'[22] And Apollo refers to them as 'gray virgins, ancient maidens, with whom no god or any among men nor any beast has intercourse'.[23] Yet their association with the female, with kinship bonds and Mother Earth, gives the Erinyes power over fertility, and this is not something that can be banished from the new patriarchal order. Only its control is called for. Accordingly, the Erinyes are placated with the offer of a special cult in Athens. If they promise to refrain from causing 'all things that bear fruit not to prosper',[24] they are promised 'sacrifice in thanks for children and the accomplishment of marriage'.[25] Their bargain is homologous with the judgement that marital relations have priority over blood bonds, in so far as women's ancient powers of fertility are retained but controlled within the restraints of a patriarchal legal order. Social advance is won only by the subjugation of the female. Freud and Engels would both see in these events a dramatization of the overthrow of matriarchy.[26]

There is yet a further dimension to this defeat, however. The female's power emanates from her ability to create new life, and this must be defused if male sovereignty and the rationality associated with it, are to be ensured. Thus when the Erinyes ask Apollo how he dares petition for Orestes' acquittal, given that he has spilt his mother's blood ('How else did she nourish you beneath her girdle, murderer?' they ask Orestes. 'Do you disown your mother's blood?'[27]), the god replies that although she might have nourished the embryo, the mother is not strictly a parent:

She who is called the child's mother is not its begetter, but the nurse of the newly sown conception. The begetter is the male, and she is a stranger for a stranger preserves the offspring[28]

As proof he cites the birth of his sister: 'There can be a father without a mother; near at hand is the witness, the child of Olympian Zeus'. Athena was 'not nurtured in the darkness of the womb, but is such an offspring as no goddess might bear'.[29] The idea of male generation that appears in *The Eumenides* evokes the mythic account given previously by Hesiod.

The belief that the male plays at least the more important role in reproduction, was to remain a popular one throughout Greek thought. It appeared in a rather different form, for example, in Plato's *Symposium*. Here, not only is spiritual love, of which men alone are held to be capable, praised as superior to carnal pleasure, but its outcome is also claimed a superior progeny:

Men whose bodies are only creative, betake themselves to women and beget children—this is the character of their love; their offspring, as they hope, will preserve their memory and give them the blessedness and immortality which they desire in the future. But creative souls—for there are men who are more creative in their souls than in their bodies—conceive that which is proper for the soul to conceive or retain. And what are these conceptions?—wisdom and virtue in general.[30]

In so far as the purpose of reproduction is immortality, the latter are superior products. The *Republic* will manage, as we shall see in the next chapter, even to eliminate women's special relationship with the generation of material beings.

It was in the new scientific theories, however, that the notion of a more important male contribution to reproduction was most literally stated. Although these theories were based on observation and deduction, it is difficult to imagine that they would have taken the form they did had they not arisen within a cultural paradigm already ascribing inferiority to things female. And they, in turn, clearly reinforced the equation. They receive their clearest expression in Aristotle's *Generation of Animals,* but this only represents a more sophisticated version of earlier themes.

For Aristotle, the respective and hierarchical functions of the two sexes are evident: 'the male as possessing the principle of movement and of generation, the female as possessing that of matter'.[31] There emerges a series of opposed terms related to the sexes: soul–body (the 'physical part, the body, comes from the female and the soul from the male'[32]); active–passive (she is the one who 'receives the semen' but is unable to discharge or shape it. Male semen is the 'active and efficient ingredient' which sets and gives form to, the female residue[33]); ability–inability (the colder female body lacks the heat needed to 'concoct' or 'act upon' her own seminal—menstrual—fluid in order to make it fertile: 'the male and female are distinguished by a certain ability and inability'[34]); form–matter ('the contribution which the female makes to generation is the *matter* used therein; semen possesses the "principle" of "form"').[35] These equations are all finally ranked as better–worse, superior–inferior. The male is the norm and the female but an 'infertile male'; a 'deformity' identified by an 'inability of a sort':[36]

And as the proximate motive cause, to which belongs the *logos* and the form, is *better* and more divine in its nature than the matter, it is *better* also that the superior one should be separate from the inferior one. This is why whenever possible and so far as is possible the male is separate from the female, since it is something *better* and more divine in that it is the principle of movement for generated things, while the female serves as their matter.[37]

While the female provides the 'stranger' receptacle that nourishes, it is thus the male who imparts life, soul and reason. Such theories, harking back to the mythical belief in the head as the organ of generation, held that seminal fluid originated in the male's head, flowing down the spine and out through the genitals.

We have already seen how Plato took this idea a stage further, claiming that the soul could actually produce a superior creation—virtue, wisdom—when unadulterated by carnal imperatives. As far as real offspring were concerned, however, Plato evidently believed in an explanation resembling that of Aristotle. Discussing the origin of the universe in the *Timaeus,* he uses the human experience as an analogy, likening the mother to the receptacle and the father to the model. The qualities of the former are that 'it continues to receive all things, and never itself takes a permanent impress from any of the things that enter it; it is a kind of neutral plastic material in which changing impressions are stamped by the things that enter it'.[38]

Finally, these mythic, dramatic and scientific equations between male and female and related oppositions, were reinforced in and by Greek philosophy. Already in the sixth century BC the Pythagoreans had seen a universe riven by dualisms. In the table they drew up to classify these, male–female was aligned with light–dark, good–bad, limited–unlimited and so on. Femaleness was linked to that which lacked form; with vagueness, indeterminacy, irregularity. It was the male principle that brought order and rational organization; that gave shape to the indeterminate, in much the same way that Aristotle's male would shape offspring out of the indeterminate female fluids, to suggest a correspondence between embryology and epistemology.

The question remains how and why a whole culture evolved such powerful symbolic associations with the sexes. Clearly, they do not rest upon simply functionalist or empirical arguments about the different physical or emotional capacities related to a sexual division of labour (although they would eventually be used to underpin these).[39] We need to explain why women were seen not merely as different but also as synonymous with a whole host of negative qualities. Our conclusions are important since the equations and deprecations traced thus far reappear in Greek political writing and achieve considerable endurance within the genre.

From the beginning women seem to have been associated with certain natural phenomena, and this is perhaps unsurprising. Their power to create new life was wondered at long before any male contribution was recognized. This power seemed to ally them with the earth and with a nature whose fecundity they shared. The early fertility cults would naturally have been presided over by female goddesses. Plato shows himself still immersed in the equation when he suggests that in conceiving and generating, women imitate the earth, such that there is a correspondence between the milk of motherhood and the grain the earth yields to men.[40] However, women's identification with the earth also seems to have suggested an allegiance with dark powers inimical to the mind (but related to the womb). Most Greek daemons were born of the earth (chthonic) and were female. They threaten their victims with madness. Thus Aeschylus has the Erinyes chant:

Over our victim/we sing this song, maddening the brain,/carrying away the sense, destroying the mind,/a hymn that comes from the Erinyes,/fettering the mind[41]

By linking woman to darkness via the earth, the Greeks associated her with insanity and also with death. The latter was in turn identified with contamination and women were seen as having an affinity with polluting forces, with which they mediated on men's behalf in religious rituals.[42] At the same time, women's fertility related them to the flesh in a culture that maintained a strict mind–body dualism and hierarchy in its thought. This had important consequences for the theories of knowledge that developed as well as for a political thought which equated the good life with the capacity to subordinate body to soul and a virtuous existence with contemplation and rational discourse.

A variety of explanations has been offered for the misogyny that accompanied this symbolism. From a political perspective it is suggested that the historical overthrow of matriarchal religion and/or matriarchy itself, was sufficiently recent for the new patriarchal order to yet be on the defensive against women's power.[43] It is evident from Homer's account of Heroic Greece that kinship bonds had only recently yielded precedence to the authority of the city-state, and the women associated with familial loyalties are still greeted with suspicion by Plato several centuries later.

City-states first appeared in Greece around the seventh century BC, bringing with them a decline in tribal and familial authority. Civic republics of a small and intimate nature, they drew no distinction between society and state, fulfilling equally both moral and material needs. They aspired to a harmonious existence; to a community wherein values and destinies were shared, shaped by the rational discourse of virtuous citizens who inhabited the public realm. Citizenship was nevertheless extended only to a minority: women, as well as slaves and foreign residents, were excluded. It brought with it both a sense of membership and a right to participate, in what was perceived as the highest association known to humanity; an association which transcended and bestowed meaning upon lesser groupings such as the family. Since the *polis* defined and facilitated the good life, there was no room for a counter-realm of privacy into which one might retreat. Liberty meant the political autonomy of the republic rather than the rights of individuals within it; justice meant performing the civic role associated with one's station, in order to strengthen the whole. Law meant an escape from arbitrary or customary decrees; an impartial and rational expression of what was objectively right. Against this background, the *oikos* could only represent threats of factionlism, partiality, privacy and avarice.

Engels would associate the Heroic family form with a transition to father-right, engendered by the development of new wealth, private property and a desire by husbands to bequeath that property to legitimate sons, which required rigorous policing of women's sexuality.[44] Certainly, Solon's reforms in the sixth century achieved the latter, while simultaneously freeing individual property from clan control.

As well as the Marxist account, which anchors misogyny in the development of private property, there is a more Hegelian theme implicit in the work of many scholars. This suggests that reason itself could not have emerged in political or philosophical form, without the suppression of all that women had come to represent.[45] Certainly, the Greeks themselves seem to have proffered such a view and it is impossible to conceive whether this type of judgement would even be possible for us, had they not started philosophy off on a course that associated reason with the subjection of a flesh identified with woman.

Genevieve Lloyd develops this theme when she argues that the Greeks associated femaleness with that which reason must leave behind: the vagueness and unboundedness equated with the female were seen as anathema to the clear and ordered thought identified with reason and the male. Although this did not *necessarily* imply that women themselves lacked reason, 'the very nature of knowledge was implicitly associated with the extrusion of what was symbolically associated with the feminine'.[46] With Aristotle the association becomes explicit and it is tempting to discern it, too, in Plato's allegory of the cave. For the cavernous domicile of the uninitiated has a certain affinity with the darkness/earth/womb metaphors equated with woman, while the state of enlightenment is quite literally that: its protagonists escape into the sunlight of knowledge (light/head/sky/male).[47]

A variety of analogous explanations, similarly equating women with phenomena to be transcended in the name of historical progress, has proliferated. Thus it is claimed that the emotion and sexuality linked with the female were perceived as a threat to the *polis;* that their closeness to biological rhythms associated them with the seasons, with birth and death (transitional processes that threatened the desire for permanence, independence and autonomy); that women threatened the clear antimonies (like nature/culture, barbarian/civilization) so dear to the Greek mind.[48] The homosexual practices of the upper classes are also offered as a reason for widespread misogyny,[49] although it is difficult here to disentangle cause from effect. Finally, Simone de Beauvoir suggests that, among other things, men might simply have railed against 'the adversities of married life'.[50]

Perhaps there is some truth in all of these speculations, for as Greek society evolved, so religious, sexual, literary, philosophic, scientific and political attitudes towards women reinforced one another until a coherent dialectical unity, characterized by misogyny, crystallized. The question would then arise as to whether this ideology served some underlying economic purpose, and with this in mind it is salient to look briefly at the socioeconomic conditions under which Greek women lived. Before doing so, however, it should be noted that none of the above accounts of misogyny suggests a simple desire by men to dominate women, although the very fact that the culture described was one devised by men should alert us to women's powerlessness in defining a more positive image of themselves. Women have left virtually no record of their own attitudes and aspirations, apart from the work of a rare poet like the sixth-century Sappho. This is unsurprising since, as we will see below, women in ancient Greece, and especially in the Classical Age, when the arts flourished, had little opportunity for public expression.

Since it was in classical Athens that political thought reached its zenith, it is most useful to concentrate on arrangements here. The position of women can perhaps be understood best if we think of them merely as functionaries of a state conceived as a simply male institution. Their role was to produce legitimate sons who would carry on the family cult and property of the *oikos*, and also to provide the *polis* with new citizens and warriors. They did therefore perform a civic duty, but from within the privacy of the family and with none of the privileges accorded to male citizens. By marrying, women were simply being used as a medium of exchange between men of different households. They were ideally married off at the age of 18, when their father would select a suitable husband and pay him a dowry for his new wife's keep. Divorce was easy for a man provided he returned the dowry, along with his bride, to her father. Husbands might also give their wives to another or fathers might themselves decide to terminate a marriage. Thus women could be transferred to several households during their lives, engendering suspicions among men that their loyalty was suspect.

During this process, women remained under the guardianship of the male to whose *oikos* they currently belonged; they were permanent legal minors. Although they might inherit property, they could not own it. If her father had no sons, then the household property went to the daughter, but only as a means of transmission to another male. For a female heiress, an *epikleros*, was obliged to marry her oldest male relative on her father's side so that the property might remain within the family. Such an arrangement must have had an important economic function in preserving the household property against subdivision.[51]

For the women, one household must have been much like another. Whether young girls or married citizens, they were confined together in the women's quarters, the *gynaeceum*. They were not allowed into the inner courtyard lest they be espied by male relatives; they went out rarely, and then never unescorted. Family festivals offered infrequent opportunities to meet with male kin. There was little education for such persons beyond the learning of skills from older women. These, of course, focused on domestic labours: cooking, cleaning, weaving, childbearing. All of a woman's relationships thus revolved around the home, but these remained strictly limited. There remains no evidence of the sort of relations they might have enjoyed with one another, although the familiar stories of women's love of gossip circulated among the men.[52] In fact, however, it was the men who met for discussion and enjoyed public life. They spent little time at home but visited the market, the assembly, the gymnasium or the symposium, for civic discussion, feasting and drinking. Women were allotted no political responsibilities or privileges; they had no access to the assembly. The only virtue available to Athenian women was *sophrosyne,* meaning modesty, self-restraint, especially over their passions.[53] Strict monogamy was demanded, though rape was seen as an insult to the husband and retribution was settled between the men involved.

This picture of the secluded Athenian woman nevertheless fails to tell the whole story. Female slaves were sent into public places to perform necessary functions (often including sexual availability to the master). Then there were the wives of metics—the foreign residents who worked in Athens—who were obliged to seek employment. Records tell of freewomen in a number of professions: sesame seed-seller; wet-nurse; wool-worker; groceress; harpist; horsetender; pulse vendor; *aulos*-player; honey-seller.[54] Moving down the social scale, the differences between the lives and status of the sexes undoubtedly diminished.[55] There were also large numbers of prostitutes, many of whom worked in state brothels and received wages from the public purse. And there were free courtesans, among them the *hetairas* who might strike up relationships with important men (even with Socrates himself) and who might alone acquire the intellectual skills and personal property that would make them welcome in male company. Athenian men, it follows, were bound by no monogamous restraints. As one fourth-century representative put it, 'we have courtesans for pleasure, concubines to perform our domestic chores, and wives to bear us legitimate children and be the faithful guardians of our homes'.[56] They also had young boys for homosexual relations and older male friends for intellectual discussion. As one author sums up the situation: public life in Athens was a 'men's club'.[57]

The classical situation was far more oppressive than anything portrayed in Homer and had largely resulted from reforms enacted by Solon in the sixth century. It would therefore be wrong to suggest that no alternative was imaginable, and this is especially true since different practices pertained in some of the other Greek city-states. In Sparta, for example, women had much more freedom and public presence. Eugenics rather than legitimacy was the concern of this society with its communal property and military ambition. Thus girls exercised in public to become fit, and clandestine marriages were practised to ensure that a partnership would be a fecund one. Satires like Aristophanes' play the *Ecclesiazusae,* in which the women take over the assembly to institute common property, wives and children, further suggest a familiarity among the theatre-going public with questions of gender relations. There is some evidence to suggest that the woman question was even then in the air.

In conclusion, it is evident that women's social and political position was fully consonant with the misogyny manifest in Greek culture. How far that ideology might have been used to legitimize an arrangement whose true *raison d'être* was an economic one, is hard to say. The greater liberty and esteem accorded to Spartan women in a society that sustained communal property, might be compared with the confinement of Athenian women in a culture favouring private property, to support this view. On the other hand, it is undoubtedly true that male Athenians, *qua* men, reaped benefits from the sexual division. And it would certainly be grossly reductive to suggest that the interlocking facets of Greek culture, with their elaborate images of woman, were but a reflection of economic imperatives. A certain autonomy must surely be granted to the ideas that gave birth to Western thought and that were destined to endure across the millennia, even if they did help to sustain a system of which both men and the institution of private property were beneficiaries. As I said at the beginning of the chapter, delving into the first references to women in Western thought cannot yield a definitive explanation of their oppression. It can, however, disclose the origins of a symbolism of gender, and it is now necessary to see how far this was adopted by early political thinkers.

2 Plato and Aristotle: The Status of Women in the Just State

A comparison of the *Politics* with the *Republic* seems at first sight to suggest that Aristotle reverted to, and reinforced, gender distinctions that had been transcended by Plato. In this chapter, however, I shall argue that Plato sustained a belief in the inferiority of female characteristics and even that it was these which the *Republic* and the *Laws* were partially designed to suppress. At the same time, I will suggest that there are some valuable aspects of Aristotle's thought as far as women are concerned. A simple distinction between an egalitarian Plato and a hierarchical Aristotle is therefore less useful than some of their critics would have us suppose.

Nevertheless, there are important distinctions between the two thinkers that point in this direction. Plato's approach is a rationalist one: he believes in the power of reason to devise and order an ideal political organization. The most desirable relationship between the sexes has therefore only to be conceived, willed. Aristotle, on the other hand, adopts a naturalist approach: political arrangements must conform with a pre-existing configuration that can only be observed and classified. The given order of things is overturned at citizens' peril and so the natural relationship pertaining between man and woman must find reflection in the *polis*. While the Platonic method favours radical change, its Aristotelian successor offers a conservative argument predicated upon naturalist and functionalist premises. The former, with its stress on the educability and (in principle) equality of souls, would strike a greater resonance in the liberal and socialist approaches of the modern world. But as we will see, it was the structure of the Aristotelian claim of natural sexual distinction, that would dominate well into the eighteenth century. To this extent it would be correct to see Plato as a progenitor of radical sexual politics and Aristotle as the harbinger of women's oppression.

Political ideas and discussions abounded in democratic Athens from the sixth century BC on. The clan had by then been rendered largely impotent as far as politics was concerned, and the city-state had become the main nexus of social relations. Good order was a major concern following decades of instability, but none of the new interest in politics was systematized until Socrates taught in the fifth century.

Socrates argued on behalf of a universal virtue, which required knowledge for its appreciation and could therefore be learnt. In this he opposed any suggestion that virtue might be relative to one's age, sex or social position and so his arguments were relevant to questions of gender. He was thoroughly opposed to the moral relativism espoused by the Sophists. It is through the work of his student, Plato, that Socrates' thought endures for us, captured in the dialogues in which he is cast as chief protagonist. In so far as Plato himself is credited with sympathies for female equality, these can generally be traced back to Socrates when he spoke of one virtue and type of soul, regardless of sex. Plato records the relevant discussion in his *Meno,* and it is worth looking at this to discern exactly what is and what is not being claimed here.

When Socrates refuses to speculate on the origin of virtue, Meno obliges with a definition. He contends that there are actually several virtues, their applicability depending for example on whether one is young or old, bond or free. His main division is, however, a sexual one: a man's virtue lies in knowing how to administer the state while a woman's is 'to order her house, and keep what is indoors, and obey her husband'.[1] Socrates is unhappy with this diversity of values; he establishes that health and strength are subject to the same criteria in either sex and that virtue must be similarly universal since state and household both demand temperance and justice for their good ordering. Meno must therefore accede to Socrates' rhetorical question: 'then both men and women, if they are to be good men and women, must have the same

virtues of temperance and justice?'[2] This conclusion is
progressive in its denial of any natural distinction between
inferior and superior souls or types of virtue. However, it does
not necessarily follow that women are in fact as virtuous as
men, nor does it challenge the original suggestion that
women's domain is the household and men's the state. It
claims only that each sex performs its duties well in so far as it
fulfils a single criterion of virtue. It is the ambivalence of this
position that haunts the *Republic*.

Comments about women are scattered throughout Plato's
writings and suggest that he generally found them weak,
emotional, complaining and lacking in virtue.[3] In the *Republic*
and the *Laws*, when he turns to arrangements for the best and
second-best states, respectively, he nevertheless offers detailed
suggestions for the organizing of women, children and family
that have prompted some critics to foster a myth of Plato's
feminism.[4] It is necessary to disentangle the arguments here in
order to see what Plato is actually claiming on women's behalf.

The aim of the *Republic* is to give an account of the just
state. What emerges is a hierarchical and stable edifice in which
each performs the functions for which his or her nature is best
suited. Three major functions must be carried out according to
Plato, these being deliberative, executive and productive. They
yield three classes of functionary: rulers and auxiliaries (both
constitutive of the élite group of guardians) and producers.
Corresponding to this account of the tripartite state is one of
the just soul, similarly divided into three parts: reason, spirit
and appetite.[5] Spirit, or courage, mediates between reason and
appetite, but it is actually allied with the former (just as the
auxiliaries who defend the state are allied with its rulers, the
two classes having souls with a predominance of spirit and
reason, respectively). Thus the overall structure is a dualist one
and the state–soul analogy rests on the idea that appetite, the
irrational part of the soul driven by corporeal imperatives,
must be controlled by reason.[6] Accordingly, the lowest echelon
of the state is made up of that class whose members' souls
reveal a preponderance of appetite and whose work is
characterized by material production; the philosopher kings at
the pinnacle are motivated by reason. Because the latter can
control their own appetites, they do not threaten the *polis* with
personal greed and their rule contributes to a just state

because, like their souls, such a state is dominated by what is rational. It is therefore just that they should rule over the producing classes in the same way as in a just soul, reason rules appetite and hence the flesh. The philosopher kings' lives are spent in the ethereal realms of philosophy since Plato believes that the Good is absolute and embodied in ideal Forms, known only by the few who move through the requisite levels of education. Virtue is knowledge; there is no personal, subjective decision-making by the rulers but an application of objective values on behalf of the state.

In the light of the preceding discussion of Greek misogyny, we might anticipate women's being simply equated with the appetitive and irrational stratum of which the *Republic* says little beyond its need for control. And indeed, there is some evidence that Plato did favour such an equation, as when he states that 'the great mass of multifarious appetites and pleasures and pains will be found to occur chiefly in children and women and slaves, and among free men so called, in the inferior multitude'.[7] However, the formal structure of his argument is quite otherwise.

The constructing of the ideal state begins with the recognition that since no one is self-sufficient, a division of labour and mutual assistance must ensue. Plato's suggestion that there are *innate differences* equipping persons for different occupations,[8] apparently contradicts the later assertion that it is education and nurture which differentiate, since they affect the soul which is the crucial factor. But in the lower class, which is described first, it is biological qualities which are important owing to the physical nature of the work involved. We must also assume that persons with a predominance of appetite are less likely to have the self-discipline needed to benefit from learning. Education will therefore attain significance only for those already possessing a natural predisposition to a just soul, and Plato generally inclines to the view that the élite are those 'with the best inborn dispositions and the best educated'.[9]

During the early phase of the state's construction, all the occupations mentioned are productive ones. There is no reference to reproduction nor to a differentiation of function according to the differences between male and female anatomy. But on the other hand, since the private family and property are to endure among producers, this most populous of classes, we must assume that Plato would have continued the Athenian sexual division of labour within this stratum where innate and physical differences still count. The argument concerning sexual equality therefore refers only to the minority who are suitable for guardianship.

The guardians are required once we move to a more developed state. Here the condition of one's soul does determine function and this obliges Plato to discard any bodily distinction as a criterion for allocation. Since it is nurture that shapes the soul, there is no reason to assume that it is differentiated according to sex, nor to doubt that women's souls will be less improved by the right education than are those of men. Plato accepts such implications in the logic of his argument and it is this that leads to his apparently egalitarian treatment of women.

The argument concerning women's contribution to the state begins with an analogy. When the need for guardians was first deduced from the possibility of war, the temperament required of such persons was derived from those qualities identified with the well-bred watch-dog.[10] Plato now returns to the parallel: female watch-dogs are not exempt from the 'hard work' of guarding and hunting, nor declared fit for 'no more' than bearing and feeding puppies; they are expected to take their fair share of tasks in so far as their strength permits. Since similar work requires an equivalent upbringing and education, it follows that 'if we are to set women the same tasks as men, we must teach them the same things. They must have the same two branches of training for mind and body and also be taught the art of war, and they must receive the same treatment'.[11] Women are not, then, to be pampered with merely domestic functions in the just state (here we might recall Hesiod's references to them as parasitic drones as well as Spartan practices regarding women's training).

The obvious rejoinder to this contention is anticipated: if justice means performing one's natural function, do not men's and women's natures befit them for different roles? The answer hinges on the question of relevant criteria and 'if the only difference appears to be that the male begets and the female brings forth, we shall conclude that no difference between man and woman has yet been produced that is relevant to our purpose'.[12] Now, it is agreed among the discussants that 'in almost everything one sex is easily beaten by the other'.[13] And men are seen as especially superior in terms of 'natural talent'—a gift for learning easily and subordinating body to mind.[14] But since it is spurious to argue from general classes of people to specific individuals, it follows that particular women might be better at a certain task than particular men, and they should be obliged to compete even if statistically they stand less chance of succeeding. The structure of the argument is thus similar to that used in the *Meno,* where although standards of virtue are the same for each sex, the possibility that one may fail to fulfil its criteria is not precluded. While there is no logical reason for excluding women from the guardian class, then, it is unlikely, given his remarks about the nature of their souls elsewhere, that Plato believed many would attain such a status.

Moreover, the argument used here is a strange one: Plato sets himself the task of showing that no occupation concerned with the management of social affairs is peculiar to a *woman.* Yet as Julia Annas points out, the burden of proof should surely have rested on showing that no function is the monopoly of *men,* since it is their exclusive claim to certain tasks that is being challenged.[15]

The argument thereafter becomes rather circuitous and it is tempting to surmise that this results from a refusal to acknowledge that women might actually be men's equal in intellectual powers. While the case for equal treatment hinges on the contention that bodily differences are irrelevant to functions that rely on the quality of the soul, many of the tasks that fall to the guardians do require physical prowess and Plato has already allowed Glaucon's qualification that females will not do their full share because they are 'not quite so strong'.[16] This seems to provide legitimate grounds for discrimination, and Plato concentrates on showing that women do nevertheless possess sufficient strength to participate. Yet the more obvious possibility of their having an equal intellectual capacity, which is also the more important criterion for entry into the guardian class, is ignored. Indeed, when the discussion later turns to the selection of the highest class, that of the philosopher kings who are the most truly rational, Plato opens with the claim that he has 'now disposed of the women and children' and must begin again with the training of rulers (by implication, all male).[17] If he concludes the account with a reminder that it 'applies just as much to any women who are found to have the necessary gifts',[18] this seems to be an after-thought whose main purpose is logical consistency. For Plato has already identified the philosophical nature with a love of wisdom that suppresses bodily desires[19]—precisely the 'natural talent' in which he found women especially inferior.

This 'first wave' of the argument for sexual equality thus relies, on the one hand, on the demands of logic and, on the other, on the claim that justice can accommodate discrimination only on the basis of relevant criteria. Beyond these purely formal propositions there lies a belief that the *polis* should benefit from the abilities of its members, and so any women who are capable should put their talents at its disposal. But underlying these principles is a belief that women are in fact less capable of virtue, less rational and less ready to learn than their male counterparts. The levels of fitness achieved by energetic Spartan women might well have convinced Plato of the potential of the female body, but he evinces little equivalent faith in the potential of the female soul.

In any case, it is the 'second wave' of Plato's argument about women that is more significant for arrangements in the just *polis*. He now explains that among the guardians, wives and children must be held in common. No child is to know its parents or vice versa, and so there will be no private houses or families, nor is there to be private property. Common dwellings, shared tables, unrestricted meetings and public crèches must replace them. Sexual unions are ostensibly to be decided by lot but will actually be manipulated by the rulers for the purpose of breeding healthy offspring.[20] With no property to be inherited, eugenics rather than legitimacy is to dictate with whom women may mate.

These arrangements make most sense if we ask what functions they might perform in the just community, and Plato suggests two. First is the eugenics argument: if parents are matched according to their suitability and optimum ages, then good human stock will be bred 'for the commonwealth',[21] while population size will also be kept to its optimal level. And second, Plato argues that the abolition of the family and its property will enhance unity in the state.

Now, we have already seen that Greek drama was obsessed with the conflict between kinship and political loyalties and also that the *polis* had only relatively recently established its dominance. Plato was eager to allow no factions that might destroy the unity of his Utopia and he saw that the family posed a major threat here, inspiring greed, private loyalties and a selfish concern for one's own children's advance.[22] Thus his guardians 'will not render the community asunder by each applying that word "mine" to different things and dragging off whatever he can get for himself in a private home, where he will have his separate family, forming a centre of exclusive joys and sorrows'.[23] Plato recognizes a connection between family, monogamy and private property, but it is also evident from the *Laws* that he found women particularly susceptible to the anti-social tendencies it induced and therefore in need of ejection from the home.[24] His perception of wives as 'possessions' also probably led him to see women themselves as a source of jealousy, hence conflict: another reason for de-privatising them. Furthermore, the unity of the state could now be enhanced by transferring to it the powerful language and sentiments of kinship bonds. Guardians must act as a 'real family' and address one another as brothers and sisters, which indeed they may well be, given the anonymity of communal parenting. Having stressed the significance of education, too, it is important that this not be left to the family and that the values taught be those of fidelity and service to the state. The *oikos–polis* conflict is therefore to be healed by abolishing the family while harnessing its loyalties and emotional bonds to the city; by rendering all private life, public.

An additional function of both the eugenics and the unity arguments, and one unstated by Plato though intrinsic to his overall purpose, is that it subordinates irrational and exclusive passions (spontaneous copulation, kinship bias, acquisitiveness, women themselves) to the rational controls of the state. The emotions and sexuality that threaten stability and order can be thereby banished from the *polis,* once they are rationally organized according to the dictates of absolute knowledge.

Now, this is of special significance in the case of women. We have seen that an aura of mystery and a supposed affinity with dark forces accrued to the female by virtue of her reproductive abilities and that these were challenged by theories granting men the more significant role in generation. Plato's solution for reproduction goes further in virtually eliminating gender, but it is the functions and virtues associated with women, rather than men, which are to disappear. The mother–child bond is to be broken and women's fertility controlled by a rigorous regulation of sexual contact and hence pregnancy. The natural world of fertility is to be brought firmly within the ambit of reason, and women's power is consequently demystified, rationalized. Plato is at pains to instil an equivalent ethos even among the lower order, and he achieves this by the allegory of the metals. In order to persuade all classes that their functions and positions are innate (hence immutable) rather than the result of nurture, the community is to be told that each was born with iron, silver or gold in their soul, this determining subsequent class membership. Additionally, however, the allegory serves to deny the role of the mother. Education and upbringing are to be explained away as a dream and people are to be convinced that they sprang ready-made from the earth: 'at last, when they were complete, the earth sent them up from her womb into the light of day'.[25] These autochthonous persons are to feel for the earth as they would for a mother, thus giving to the territorial base of the state the love normally felt for the family and the mother who produced them. And again, each is to see the others as kin, since all sprang from the same origin.

We have seen that Greek culture associated women with birth and death, and these are also to be pushed aside in the *Republic* because of the transience they betoken. Instead of individuals who come to be and pass away, loved and mourned by relations, there will be a permanent community in constant renewal (Plato argues that men of high character will not bewail comrades' deaths because death will hold no terrors for them, while autonomous individuals will never fear the death of loved ones[26]). These highly personal experiences, which manifest the temporary nature of life and reason, are to be eliminated in favour of a process of civic immortality.

Plato wrote his *Laws* some thirty years after the *Republic*,[27] to offer a more practical programme for just rule. Although the most virtuous state remains one where 'friends have all things in common',[28] persons not yet ready for such a life can still live virtuously in the second-best state described here, where good laws instil the requisite qualities over time. Private family life and property are now retained for all classes, but Plato is no less eager to bring them under the rule of reason and control than he was in the *Republic*. His interest in eugenics and unity is similarly to the fore in the detailed regulations of private life that he advocates.

Having stipulated an ideal population size (5,040), Plato must provide for strict controls over women's fertility if the number is to be sustained. Roughly equal lots are to be allocated to each family, and to maintain this distribution, one child will inherit all the family property: if there are others, girls will be given in marriage and sons to citizens without children. Those who are especially fertile will be induced to abstain from sexual activity and rewards or sanctions used to this end. Men who fail to marry will be fined. Plato's concern thus lies with the quantity as well as the quality of births. In choosing a marriage partner, a man must select not she who pleases him most but 'that which is most beneficial to the state'.[29]

Detailed provisions are to regulate conception, to 'teach persons in what way they shall beget children, threatening them, if they disobey, with the terrors of the law'. For a couple must 'produce for the state the best and fairest specimens of children which they can'.[30] Female overseers will have access to private homes to admonish and threaten those who abuse the law; women are to be available for marriage only between the ages of 16 and 20 and to conceive for no more than ten years. Strict monogamy is to be enforced. Once born, the nurture and education of offspring is similarly to suffer minute regulation. While it is true that this education is to be compulsory and similar for both sexes—for Plato is still eager that the state should benefit from any abilities women might manifest, as well as wishing to subsume them beneath a system of rational education—he no longer makes any claim that equivalent souls are being nurtured. In discussing music, for example, he has the Athenian assert that different melodies and rhythms are identified with, and suitable for, the different sexes: 'The grand, and that which tends to courage, may be fairly called manly; but that which inclines to moderation and temperance, may be declared both in law and in ordinary speech to be the more womanly quality'.[31]

Again, reproduction is rendered a purely civic affair and woman's contribution is to be regulated for purposes of state. Plato's awareness of the property–family relationship in promoting anti-social sentiments is still evident, too. Excess wealth causes civil strife and so he 'would not have anyone fond of heaping up riches for the sake of his children, in order that he may leave them as rich as possible'.[32] Fertility must be controlled so that broadly equal property distribution endures, but Plato is aware that it is largely the family which motivates the acquisitiveness and greed that necessitate laws limiting accumulation.

The laws that control family life have a further purpose, however, in that like the arrangements for the guardians in the *Republic,* they drag private life into the full glare of the community. Plato especially associates women with an equation between privacy and sedition and a powerful symbolic opposition between light and darkness operates here. Inhabitants must meet regularly, he insists, so that they get to know each other and appropriate honour and justice can be assigned: light, rather than darkness, must govern daily relations.[33] The statesman who imagines that individuals passing the days as they please will then act lawfully in their public life, is making a great error, especially dangerous if extended to women:

They have no similar institution of public tables in the light of day, and just that part of the human race which is by nature prone to secrecy and stealth on account of their weakness—I mean the female sex—has been left without legislation by the legislator, which is a great mistake.[34]

Women's lesser virtue makes their potential threat to the state stronger than men's if they remain unregulated, but Plato fears objections from them since 'women are accustomed to creep into dark places and, when dragged out into the light they will exert their utmost powers of resistance, and be far too much for the legislator'.[35] If they can be successfully brought out into the light, they may enter the realm of wisdom, law and knowledge, however. One is again reminded of the cave allegory in the *Republic,* where recalcitrants cling to the darkness of their subterranean caverns.

To conclude this section on Plato, I think it would be difficult, on the strength of the argument in the *Republic* and the *Laws,* to maintain that he had any feminist sympathies (an anachronistic argument in any case). It is obvious from the general corpus of his work that he did not have a high opinion of women's nature and capacities and this is scarcely surprising, given the culture and social practices in whose context he wrote. While it is true that he offers them a formal opportunity for equality in the *Republic,* the main thrust of the argument is that womanly qualities should be eliminated. Rousseau recognizes this when he observes that following the elimination of the family, Plato no longer has a place for women in his system and so 'he is forced to turn them into men'.[36] Women themselves succeed only to the extent that they achieve this bizarre status. The project accords with the more general desire to subordinate all that is irrational and appetitive to reason and order, which is also apparent in the *Laws.* Any benefits that might accrue to women are entirely incidental except in so far as they are members of the community, for it is its well-being with which the texts are concerned. Yet it is important to recognize that for Plato this is a just resolution; it is not appropriate to chastize him for failing to fulfil the demands of a later liberal age when justice, equality and rights would relate to self-determining and autonomous persons. His problem was a different one. Personal happiness or expression was not a consideration in ancient thought, but then neither was the experience of alienation from the state nor isolation from a shared community. Justice was a civic virtue and all were to benefit from living in so harmonious an order.

Some final implications for women might be drawn from Plato's position. The claim that women's souls and virtue are the same as men's, which he inherited from Socrates, challenged arguments regarding inherent differentiation and the natural wickedness of women (despite some inconsistency in the application of this point). But the belief in immutable truths known only by a highly educated élite, offered a dangerous precedent for those who claimed to speak on others' behalf. For in so far as women remained in the private household, as a majority would even in the *Republic,* their voices were discounted as mere opinion rather than knowledge and their own experience was thereby discredited.[37] Although

Plato himself was willing to allow women into the ruling class, he never overcame the images identified with the female in Greek culture, and so women's association with dimensions outside of the rational political order, endured. It is true that they were to be rendered more explicit in the work of his successor, Aristotle, but the difference is one of degree and explicitness only. The earliest writings in political thought seem to be motivated in part by an inordinate fear of woman and a determination to subdue her power at all costs.

Aristotle is more concerned than Plato to produce practical guidelines for a feasible just state. He therefore devises no elaborate plan for an ideal *polis* or for women's role therein. He does, however, offer some criticisms of the Platonic republic and some of these focus on the shortcomings of a communality of wives and children.

Aristotle fears that rather than adding unity to the state by transferring familial loyalties to it, Plato will merely devolve the *polis* into a large household. This is inappropriate because quite different authority relations endure in the two institutions and their boundary must therefore remain clear. Moreover, instead of mobilizing domestic loyalties for political ends, he thinks that Plato has merely offered a recipe for diluting them. All that would survive would be 'a watery sort of fraternity',[38] while the demise of the married couple in the *Republic* denies to men an important avenue of moral expression, namely avoidance of adultery.[39] It is not private ownership that engenders anti-social sentiments, he concludes, but the wickedness of human nature. As far as Aristotle is concerned, natural phenomena must always be borne in mind when political arrangements are being advocated, and Platonic rationalism flies in the face of these. It is because women and the household have a specific role to play in the natural order of things that their functions should not be tampered with. When Aristotle discusses women, it is accordingly as an integral part of his overall philosophy and they are accorded no separate treatment.

We have already seen how Aristotle ranked male and female contributions to reproduction and his treatment of this activity is symptomatic of his whole approach. This rests on a number of related concepts pertaining to function, nature, hierarchy and teleology: their interplay yields the designation of women as imperfectly rational and virtuous relative to the male norm. The argument can be extrapolated in large part from Book I of the *Politics* (lines 1252a–60a), where Aristotle offers his theory of the household.

The aim here is to distinguish between different forms of authority, notably between those in household and polity, although further variations are apparent within the former. In order to make this distinction, Aristotle relies on two different modes of analysis: genetic and teleological. The first method traces the historical development from household, via village, to *polis*. It thus looks back to that Homeric situation where political relations were still modelled on those of kin, with kingship in the village readily patterned on the patriarchal rule of the eldest male in the family. A prior association is, however, the male–female one, and Aristotle explains that this derives from 'natural impulse' rather than 'deliberate intention'.[40] The implication is that this primary relation is natural in the sense of being close to the biological rhythms of the species. However, this is not Aristotle's usual meaning of the term 'natural'. The second type of relationship that he finds in the household, between master and slave, is natural in a different way and one that must invoke the teleological approach if we are to make sense of the claim that it is the union of the 'naturally' ruling and ruled elements.

According to Aristotle, the universe adheres to a natural order organized along strictly hierarchical lines and within which each being moves towards fulfilment of its own particular end. At the apex of the hierarchy lies the unmoved mover—thought thinking itself—towards which all beings gravitate. A higher ratio of rationality to merely material being positions something higher up the scale such that inanimate objects are at the bottom whilst the gods approach its zenith. Now, the quality that distinguishes humanity is precisely its reason, such that the proficient exercise of rational powers marks the end, or *telos,* of man: it is that towards which he strives in order to actualize his potential and to achieve goodness and happiness (*eudaimonia*). Man is therefore best attuned to his natural state when he is most rational: reason and nature are not antithetical. And those institutions which best facilitate the exercise of rationality, and hence the good life, are similarly the most natural. The teleological approach thus looks to the end prescribed by the natural order of things, rather than at development over time which is undertaken in the genetic approach. It is not, then, an origin in some pristine, pre-social nature that yields a judgement of naturalness. The latter is an evaluative term, achieved only by those phenomena which fulfil their potential: 'the "nature" of things consists in their end or consummation; for what each thing is when its growth is completed we call the nature of the thing'.[41] And later, 'the good life is the chief end, both for the community as a whole and for each of us individually'.[42]

If we apply this teleology to associations, we discover that the *polis* is more natural than the *oikos* even though it appears later in time. The household is natural because it is the site of production and reproduction; it facilitates life, it is necessary to a well-ordered life, and may even participate in a limited expression of the good life.[43] But it exists on behalf of that higher political institution (more natural in a teleological sense) that is self-sufficient and arena of the good life itself. For in civic life, freemen who are equals in terms of their reasoning capacities, engage in self-determination through rational discourse, taking turns to rule and be ruled: they achieve their *telos*. Only those who are free can enjoy such activity, and such freedom depends on a life of leisure and plenty, on liberation from the daily round of productive and reproductive tasks. The household's natural function is therefore to fulfil the preconditions making such a life possible for the few. Women and slaves exist for the sake of rational male citizens; they remain in the realm of necessity rather than freedom, a prerequisite of the good life rather than participants in it.

Aristotle is able both to identify the *telos* of humanity with rational excellence in the *polis* and to exclude the majority of persons from such activity, because the natural order that ranks all beings also operates within humanity, not all of whom have much capacity for reason. Each is a compound of body and soul (matter and form) but the ratio differs. In superior individuals, the soul dominates the body more effectively. This is for Aristotle an innate characteristic such that certain classes within the species (male citizens) are born with a natural capacity for reason while others (barbarians, slaves, women and children) have a higher quotient of the irrational, material component. The inner life of man, whereby the soul dominates a body which is merely functional for its purposes, is to be strictly replicated in his outer life such that the natural order yields a social equivalent: the master is to rule the slave.[44] Aristotle suggests that such relations of domination are beneficial or even advantageous to the ruled party, since lacking ability to make decisions, the less rational partner benefits from fulfilling plans engendered in reason. But the natural hierarchy he speaks of is one structured in terms of functional relations such that the function of inferiors is always to fulfil ends which conduce to the realization of yet higher ends, by superiors. Aristotle is therefore more consistent when he acknowledges that 'the rule is primarily exercised with a view to the master's interest, and only incidentally with a view to that of the slave',[45] since the latter's function is merely to perform the menial tasks that will allow the master freedom for rational endeavour. The *telos* of different strata will therefore vary: some will have the potential to achieve only a very limited form of goodness and happiness.

It was Aristotle's description of the master–slave relation that would capture the imagination of later political philosophers like Hegel and Marx. But although the relationship is not identical with that which Aristotle prescribes for husband and wife, the latter is based on analogous premises of natural inequality. At the beginning of the discussion of the household, we found both sorts of relationship proliferating and I suggested that these seem to capitalize on different senses of the term natural, the male–female union appearing as natural in a biological sense and the master–slave relationship relying on a teleological account of nature. However, we also saw in the previous chapter that Aristotle's account of reproduction did evoke teleological criteria whereby the male was equated with form, soul, superiority and the female with matter, body, inferiority. We now find that the husband–wife relation is also natural in this manner: 'the relation of male to female is naturally that of the superior to the inferior—of the ruling to the ruled'.[46] Or again, the male is 'naturally fitter to command than the female'.[47] This judgement rests, like the argument for slavery, on claims about different types of soul and their relationship to the body. The natural status of both slaves and women is clearly visible from the physiognomy of their bodies. But while the slave is held to possess no faculty of deliberation and children reveal it in immature form, women are said to have it 'in a form which remains inconclusive'.[48] A different type of authority over them is therefore called for, even though in classifying certain groups as fit only for subjection, Aristotle does not distinguish sharply between reproductive and productive function. Both are physical roles and, as such, inferior to those of the rational male citizen.

The different classes of person must possess a different form and degree of moral goodness, depending upon 'the extent required for the discharge of his or her function'.[49] Aristotle takes issue here with the Socratic claim in the *Meno* that virtue is the same for both sexes. Woman's household function requires only goodness sufficient for obedience to her husband plus discharge of domestic duties, and so a more suitable dictum is Sophocles' 'A modest silence is a woman's crown'.[50] Aristotle returns to this theme in Book III, where he likens the different qualities of temperance and courage required of ruled and ruler to those found in women and men respectively, a variety of function analogously denoting a differential virtue:

A man would be thought to be cowardly if his courage were only the same as that of a courageous woman; and conversely, a woman would be thought to be forward if her modesty were no greater than that which becomes a good man. The function of the man in the household is different from that of the woman . . . It is the function of the one to acquire, and of the other to keep and store[51]

To fulfil these functions, it is necessary only that women exhibit 'right opinion' and a 'proper state of feeling'. Even when they excel, they acquire only the inferior goodness associated with the ruled and the household. Because they never rule, they do not need the moral wisdom, absolute goodness and fully fledged reason of the ruler, and since nature creates nothing in vain, they are not given them. The circularity of the argument is more than an empty tautology only if we accept Aristotle's belief in a natural order which matches up functions and capacities in each stratum of being. But the destiny he imparts to women is more potent than that granted by his predecessors precisely because it is integrated into a whole theory of universal order. Moreover, in discussing household arrangements, Aristotle is able to bring together the symbolism attached by the Greeks to the female principle, with a functional division of labour specifically tying women to the household and to the servicing of men, as their highest duty.

What, then, is the nature of men's authority over women in the household? It is no accident that in defining the different sorts of rule, Aristotle reverses the Heroic and Platonic practice of patterning political relations on those of kin, instead explaining relations in the household by reference to those in the *polis*. For it is the latter whose forms now predominate, both socially and conceptually. The husband's rule over his wife is accordingly described by analogy with that of the statesman over his fellow-citizens, while that of the father over his children is more akin to a monarch's rule over his subjects.[52] The parallel breaks down, however, because in the *polis* the statesman is one among freemen and equals who all take turns in ruling and being ruled, whereas no such matrimonial role reversal can occur in the family owing to women's natural inferiority. Yet the woman's relation to her husband is not one between master and slave, where the relative inequality is much greater (although Aristotle does suggest the freeing of slaves under some circumstances, an activity hardly applicable to women).

These fine gradations in authority relations accord with the Aristotelian notion of justice, whereby it is unjust to treat those who are unequal with equal honours and privileges. Those who are superior are entitled to more benefit from a relationship. The idea is developed further in the *Nicomachean Ethics* when Aristotle deals with friendship. In so far as husbands and wives are friends, it is only right that the woman should love more than she is loved.[53] In every sort of relationship practised in the household, then, there are relations of dominance and subordination predicated on natural differences between persons. Only in the *polis* can there be reciprocity, and this is a realm reserved for the minority who are male citizens.

Although Aristotle draws on associations with the female that had already enjoyed a long history in Greek culture, he relates them more specifically to woman as such and to the organization of everyday life. His ethical position is regressive in so far as he renounces the Socratic description of a single virtue and reverts to the Heroic equation between social status, function and type of virtue, now wrapping it in a whole philosophy of natural order which finds an absolute distinction between male and female. Precisely because his hierarchical thought posits an ontological distinction between the sexes, it offers no universalist claims that might be turned against it or that might provide a vocabulary for women demanding the same opportunities as men in the name of consistency. On the other hand, Aristotle achieves this only by introducing a certain hiatus into his account: the very quality that is used to define humanity (reason) is denied to its majority.

Although Aristotle's work is in some respects even more unsympathetic to women's position than Plato's, there are aspects of it that are nevertheless less devastating for the feminine in the long run. He does not, for example, share Plato's desire to subordinate every activity to rational control. Aristotle accepts natural functions that accrue to different classes of individual and so he at least leaves women a role and an identity (albeit of a poor kind) rather than aspiring to dissolve womanhood into a male norm and gender into a sexually neutral category of servicers of the state. If he defines women solely in terms of the household, he does leave them a space in society: their status is an inferior one and their reason is imperfect, but they are not neutralized as inimical to reason itself.

This does not mean that marital and womanly affairs can remain unregulated. Aristotle is highly critical of the Spartan constitution precisely because it indulges women. Failure to use law to regulate their lives results in a flirtation with licence and luxury; a whole culture corrupted by avarice. Again, there is the reference to women's insubordination: when Lycurgus tried to legislate for women, 'they opposed him, and he had to abandon the attempt'.[54] But Aristotle's main concern lies in healthy progeny. The relative ages of partners must be controlled since young parents produce imperfect offspring—that is, small and 'of the female sex'. Besides, girls who experience sexual intercourse too early are 'supposed to be more intemperate', so maturity upon marriage encourages sexual restraint (a good thing).[55] Eighteen is the ideal age. Once pregnant, the woman should follow a regimen of physical exercise and mental lethargy. If she has too many pregnancies, induced miscarriage is preferable to exposure, as a means of population control.[56] Yet despite such regulations, Aristotle's strictures avoid the Platonic implication that all things female must be subdued. Women's functions are to be controlled rather than defeminized or eliminated.

Aristotle also offers an ideal of participatory citizenship that differs from the Platonic variety. Rather than rule by the few who have acquired knowledge of the Good and can speak on others' behalf, citizens are involved in forging a collective identity wherein equals define their community. Although Aristotle's participants remain a male minority, such a configuration might offer, as Elshtain argues, a valuable political model for feminists of a later age.[57] Nevertheless, while it may now be instructive for feminists to look back to the fourth century BC for ideals of civic virtue, many centuries would pass before women were in a position seriously to question the natural inequalities ascribed to them by Aristotle.

We have seen over the last two chapters how political thought evolved within a context of misogyny, and incorporated fear, distrust and dislike of women into its foundations. Aristotle made women's inferiority and domestic role an integral part of his philosophy, thereby granting to such ideas a legitimacy they could never have derived from merely gratuitous comments. Ancient ideas about women were subsequently incorporated into medieval notions and thereby preserved long after the Greek city-state and the culture which had given birth to them, had disappeared.

3 Women in Medieval Thought:
Transitions from Antiquity to the Renaissance

An account of medieval theories of woman must inevitably focus on religion, since it was this form that serious discussion of human qualities and purposes took until the Renaissance. Accordingly, this chapter will examine some of the significant writings in the Judeo-Christian tradition. Yet women remained a marginal concern for religious thinkers, and references to them are hardly profuse. Moreover, despite changes in the mode of discourse, the sentiments expressed are rarely original either. The Middle Ages may literally be seen as a middle period between ancient and modern times (very roughly, the fourth to the fourteenth centuries), and the culture that spans them retains poweful elements of an earlier era. Indeed, it will be my contention that medieval Christianity acted as a means of transmission for ancient misogyny, carrying it across dark and more enlightened ages alike, into the modern world. As Perry Anderson writes of the Church generally, it was 'the main, frail aqueduct across which the cultural reservoirs of the classical world . . . passed to the new universe of feudal Europe'.[1] Although the Middle Ages produced little that would qualify as political thought and thus lacked a political theory of women, they did therefore preserve certain images of their inferiority and unreliability which would regain political relevance at a later stage. Before discussing these ideas, as well as some more positive contributions which the new religion made to perceptions of women, something must however be said of the conditions under which they lived. For there appears to have been both a dialectical reinforcement and a certain disjunction between medieval women's lives and ideological representations of them.

When Aristotle wrote, the city-state was already crumbling and Greek civilization subsequently found a new centre in the Hellenistic Empires, themselves eventually eclipsed by the imperial might of Rome. By the first century AD, Roman rule had extended westward to the Celtic fringe of Britain. Germanic invaders finally toppled the Empire during the fifth century, heralding the Dark Ages of barbarism, during which insecurity drove populations under the protection of local military leaders. By the ninth century, these protective relations had hardened into a feudal system whose zenith was reached during the twelfth and thirteenth centuries, that high period of the Middle Ages which was marked by a renaissance of culture and learning.

It is not easy to establish within this huge and ill-recorded drama how the fortunes of women fared, but they undoubtedly began at a low ebb. The Twelve Tables which formed the basis of Roman Civil Law committed women to male guardianship as perpetual minors due, amongst other reasons, to their 'levity of mind'. The power of the father over his household, the *Patria Potestas,* remained a fundamental principle of Roman Law. Adultery, even the consumption of wine, brought harsh reprisals for his wife.[2]

Although the Germanic tribes which overthrew the Empire were culturally and economically primitive in comparison with its Latin inhabitants, they had not yet fully enacted, in Engels' famous phrase, the world-historical defeat of the female sex. When the Romans had first encountered them in Caesar's time, many of their clans were matrilineal and the women appear to have been influential in public affairs.[3] Despite the attenuation of such traditions by the time of the invasions, the exigencies of ruling the vast domains of the former Empire seem to have produced a conflict between familial and political authority similar to that already encountered in ancient Greece: 'the authority of the new royal states had to be built up against the tenacious influence of these older kindred patterns'.[4] Perhaps because the new rulers lacked the cultural apparatus to do so, the struggle did not this time result in a general denigration of women and all that they represented.

Engels certainly perceived a more harmonious resolution:

The new monogamy which now developed out of the mingling of races on the ruins of the Roman world clothed the domination of the men in milder forms and permitted women to occupy, at least with regard to externals, a far freer and more respected position than classical antiquity had ever known.[5]

Anglo-Saxon marital customs in England, like protective relations generally, do seem to have been quite flexible and readily terminated by either party.[6] The arrival of both the Church and feudalism must have eroded women's position there. The former brought from the East a belief in their subjection to husbands and more rigid notions of matrimony. The latter, introduced as a centrally organized system for the first time by the Normans, imposed a strict hierarchy on all relationships and thereby reinforced sexual subordination.

Within feudalism two related phenomena can be discerned: vassalage and serfdom. Both associated the holding of land with the performing of certain services: military and economic, respectively. Although the former was more short-lived, notions of military obligation clung to the land long after its demise. More common, however, were labour services owed to lords by a peasantry which poverty, insecurity and brute force had driven *en masse* into serfdom by the eleventh century. The effect on women relative to men varied according to the type of service extracted and must have been greater among the nobility. For in a society organized for war, where upper-class women could perform as neither overlords nor knights, they lacked a function in terms of society's *raison d'être*. Instead, they must seek their own protector. As Bloch writes of marriage, 'it was often quite frankly a mere combining of interests and, for women, a protective institution'.[7] Women were accordingly married off early; child brides were common. Widows were obliged to remarry if they were landholders because of the difficulties of fulfilling the terms of service alone, and this applied even among the peasantry.[8]

As the military fief passed into the hereditary caste around the twelfth century, a strict form of primo-geniture—inheritance by the eldest son—quickly followed, making it difficult for women to inherit. Primogeniture performed a function similar to that of the Greek institution of the *Epikleros* in preventing the subdivision of estates. But in any case, the son would have appeared a more natural heir than a daughter, where military obligations were still involved.[9]

Unmarried or widowed women did possess rights and duties equivalent of men's: they could make wills, contracts, sue and be sued. Once married their land passed to the husband for the duration of the marriage, but on the termination of marriage, much of the property would revert to them.[10] And where there were no male relatives, there was nothing to stop them inheriting. Some did have large estates and the power that went with them, while even married noble women played an important role in managing the estate in their husband's absence and transacting his business while he was at war. Yet once inheritance was introduced, marriage became an important means of linking bloodlines and estates; women's virginity became an important commodity—a point on which feudalism and the Church concurred—to protect patrimony and produce a legitimate and undisputed heir.[11] While the Church asked that consent be given to marriage, there was no conception of free choice in a society where fathers and lords negotiated a suitable match. As one writer put it, 'fiefs marry'.[12] Nor did feudal society have any place for the unmarried woman. Those that existed would join nunneries if they could afford it; if not, they might become artisans or enter the labour market, but their lot must have been a hard one. If every man in feudal society must have his master, every women must have hers, too.[13]

The majority of women were not of course noble and where economic, rather than military, considerations were paramount, we might expect them to have played a role that was less differentiated from that of men. Among the peasantry, there was too little surplus to allow the option of idleness for one sex; everyone was involved in socially productive labour. The household was the unit of production, providing for its own needs as well as owing rent or labour services to the lord. Although markets grew in importance over time, production was mainly for use; food had to be grown and prepared, clothing and textiles made. Thus no real distinction existed between domestic and social production, nor was there any separation between home and workplace. While women's labour was a necessary and integral part of the household economy however, a rudimentary division of labour did undoubtedly exist. Women might perform any task that a man did, apart from heavy ploughing,[14] but they were usually employed in particular types of work: tending the vegetable garden, orchard, dairy and poultry. In their cottages, they span wool, flax and cotton for family garments and later for the textile industry. Cooking, cleaning, washing and child-care also seem to have fallen to them, although housework as such remained undifferentiated and no conception of either family or childhood existed in the medieval household—that congeries of transients which Stone likens to a birds' nest.[15] Middleton nevertheless concludes that, 'whilst occupational specialisation was still rudimentary, sex did constitute a major principle of demarcation where it existed'.[16]

With the development of towns from the twelfth century on, women began to enter trades. Many unmarried women supported themselves thus, and where married women were so engaged, they were often treated as single persons trading in their own right. Records show such women working as butchers, innkeepers, shopkeepers, fishwives, millers, pawnbrokers, smiths, moneylenders. While most skilled trades were controlled by guilds, women were accepted as apprentices and often inherited their husbands' rights when they died. There are even records of women masters. Yet for all this, women were on the whole seen as their husbands' helpers, and many of the guilds remained closed to them by any other route. As Power points out, too, it is strange that trades exclusively run by women, like the silk trade, were not recognized as a craft and lacked a guild, especially since jobs where women dominated seem to have been worse paid.[17]

To conclude, the formal picture that emerges of the noble women under feudalism suggests that the military and inheritance principles structuring the society, prescribed for her a role but one that was very much subordinated to male needs. Within that role, however, she seems to have played an important social and economic part; some noble women even became patrons of culture. Among the peasantry there was a greater similarity of function between the sexes even if it was not undifferentiated. Yet all women were recognized as subordinate to husbands, who were quite entitled to beat and generally govern them. In a culture which structured all its relations in terms of subordination and domination, this would not have stood out as an anomaly. But it does need explaining, especially in the light of women's economic importance. The demands of conjugal fidelity which accompanied the desire of the landed for legitimate heirs do not seem adequate to explain the contempt in which women were often held, especially among the lower ranks. It is with this in mind that we must turn to the sexual ideology of the Middle Ages.

Following the degeneration of the Greek *polis* and the clan, communities where a sense of unity was high, individuals had been cut adrift, estranged from distant imperial rulers and citizen masses. Christianity eventually facilitated their return to a sense of belonging, but it was within a universal community of the faithful which transcended the territorial boundaries and corruption of the world. Their faith reconciled individuals to their alienation by preaching brotherly love and spiritual equality, anticipating salvation in the bosom of the heavenly family through the grace of God the Father. Much of the moral and revolutionary force of early Christian doctrine was lost as a Church bureaucracy developed and dogma hardened, but it never abandoned this familial imagery.

The new religion was susceptible to misogynous influences from the beginning. The patriarchal practices of the Hebrew and Roman societies in which the Old and New Testaments were written were generally reflected in the Bible, thus endowing specific socio-historical values and customs with an aura of divine revelation. Christianity also drew heavily on a Greek thought whose misogynous credentials have already been established, such that 'two cultures, classical and Judaic, flowed together . . ., bearing a heavy burden of long prejudice against women'.[18]

This flowing together occurred via both assimilation and conscious adoption. Many Greek ideas were undoubtedly incorporated into the Bible simply as part of contemporary wisdom. But from the first to the fifth centuries, thinkers from Philo to Augustine worked towards a synthesis of biblical interpretation and Greek philosophy, retaining there a strongly Platonic metaphysics. Until the thirteenth century, it was the doctrine of Augustine that held most sway, and as one commentator says of him, 'his mind had encompassed almost all the learning of ancient times, and through him, to a very large extent, it was transmitted to the Middle Ages'.[19] And when Aquinas finally developed a restatement of Christian orthodoxy, it would be under the impetus of rediscovering Aristotle, whose beliefs concerning women would henceforth find resonance well into the Renaissance.

Christianity became the established religion of the Roman Empire in the fourth century, spreading across Europe to England by the seventh. Thereafter, it dominated the minds and beliefs of Europeans well into modern times. Of course, the beliefs of the masses were unsophisticated in comparison with those of theologians, especially since few were either educated or familiar with the Latin tongue in which religious debate was conducted. But the main ideas filtered down to them via plays, stories, iconography and the pulpit. Religion provided a horizon for all thought, and even where temporal rulers came into conflict with the Church, they played it out as actors within a Christian community, using the religious arguments which were the only ones available to them. Spiritual concerns thus remained uppermost, supernatural and mystical beliefs pervading every facet of existence. Anticipation of the next world, of salvation or damnation, was the abiding concern of this one.

It is not suprising, then, that when thinkers turned to the question of woman, their main concern lay in the status of her origin and in the type of destiny this presaged. Although there was some debate as to woman's role in a Christian Commonwealth or in the Church, the conclusions were contigent on prior considerations of her nature, her relation to God and her place in the divine order. The important questions were whether she might find Grace and whether she was not intrinsically sinful. But out of the answers given there also arose grounds for declaring her wordly subjection to men. In examining such debates, I will focus on three phases: biblical, with emphasis on the Old Testament creation story in Genesis and on the New Testament Epistles of St Paul; Patristic, notably the thought of St Augustine; and Scholastic, as represented by St Thomas Aquinas.

The story of the Creation and Fall with which the Bible opens, was the most significant piece of guidance to woman's nature and status as far as medieval thinkers were concerned. The conclusions they reached about her were therefore predicated on interpretations of the ambiguities and allusions within a text of supposedly divine inspiration, not on any empirical evidence about actual women's behaviour.

The sequence of significant events is recounted briefly across the first three chapters of Genesis. First comes the Creation. God makes heaven and earth; out of the dark and shapeless waters of the latter He forms dry land, lit by the heavenly bodies and colonized by self-generating vegetable and animal life. On the sixth day He decides, 'Let us make man in our image, after our likeness and let them have dominion . . . over all the earth' (Genesis 1:26).[20] The text continues, 'So God created man in his own image, in the image of God created he him; male and female created he them' (Genesis 1:27). Like the fish and fowl, these novice homo sapiens are bidden go forth and multiply, although they are to subdue, as well as replenish, the earth.

In the second chapter, the creation of man and woman is retold in more graphic but not quite consistent, detail. God forms man 'out of the dust of the ground', breathes life into his nostrils and places him in Eden. He surmises that 'It is not good that man should be alone; I will make him an helpmeet for him' (Genesis 2:18). First, however, He brings all the creatures for Adam to name, only subsequently putting him to sleep and removing the fateful bone: 'And the rib, which the Lord God had taken from man, made he a woman, and brought her unto the man' (Genesis 2:22). Adam immediately acknowledges their unity and identity: she is of his flesh and bone; he names her woman to signify her origin in him and announces that man shall 'cleave unto his wife: and they shall be one flesh' (Genesis 2:24). Each is naked and unashamed, but the Fall soon follows.

A serpent persuades Eve to eat of the forbidden tree, whose fruit will yield knowledge of good and evil. She consumes some then persuades Adam to do likewise. The immediate result of their newly found knowledge is awareness of their naked condition, and specifically of their genitals, their shame alerting God to the deed done. Adam at once blames Eve: 'The woman whom thou gavest to be with me, she gave me of the tree, and I did eat' (Genesis 3:12). Eve blames the serpent. God punishes them all. Condemned to hard labour in their respective roles, Eve is additionally subjected to her husband. To her God announces, 'I will greatly multiply thy sorrow and thy conception; in sorrow thou shalt bring forth children; and thy desire shall be to thy husband, and he shall rule over thee' (Genesis 3:16). Adam must henceforth produce bread by the sweat of his brow.

Some interesting points at once arise. There appear to be in Genesis two accounts of creation, and this is indeed the case. The story of the seven-day creation which appears first, actually originated several centuries after the account of the transmogrification of Adam's rib.[21] Now, this latter (though historically earlier) explanation of woman's appearance connotes a quite different relationship between the sexes. Instead of the simple creation of man and woman in his own likeness, God makes woman after man, out of man and in order to help man. Adam has already named the creatures and it is he who names his wife. The implication thus emerges that Eve is in some sense in man's rather than God's image and that her purpose is defined in relation to man's needs—suggestions that would be debated, but largely accepted, by future theologians who would invariably look to the second, rather than the first, chapter of Genesis (although a minority would point out that Eve was made of an ostensibly superior substance—of man rather than dirt—and in a superior place—Paradise. Later still, feminists would suggest that when God made Adam, She was only practising). The inference is that Eve was Adam's inferior even before the Fall. Yet she must also have been sufficiently powerful to seduce her mate into participation in the fruitarian transgression, and although Adam freely accedes to the act, woman's duplicity, her responsibility for the Fall and hence for sin and mortality, would be deemed to follow. Even Eve's conversation with the serpent which initiated the original travesty, would be used to convey woman as dangerously garrulous thereby reinforcing traditional condemnations of her gossiping, which are by no means absent from the Bible.[22]

A further consequence of this train of events is that God's curse sanctions a sexual division of labour (although there is no suggestion that the division is itself a result of divine retribution). The man is to work the land (although later in the Bible, the hard-working wife who, among other things, plants vineyards, is praised (Proverbs 31:10–31); the woman is to bear children. From her association with the latter, various ideas will follow. When Genesis is interpreted allegorically, woman the childbearer will be identified with the flesh, itself a threat to devotion and purity, thus reinforcing her ascribed role as temptress. Marriage, the sacrament which subjects passion to reason, will therefore properly subject woman to her husband. The bearing of children would also be associated with all the other aspects of woman's generative capacity: the pain suffered during menstruation, pregnancy and birth would all be taken as symptoms of her sinfulness, now mingling with ideas of the pollution and uncleanliness of such processes which proliferated during biblical times.[23]

The Genesis account is also interesting if we recall another creation myth: Hesiod's *Theogony,* with its frabrication of Pandora. Both emerged within a similar period and tradition and they bear a certain resemblance. Pandora, too, is referred to as a helpmate. Although her arrival is an infliction of punishment for a prior act (theft), rather than the cause of it, in both cases it is woman who unleashes death and suffering into a previously paradisaic male world. The birth of woman from man in the Bible also rehearses Greek myths concerning male generation. As Eva Figes notes, 'Far from being the mother of all races of men, the natural order has been reversed, and woman is born out of man, no more than a single male rib'.[24] Perhaps we might even recall the Erinyes from the *Oresteia*: like Eve, they are needed for the fertility they bring but like her, they are to be subjected to man in a severely circumscribed role. The Bible, in short, was not alone in articulating creation myths which alluded to woman's emergence as regrettable.

Together with Genesis itself, it was St Paul's allusions to it in his Epistles which would most influence the Church Fathers and medieval churchmen. Paul uses the Creation myth to address the question of woman's relationship to her husband, and he leaves no doubt as to her lesser status. In looking to the order of creation, it is the Adam's rib version which he draws upon: 'Adam was first formed, then Eve' (1 Timothy 2:13); 'the man is not of the woman; but the woman of the man' (1

Corinthians 11:7–8). From this he concludes that women, but not men, should cover their heads in church as a sign of submission, since 'he is the image and glory of God: but the woman is the glory of man' (1 Corinthians 11:7).[25] Further implications become clear elsewhere:

Wives, submit yourselves unto your own husbands, as unto the Lord. For the husband is the head of the wife, even as Christ is the head of the church; and he is the saviour of the body. Therefore as the church is subject unto Christ, so let the wives be subject unto their husbands in everything.

(Ephesians 5:22–4)

The allegorical relationship between woman's relation to her husband and the relation of the Church to Christ bears the message that women should be loved and cared for by men since the two are indivisible, but like Christ the man is the head and that for the sake of which the body (Christ's temple) exists. Not only must the woman cover her head in church to signify this, but she must also remain silent there and ask any question of her husband at home. 'Let the woman learn in silence with all subjection'. She is not to teach because she must not usurp male authority (1 Timothy 2:11–12; 1 Corinthians 12:34–5). The silence that is expected of her is perhaps a legacy of Eve's conversation with the serpent, mentioned above; certainly Paul is critical of women's talk as when he condemns young widows who learn to be idle, tattlers and busybodies (1 Timothy 5:13). In a similar spirit, we find him calling on them to dress with modesty, shamefacedness and sobriety (1 Timothy 2:9). For he never doubts that woman tempts man into sin, just as it was in the beginning: 'Adam was not deceived, but the woman being deceived was in the transgression' (1 Timothy 2:14).

It is in this light that Paul addresses the question of marital relations, and we might well have expected him simply to advise men against contamination by women. Yet he neither condemns it outright nor does he counsel chastity within it, despite his preference for such a state. He sees marriage as acceptable, if not desirable, precisely because of the sinfulness of fornication. Since the body belongs to the Lord, it is not one's own (to abuse) (1 Corinthians 1:9–19), so it 'is good for a man not to touch a woman' (1 Corinthians 7:1). But since it is not easy either, it is better to wed than to fornicate: in Paul's words, 'if they cannot contain, let them marry: for it is better to marry than to burn' (1 Corinthians 7:9). Although he admits that he has no divine commandment in favour of virginity, he concludes that it must be a better state since the married must care for their spouses and their situation brings 'trouble in the flesh'—worldly concerns. Only the chaste can devote themselves to things of the spirit, hence to the Lord (1 Corinthians 7:25–40). He counsels the unmarried and the widowed to sustain their state wherever possible.

For women this is an ambiguous message. Paul adds to Genesis the suggestion that they might actually be saved by childbearing as long as they continue in faith, holiness and sobriety (1 Timothy 2:15). As Harris notes, he thereby introduces the notion that the infertile cannot be thus saved, that barrenness is a curse.[26] But it is also from Paul that the idea of marriage as a sacrament—an act signalling the attainment of spiritual grace—is drawn, which will culminate in the Church's eventually taking over the marriage ceremony. And it is true that the emphasis on conjugal love will eventually have a humanizing role there, especially if we compare it with the pragmatic nuptials of feudal society.

Overall, then, Paul's message is that women are inferior to their husbands and rightly in subjection to them, for they were made of and for them, resembling God once removed. They carry the burden of the Fall and are not to be trusted; their chatter and self-ornamentation make them dangerous and are to be suppressed. Yet for those who do remain aloof from temptation, Paul holds out the hope of equality in spirit: once baptized into the faith, there is 'neither Jew nor Greek, there is neither bond nor free, there is neither male nor female: for ye are all one in Jesus Christ' (Galatians 3:28). It would be the difficulty of interpreting and reconciling this spiritual equality with woman's subjection, that would stimulate much subsequent religious debate. But it did open up a possibility that had been denied women in antiquity (with the ambiguous exception of Plato), where only males were considered capable of the contemplative life.

The Church Fathers were those men who formulated early Christian doctrine. St Ambrose, St Jerome, St Augustine and St Gregory all wrote between the fourth and sixth centuries. It was their thought, and most notably that of Augustine, which would carry the Christian message across the Dark Ages.

During its Patristic phase, asceticism (a legacy of Stoicism) became firmly entrenched in the evolving religion. The virginity tract became something of a genre,[27] and sexuality, the primary sign of contamination. Ambrose, for example, made the very Platonic claim that spiritual progeny are superior to material ones;[28] like Jerome, he finds in woman the origin of all evil, associating her with lust and pleasure. While she can find salvation by renouncing her body, in that case she becomes no longer female: 'As long as a woman is for birth and children, she is different from man as body is from soul. But when she wishes to serve Christ more than the world, then she will cease to be a woman, and will be called man'.[29] Platonic ideas about the distractions posed by sense perception and appetite to a rational knowledge of abstract absolutes, thus became deeply rooted in Christianity in the guise of an opposition between the temptations of carnality and spiritual devotion. The ascetic life, the control of appetite by will and of body by mind, was the road to salvation. Greek fears that passion would stifle reason were now mixed with beliefs in original sin and redemption, the latter adopting pre-existing symbolic notions of woman which were encouraged by the tendency to allegorical interpretations of the Bible.

In the work of Augustine (AD 354–430), and especially in his *City of God,* the relations between body and soul are central to an understanding of the distinction between the earthly and heavenly cities and to women's place therein. The two cities are co-mingled in this world since man, a compound of body and soul, is drawn by both mundane and spiritual interests. Through his spiritual development, however, he moves towards the heavenly city, leaving behind its earthly counterpart where appetite and his lower nature hold sway. Although it is the Fall that makes them necessary, this does not mean that all temporal institutions are bad. In the divine order all things seek peace, and although this can never be fully realized in the worldly domain, institutions there can be reformed to promote such peace. Civic and domestic institutions are both important in this regard and must therefore be rightly ordered, with proper relations of subordination among their constituent parts. Accordingly, the

Christian father must rule over his wife and children as the soul governs in the just man.

Augustine does not, however, present a simple dichotomy of body and mind, equate it with female and male, and counsel the former's subjection on this basis. His ontology is more akin to the Platonic distinction between the higher and lower parts of the soul. It is pride, rather than carnal activity as such, which he equates with the Fall. It is not that the flesh is itself corrupt but that it becomes so when we lose control over its demands. Lust is especially imperious, revealing the disobedience of the flesh and the misery and injustice of the human condition, whereby that right order of things wherein will governs desire, is reversed. Passion, in short, is the *result* of sin; if sexual activity existed before the Fall, it must have been without lust and will again become so in heaven, where woman will be resurrected but without the travails of marriage or childbirth.[30] Although Augustine accepts Paul's view that marriage is sacramental, facilitating procreation whilst eliminating infidelity, he differs from his predecessor in looking to continence even within it.[31]

Within this conceptual framework, Augustine is nevertheless eager to refute claims that womanhood is an intrinsically evil phenomenon. As part of God's plan her status must be preserved and this leads him into the difficult claim that woman is both equal and unequal to man; that there is similarity and difference. To establish this position he must grapple with Pauline statements whose aim, though undeveloped, seems similar. He recognizes that the key is to distinguish between literal and symbolic accounts of woman.

If God is spirit then it follows that man can be in His image only in this sense, and since the spirit is asexual, it must be a likeness shared by all who possess it. Yet humans are also corporeal and cannot share in God's image in this capacity, which is the one in which they are sexed: 'man was not made in the image of God according to the shape of his body, but according to his rational mind'.[32] It is not even in all spiritual aspects that humans resemble God, but only in the use of the higher, rational part of their soul. It is this part which engages in spiritual devotion to the Lord and at such times, both men and women are equally in His likeness: they transcend gender. 'Who is there, then, who will hold women to be alien from his fellowship, whereas they are fellow-heirs of grace with us . . .?'[33] It is for this reason that continence, a turning away from wordly concerns, is advised: the pious woman can be saved.

It would seem to follow from this line of argument that the distractions of the flesh must haunt both sexes alike, but Augustine persists in a *symbolic* association between appetite and woman. Referring to Paul's claim, he says that 'because she differs from man in bodily sex, it was possible rightly to represent under her bodily covering that part of her reason which is diverted to the government of temporal things'.[34] Although both man and woman can attain rationality, it is man alone in whom it is symbolized; woman only attains the condition when she struggles to surmount that purpose for which Eve was created: man's helpmate.

the woman together with her own husband is the image of God, so that that whole substance may be one image; but when she is referred separately to her quality of *help-meet,* which regards the woman herself alone, then she is not the image of God; but as regards the man alone, he is the image of God as fully and completely as when the woman too is joined with him in one.[35]

It is in practical activity that woman performs her helpmate role and she cannot resemble God in such worldly pursuits, involving as they do the lower part of her nature. But she can thereby represent a source of distraction requiring restraint. It is this, Augustine concludes, that underlies Paul's contention that woman must cover her head in church:

too great a progression towards inferior things is dangerous to that rational cognition that is conversant with things corporeal and temporal; this ought to have power on its head, which the covering indicates, by which it is signified that it ought to be restrained.[36]

Augustine is thus obliged to pursue a paradox: that the very purpose for which woman was made condemns her to a lesser status, which she must endeavour to surmount. Yet to transcend her state is to suppress her very definition as woman—a problem avoided by men whose spiritual destiny 'naturally' accords with their definition. The resolution is little different from Plato's, despite its religious trappings. It is not then that women are identified inextricably with the body, but that their role associates them with a subversive appetite. And although the equation remains in one sense merely symbolic, this does not prevent Augustine from going on to argue for their literal subjection:

And as in his soul there is one power which rules by directing, another made subject that it might obey, so also for the man was corporeally made a woman, who, in the mind of her rational understanding should also have a like nature, in the sex, however, of her body should be in like manner subject to the sex of her husband, as the appetite of action is subjected by reason of the mind, to conceive the skill of acting rightly.[37]

In conclusion then, Augustine's position on women remains an ambivalent one. He sustains the Pauline allusion to spiritual equality, and he locates woman within the bounds of reason. Elshtain concludes from this that he is 'one of the great undoers of Greek misogyny'.[38] Yet as Lloyd points out, 'despite his good intentions, his own symbolism pulls against his explicit doctrine of sexual equality with respect to the possession of Reason'.[39] Woman is upgraded in being seen as man's equal in reason, but the symbolism in which Augustine envelops her must make reason's appearance there seem precarious, while her association with appetite implies her culpability for that loss of rational control which demonstrates the sinfulness of the race. It is not therefore gratuitous that he warns against the subordination of virtue to 'Lady Pleasure', whom he describes as an 'imperious and dishonest woman'.

Formally equal in things spiritual, woman thus remains man's inferior in things mundane, owing to her symbolic equation with the lesser, mundane realm itself. Between her practical bent as helpmate and her identification with corruption, there is only the thinnest of lines. The Platonist metaphysics underlying Augustine's thought therefore works against woman. In the practical affairs that proliferate in the familial and civic domain, she must be subjected to male authority, the basis of this contention lying in Platonic claims regarding the right ordering of parts of the soul, now symbolically associated with gender.

During the High Middle Ages there was a renaissance of intellectual activity across Europe. The rediscovery of Aristotle's work, of which only the *Logic* had previously been known in the West, was a major factor in this wave of enlightenment. As Ullmann notes, the 'influence of Aristotle from the second half of the thirteenth century onwards wrought a transmutation in thought that amounts to a complete revolution'.[40] One of the most significant aspects of this influence was Aristotle's definition of the state as a natural community of citizens pursuing the good life: the *Politics* was translated into Latin in AD 1260. It would eventually reinforce a sense of political autonomy which was already developing with the emergence of towns, most notably in the communes of northern Italy. However, it would not be until the fourteenth century that the implications of Aristotle's politics really bore fruit in a revival of political theory; in the thirteenth century, it was its metaphysical underpinning that was important, and this received its most significant treatment in the work of St Thomas Aquinas (1227–74).

In Aquinas' work, notably his *Summa Theologica,* we find a unified synthesis of ancient and medieval thought. Where the Patristic synthesis had remained largely implicit and Platonic, this Scholastic version was explicit and thoroughly Aristotelian. Aristotle's influence was in many ways a progressive one. It revived notions of the power of reason as opposed to revelation; of natural over divine order. In Aquinas' work, however, these levels were brought together. He accepted the holistic, all-embracing nature of Aristotle's project, but incorporated a divine hierarchy into the ancient's natural one. In adopting this approach, it became unavoidable that Aquinas, like his predecessor, should treat women and their purpose as an integral part of his system. In this sense the Aristotelian revival was not a progressive one since it reintroduced ideas of women's natural inferiority. The theme was only reinforced by a contemporaneous recovery of an accurate account of Roman Law, itself a vehicle for contentions regarding women's minor status.

Aquinas took over the whole panoply of Aristotelian natural order. Revived was the notion of a hierarchy in which the more rational ruled the more material and hence the claims regarding inequality. At the apex was God, from whom this order flowed as a divine plan. Each being had its own nature from which derived its particular purpose and the perfection for which it aimed; together the constituent elements aimed towards the

peace and harmony of the whole. We have already discussed
Aristotle's application of this philosphy to women; it is now
necessary to see how Aquinas used it to interpret Genesis and
the by now familiar Christian questions regarding women's
image and status in relation to God and men.

Aquinas accepts the Aristotelian account of generation and
with it the claims both that the female as the more passive
partner plays a lesser role, and that the reproduction of new
females is the result of an inferior process.[41] However, this
cannot mean that woman is a mistake: as part of the divine
order, she must have been produced by God for a purpose, and
indeed she was. When Genesis refers to woman as man's
helpmate, it is a statement of this purpose, and its nature is
quite specific: 'it was necessary for woman to be made, as the
Scripture says, as a *helper* to man; not, indeed, as a helpmate in
other works, as some say, since man can be more efficiently
helped by another man in other works; but as a helper in the
work of generation'.[42] It must follow from this that woman's
purpose, though valuable, is a lesser one *vis-à-vis* humanity's
end, than is man's. For it is rationality, the perfection of the
soul, which is mankind's special and divinely ordained *telos,*
and the generative function, with its materiality, cannot fulfil
this. There is 'a vital operation nobler than generation, to
which their life is principally directed . . . man is yet further
ordered to a still nobler vital action, and that is intellectual
operation'.[43] Woman's purpose is thus to help perpetuate a
species whose principle lies in man (and even in this role she
plays the less active part). In this sense it is he alone who is in
God's likeness. It is to convey this idea that Eve is made
subsequent to Adam in the Creation: 'to give the first man a
certain dignity consisting in this, that as God is the principle of
the whole universe, so the first man, in likeness to God, was the
principle of the whole human race'.[44] Note, then, that the order
of creation did not create man's dominion; it only symbolized
that which pre-existed it as a natural relationship.

Aquinas draws a further conclusion from the order of
creation. Woman's being fashioned from man enhances his
love for her, necessary because they must cohabit 'together for
life'. But cohabitation has a function beyond periodic
reproduction: it is also 'for the purpose of domestic life, in
which each has his or her particular duty, and in which the man

is the head of the woman'.[45] Woman's natural function is procreation, and similarly, her subjection to her husband is not merely a result of Eve's malediction but a function of the natural order. Aquinas establishes this last point by drawing on Aristotle's rather inconsistent claims regarding the beneficiaries of servility and giving them a religious gloss:

Subjection is twofold. One is servile, by virtue of which a superior makes use of a subject for his own benefit; and this kind of subjection began after sin. There is another kind of subjection, which is called economic or civil, whereby the superior makes use of his subjects for their own benefit or good; and this kind of subjection existed before sin. For good order would have been wanting in the human family if some were not governed by others wiser than themselves. So by such a kind of subjection woman is naturally (i.e. by nature) subject to man, because in man the discretion of reason predominates.[46]

The same argument is reiterated in abbreviated form: 'Now a woman is subject by her nature, whereas a slave is not'; 'Woman is subject to man on account of the frailty of nature, as regards both vigour of soul and strength of body'.[47] The argument for woman's subjection is thus abstract, but it is not symbolic; take away the religious elements of the argument and the allegorical accounts of Genesis, and her natural inferiority, unlike that of the slave, remains. The status that Aquinas accords her is more akin to feudal notions of protection than to slavery, however, and this is symbolized for him by the fact that woman is taken from man's side and not from his feet.[48]

Aquinas is no less eager than Augustine had been, to stress an equality of souls in the spiritual realm beyond sexual identity. In 'matters pertaining to the soul woman does not differ from man as to the thing (for sometimes a woman is found to be better than many men as regards the soul)'.[49] But in mundane affairs she has an inferior purpose which condemns her to subjection. Aquinas ends up with the same conclusion as Paul and Augustine, but for him woman's lesser position is more literal and is founded on a fully developed theory which is no longer dependent on biblical texts and symbols. While women might achieve rational, hence spiritual, equality, Aquinas seems to think it unlikely; he refers to them as incontinent, vacillating, a prey to passion and defective in reason.[50] Given their role as childbearers and domestic aids, it was in any case unlikely that they would have the opportunity to develop their spiritual capacities. It is no accident that theologians since Jerome had advertised one of the virtues of virginity as being independence from husbands and their worldly corollaries.[51]

To the extent that Aquinas differs from Augustine, this may almost be seen as a further replaying of the disagreements between Aristotle and Plato. As both Eleanor Commo McLaughlin and Genevieve Lloyd point out, Aquinas avoids the Patristic (Platonic) sense of a soul imprisoned in a body or of a divided soul, by accepting the Aristotelian presentation of a more integrated body–mind and a more unified soul.[52] This is why he must abandon much of the sexual imagery used by his predecessors and this has significant ramifications. In establishing a penetrating and integrated argument for woman's natural subjection, Aquinas appears to leave them in a worse position than had Augustine. But it also follows that his work carried a less sinister message. For like Aristotle, he does not see the body as intrinsically sinful and to be suppressed. It has a purpose, albeit a lowly one, and is good to the extent that it fulfils this. Accordingly, Aquinas recognizes a unique place for woman in the divine plan, as Aristotle had granted her in the *polis*. She is not evil or superfluous, nor is she but a man with additional obstacles to salvation presented by her more corporeal definition. If she does not reflect the principle of the race, at least the redemption of the race has nothing to do with the elimination of the female principle, as Plato and the Church Fathers imply. As Martha Osborne expresses it, 'while Augustine constantly urges woman to rise above her physical being, Aquinas appears much more inclined to consider her a product of her corporeal condition'.[53] This is possible because for Aquinas, woman's association with corporeity is real rather than symbolic, allowing her to fulfil a significant carnal purpose which is irreducible to images of expendable corruption.

Aquinas' synthesis did not long survive intact. The secular logic of Aristotle's position began to assert itself as political and divine aspects of the system moved apart with the recognition that the state could exist quite independently. But this did mean that the reappearance of political thought bore a markedly Aristotelian quality and the explicit political implications of his thought for women re-emerged with it, carrying ideas of sexual inequality into the heart of the earliest modern theories of the state.

Little more than a generation after Aquinas, both Marsiglio of Padua and Bartolus were developing notions of popular sovereignty which explicitly excluded women from citizenship, the former doing so on avowedly Aristotelian grounds and the latter, one of the great medieval expositors of Roman Law, on the grounds that women were incapable of giving legally relevant consent.[54] Debates concerning the *Politics* continued into the Renaissance, and as Maclean argues of that period, sympathy lay with Aristotle's condemnation of Spartan women's republican activities: 'there is near unanimity in the distaste shown for the notion of woman's involvement in politics'.[55] Nature, convention, divine and human law all conspired in giving governance to the male. This is hardly surprising. Paul, Augustine and Aquinas had all granted women a certain equality in those spiritual matters which they viewed as supra-sexual, while arguing for their subordination in wordly affairs. Once political thought severed the temporal from the divine, it looked exclusively to that realm in which women's inferiority had never been questioned.

By the fifteenth century, the Renaissance was nevertheless bringing the beginnings of an improvement in perceptions of women. Agnes Heller describes the period as 'the dawn of feminine equality', the first age to esteem women as '*whole human beings*'.[56] A new interest in wordly things and especially nature, which had been encouraged partly by Aristotle's influence, was helping to usher in more scientific approaches to woman, which began to dispel some of the mysteries and errors surrounding her. And where her mystique remained, it was to some degree given a new enchantment by Neoplatonism, which exalted a love found originating in beauty and associated with woman. In opposition to the Scholastic presentation of her as evil, her spiritual gifts and personification of virtue were portrayed lavishly in yet another replay of Platonic versus Aristotelian ideas on woman. Yet this was a double-edged sword for, ironically, woman, condemned throughout the Middle Ages for her worldliness, was now to be protected from public life lest it corrupt her. Political thought, most notably that of Machiavelli,[57] reinforced this latter trend by announcing the viciousness of the public realm, thereby anticipating the split between private and public which would open up with the development of capitalism and which would play so prominent a role in liberal defences of sexual inequality.

Throughout this chapter there has been a strong emphasis on images of woman. These might not appear to have immediately political significance, but my contention has been that, given the paucity of political thinking during the Middle Ages, they acted as transmitters, carrying ideas from ancient to modern times in religious form. They depicted woman as lacking in judgement and reason; as vain, duplicitous, capricious, seductive, weak-minded, generally inferior and, often, as downright evil. It is true that the cult of Mary periodically gained popularity, but its paradoxical image of the perfect virgin-mother only served to reinforce the inescapable impurity of real women. When political thinking re-emerged in the Renaissance, it thus took over ancient ideas of women that had been preserved through a Christian symbolism. Although Christianity had appended to them a certain view of sexual equality, this did not apply to the worldly order where woman's subjection was given renewed justification. My contention in the following chapter will be that despite the rational form taken by liberalism, these traditional associations endured, causing hiatus and inconsistency in a doctrine that had dispensed with their theoretical underpinning in a natural/divine order of sexual inequality.

4 Hobbes and Locke: Natural Right against Natural Authority

During the sixteenth century, both Church and state encouraged the growth of paternal power. The Reformation had left something of a moral vacuum with the decline of the Church and its pervasive symbolism. Puritans were eager that the male head of the household should replace priests as moral and religious instructors.[1] This was particularly important in the light of emerging notions of childhood: the strict and punitive father who led family prayers and enforced iron discipline, was ideal. Women's contribution to childhood education sanctioned a change in their status, too, from evil Catholic wife to proper Protestant mother,[2] but it was a role narrowly defined and strictly enforced.

The state's interest in reinforcing the father's power was twofold: coercive and ideological. He was a useful agent of social control at a time when society was in flux, with changing values and emerging market relations threatening social disorder. But the Crown was also struggling to gain legitimacy for its claims to absolutism, and here the analogy between authoritarian monarchy and domestic patriarchy was irresistible. There was accordingly 'a deliberately fostered increase in the power of the father within the conjugal unit, that is to say, a strengthening of patriarchy'.[3]

Patriarchy was a term destined for a lively conceptual adventure in the thought of future feminists, who would broaden and flatten its meaning to signify men's power over women. In the seventeenth century it retained a more precise sense of rule by the father, but this allowed it briefly to acquire currency as a dynamic political concept. Although it was used to further arguments about political obligations, it inadvertently raised questions about women's status in the process.

Patriarchalists found in the unlimited power of the father, a basis for the absolute sovereignty of the king: family relations were perceived as a paradigm, or metaphor, for political relations. The father was credited with natural authority over his sons: the generation of their lives gave him the right to direct or even negate them. The king, as father of his people, was then credited with an equivalent power. In both cases authority was inherited via primogeniture. When combined with scriptural references, this allowed patriarchalism to move beyond merely metaphorical relations between family and state: it traced the royal line back to Adam himself. The absolute authority which God supposedly granted him over his sons, wife and all living creatures, was literally bequeathed across the generations. From these premises the doctrine's most able exponent, Sir Robert Filmer, was able to conclude that there is a divine right of kings to absolute power; that man's natural condition is slavery, since those born in subjection to parents cannot be free, and that authority is natural and hierarchical.[4] Although the term 'natural' retains something of its teleological ancestry in these conclusions, invoking as it does the idea of a natural and preordained order, it is ultimately the biological aspect of paternity which yields to the father his natural authority.

Despite some obvious lacunae in the thesis, patriarchalism provided a horizon for all English political thought in the seventeenth century.[5] It was the attempt to refute it that gave birth to liberalism. Although Thomas Hobbes (1588–1679) also subscribed to the idea of absolute authority, he wished to place it on a more rational footing since the divine right doctrine was less than compelling during a civil war whose exigencies included regicide. John Locke (1632–1704) also wanted to justify political obligation by appeals to reason, but in order to limit the power of rulers. To accomplish their respective tasks, these thinkers developed a model which began with rational, self-interested actors. Their common assertion was that no natural authority could persist among originally free and equal individuals. Such agents would set up an artificial authority if it suited their interests, but then its legitimacy must hinge on their consent. Natural versus rational authority thus became the focus of debate between patriarchalists and contract theorists.

Although the familial relationship which most concerned protagonists was that between father and son, there were a number of reasons why the logic of liberal arguments encouraged statements concerning sexual equality. First, since patriarchal authority was predicated on the facts of paternity, the demonstration of mothers' equal responsibility for their offspring made something of a mockery of the argument. Second, the challenge to natural authority in the state inevitably spilled over into challenges to such authority in marriage. This was encouraged by the homology that patriarchalists insisted upon between familial and political relations, such that consent in one sphere must imply consent in the other.[6] And third, the model of individuals in the state of nature militated against any suggestion of sexual inequality there since this would have implied that natural distinctions underlay authority patterns. The central question that we must address to Hobbes and Locke is whether they sustained the radical implications of this approach.

The strategy of Hobbes's argument in *Leviathan* is to deconstruct civil society into its elemental units, stripping them to their basic psychology. Once this is achieved it will be possible to offer a scientific account of that political arrangement which will best satisfy them. Persons are presented as first of all bodies which, like all material objects, are governed by laws of motion. Their aim is perpetual motion (life) and their greatest fear, stasis (death). These motivations yield criteria of pleasure and pain and hence objects of desire and aversion, classified by reasoning through causal chains in order to deduce their likely effect. Competition for scarce goods and the security of their future procurement, engenders 'a perpetual and restless desire of power after power, which ceaseth only in death'.[7] Eventually reason arrives at natural (prudential) laws which disclose peace as most conducive to lasting pleasure and an absolute ruler as its most effective guarantor.

It is worth reflecting for a moment on the sexual implications of Hobbes's materialism here. According to this, it is matter which is primary. Persons are ultimately but matter in motion;

their thoughts and feelings result from motions in the brain, the result of external stimuli. Ideas cannot then be determining: rather, they are effects of, and aids to, the mechanistic pursuit of motion. Each is responsible for selecting their own means to achieve this end. A radical equality thus follows: no class of persons can be distinguished by a higher purpose; there are no teleological or moral criteria according to which some self-moving bodies might be ranked above others. All are equal in regard to rights, wants and function. Because Hobbes claims to base psychology on bodily requirements but makes no mention of reproductive needs, he avoids any suggestion of either innate mental, or relevant physical, sexual difference. His materialism thereby challenges that Aristotelian legacy which saw in certain categories of individual a natural repository of reason: everyone must strive to make those calculations which are necessary to the fulfilment of desire. Each begins with an identical natural right to all things and the potential to recognize the rational tenets of natural law. Nor does Hobbes's materialism leave room for any symbolism of gender. The logic of his argument points to purely abstract individuals for whom their sex, or sexual relations, are irrelevant.

Although there is nothing in the account to suggest any sexual differentiation, Hobbes could easily have inserted it had he wished. For although his machines are sufficiently equal in terms of physical and intellectual power that none can gain permanent advantage, they are not identical (Hobbes, *Leviathan,* Ch. XIII, p. 141; XIV, p. 155). Their passions, virtues, wits and ability to reason, vary according to bodily constitution, custom, experience, industry. Since thoughts are motivated by desire—as its 'scouts' and 'spies'—those with tepid desire necessarily manifest weak passion and poor judgement (IV, pp. 80f; V, p. 85; VIII, p. 104). Such differences must nevertheless remain random, for if they were structured according to fixed categories, they would suggest a natural criterion for power. Accordingly, there is nothing to suggest that women are less desirous than men, nor anything in the description of bodily imperatives that would lead us to suspect it. When Hobbes writes that 'if any two men desire the same thing, which nevertheless they cannot both enjoy, they become enemies' (XIII, p. 142), he acknowledged that women, too, must participate in the war of all against all. For 'there is not always that difference of strength, or prudence, between the man and woman, as that the right cannot be determined without war' (XX, p. 197).

It follows that women, as well as men, must consent to any authority over themselves and that they will do so only if it accords with their self-interest. This must be true whether familial or political arrangements are at issue. Hobbes's account thus far offers no reason why women would either wish to, or need to, subordinate themselves to husbands, nor therefore why they should be excluded from an equal voice in forming a political community. Such is the universalist and egalitarian kernel of liberalism. But does Hobbes remain faithful to it?

Two doubts might be immediately voiced regarding the account so far. First, although Hobbes's materialist logic is sexually neutral, we might ask whether the human nature that he describes is as universal as he believes. For he is in fact mistaken in claiming that he derives his psychology from his materialism. Critics since Rousseau have accused him of generalizing a psychology particular to seventeenth-century man, driven into an aggressively competitive ethos by the exigencies of civil war and nascent capitalism. The case might be taken further to suggest that although Hobbes's ascription of a nature common to both sexes is an advance, what he accredits them with is a peculiarly masculine psyche: aggressive, competitive and egoistic.[8] Indeed, Hobbes himself is aware of this, for he later acknowledges that 'there is allowance to be made for natural timorousness; not only to women, of whom no such dangerous duty [as soldiering] is expected, but also to men of feminine courage' (XXI, p. 210). But in the formal account of human nature, where women and men are indistinguishable, they do seem to be motivated according to a male norm—perhaps not surprising since Hobbes invites the reader to 'read thyself' in order, like him, to understand others' passions via introspection (Intro:, p. 60). A second suggestion that it is actually men whom Hobbes has in mind, arises from the examples he offers of gains which individuals will pursue in the state of nature. These include 'other men's persons, wives, children and cattle' (XIII, p. 143)—a strange selection for any woman to covet.

The very reference to wifely roles is in any case curious in the context of the state of nature, where Hobbes claims there are 'no laws of matrimony' (XX, p. 197). Yet he goes on to speak of the natural state as one 'where men have lived by small families, to rob and spoil one another'; of pre-civil American Indians who know of no government other than that of 'small families' (XVII, p. 173; XIII, p. 144). Are we then to infer that the state of nature is, contrary to first impressions, actually populated by families rather than by individuals? Schochet argues that we are and that this renders the state of nature a historical, rather than simply logical, edifice.[9] Yet this at least *prima facie* implies natural authority relations which do after all precede civil society, apparently raising problems for the consistency of Hobbes's individualism and for the voluntary consent which rests upon it. It is necessary to examine this matter more closely.

Much ink has been recently spilt on the question of whether Hobbes remained a patriarchalist.[10] Those contending that he did, base their claim on the fact that, like such thinkers, he saw domestic and political power as analogous. Those who deny the affinity accept that Hobbes used the analogy, but point out that rather than modelling authority in the state on the natural power of the father in the family, he described voluntaristic bonds in civil society and likened familial ties to these. He thereby challenged the whole patriarchal thesis, using the familial-political parallel only to emphasize the ubiquity of consent as the basis of *all* authority relations.[11] While we might not be directly concerned with whether or not Hobbes was a patriarchalist, the type of rule he describes in the family clearly does have important implications for women.

If families are the basic units in the state of nature, it will be they who compete with one another in the same way that states, despite their internal order, are at war in an international state of nature. Hobbes acknowledges just such a situation: 'as small families did then; so now do cities and kingdoms which are but greater families, for their own security, enlarge their own dominions' (XVII, p. 174). If the analogy holds, it implies that families must operate as security systems for their members with order being guaranteed by a sovereign equivalent. The great family in the state of nature is described in just such a manner: 'a little monarchy' where 'the father or master is the sovereign' (XX, p. 200). Even in civil society, Hobbes says, the parent should be accorded a sovereign's honour in the family since 'the father and master, being before the institution of commonwealth, absolute sovereigns in their own families', had such honour 'originally by nature' (XXII, p. 223; XXVII, p. 276). There seems little doubt, then, that he saw patriarchal power pre-existing civil authority.

It follows that the individuals who compete in the state of nature must be the male heads of households. But it does not follow that they lead a familial community united by natural bonds and an ethic contrary to the competitive ethos. The Hobbesian family is in fact an entirely utilitarian affair whose members—like those who will enter the broader political association—never surmount a fragmented self-interest to forge a higher sense of unity. They cohere for purposes of protection and if family security breaks down, as Hobbes believes it often will, members revert to the state of war (XX, p. 200). Even in the family, then, the individual is the basic component; the association remains, in Zvesper's words, 'an embryonic but abortive voluntary polity'.[12] The proliferation of *families* in the state of nature is not therefore necessarily at odds with Hobbes's individualism. But is this equally true for *patriarchal families?* In order to remain consistent, he will be obliged to offer sound prudential reasons as to why sons would consent to parental dominion and why women, if they are not equal partners, would voluntarily submit to a husband's authority.

Hobbes's main concern in discussing the family is precisely to show that its relations arise from consent and therefore that it is an artificial, or political, association. He aims thereby to strike patriarchalism at its heart by demonstrating that natural authority nowhere exists. To drive his point home, it is the father–son relation which he must focus upon, but in developing the argument, he invokes the power of mothers. Although such persons remain shadowy figures of obscure status,[13] it is still possible to elicit some sense of their position in his overall schema.

Hobbes recognizes two routes to sovereignty. The first, that of institution, is the logical culmination of his original analysis of free and equal individuals. Fearing one another and sufficiently equal to establish no enduring power among themselves, they contract together, agreeing to lay down their natural right and create a sovereign who will govern them. However, he realizes that commonwealths do not usually originate in this manner; dominion is more commonly the result of acquisition. This appears to be a natural relationship since it arises from superior strength, but force in a world of virtual equals yields too unstable an order to eliminate war. Reliable authority can endure only where the agreement of the governed exists and so Hobbes rationalizes the natural origin of conquest by transforming it into a relationship of consent:

> dominion is then acquired to the victor, when the vanquished to avoid the present stroke of death, covenanteth either in express words, or by other sufficient signs of the will, that so long as his life, and the liberty of his body is allowed him, the victor shall have the use thereof, as his pleasure.
>
> (XX. p. 199)

Subjection by natural means thus becomes artificial as it is institutionalized by compact; equality passes into a relationship of stable and legitimate subordination. Hobbes argues, on this basis, that both types of sovereignty are ultimately equivalent. Both originate in fear, either of one's peers or of a conqueror, and each exemplifies an exchange whereby mutual self-interest is satisfied, one party gaining unqualified power and the other, peace and protection against death.

Hobbes goes on to identify two, structurally similar, ways in which dominion by acquisition might arise: by generation and by conquest, that is 'by natural force; as when a man maketh his children, to submit themselves, and their children to his government, as being able to destroy them if they refuse; or by war subdueth his enemies to his will, giving them their lives on that condition' (XX, p. 177). Relations between children and parents must follow the route of dominion by acquisition, since there is no doubt that the child is physically inferior. The parent's power over infants is absolute in the state of nature: he/she may sell or give them to others; pawn, sacrifice or kill them,[14] for in that state each has a natural right to use others in any way which will aid their own preservation. But this too is an unstable relationship, since the child will grow to become an enemy. It is in the parent's interest to win the child's consent in the continual search of allies, and the child is obliged to give it to those who nurture and preserve it in its youthful dependence. Parental dominion, in short, neither arises from begetting the child nor does it rest on naked force. It relies upon 'the child's consent, either express, or by other sufficient arguments declared' (XX, p. 197).

How exactly the child is to declare this consent remains something of a mystery. Hobbes several times goes out of his way in other contexts to exclude children from his arguments, on the grounds that they do not yet possess the reason necessary for consent. They are unable to follow through the logical chains of reasoning required to deduce the natural laws which are a requirement of peace. Instead, they rely on parental rule and habit; they are excused offences against natural law (V, p. 86; XI, p. 127; XVI, p. 170; XXVII, p. 271). It may be that consent can only be *assumed* until maturity, but that the family plays an important educational role in teaching the child that its acquiescence does so rest.[15] Or it may be that *de facto* submission suffices as a form of tacit consent, resting on the fourth law of nature, which calls for gratitude for gifts received.[16] Thomas concludes that in fact infants can never be said to consent to anything and that Hobbes's efforts here reveal a failure to base the family solely on utility. The rights and duties he imposes on parents and children remain patriarchal ideals.[17]

Whatever the problems arising from childhood consent, it is clearly a necessary strategy if Hobbes is to contest all aspects of natural authority. But from our perspective a greater dilemma emerges. Hobbes no more believes that dual authority can persist in the family than it can in the state, so the question arises as to which parent is to exercise dominion. The answer to this will determine not only conjugal relations but also credentials for a role in political society.

We have already seen that Hobbes declares men and women equal in the state of nature, in so far as attaining power is concerned. This status appears to be maintained when Hobbes introduces the question of parental authority: 'For as to the generation, God hath ordained to man a helper; and there be always two that are equally parents: the dominion therefore over the child, *should* belong equally to both; and he be equally subject to both' (XX, p. 197; emphasis added). Nevertheless, I think that we need to be careful in interpreting this passage. Hobbes does not usually base his claims on divine intervention, and its invocation here must surely signify an attack on patriarchalists who did. If two parents have natural dominion over their offspring, then paternity cannot carry special privileges. But the tense Hobbes uses here is a subjunctive one. He does not actually believe that generation yields dominion and therefore no parental powers, equal or otherwise, can derive from it. The real discussion focuses on the relations of consent that might develop between man and woman, given the proviso that 'no man can obey two masters' (XX, p. 197). It is at this juncture that Hobbes refers back to his individualist model with its renunciation of natural authority and its claim that men and women cannot determine the issue of superiority without war.

If the sexes remain in a state of nature with each other and make no contractual arrangement, then Hobbes accepts that dominion lies with the mother. For in the absence of marriage laws, the father may well remain unknown and it is the woman who has power of life and death over the infant. If she preserves it, it is to her that it owes its life and hence its subjection: 'every woman that bears children, becomes both a *mother* and a *lord*'.[18] If on the other hand a contract is made, its outcome is in principle contingent.

To illustrate this, Hobbes cites the Amazons, where dominion is distributed in a most egalitarian fashion, daughters remaining with their mothers and sons returning to fathers (XX, pp. 197f). The example is an interesting one and not, I would argue, to be taken at face value. For, on the one hand, it is a most unusual case because it refers to societies that are sexually segregated; its solution would not be available under circumstances of cohabitation. And on the other, it is not gratuitous that the instance Hobbes cites in which women have made so egalitarian a deal, is one where the women in question had a reputation for strength and pugnacity. The significance of this will become clear shortly. But clearly this is a most unrepresentative case, and if it shows that the contract is variable in principle, it does little to suggest that a beneficial outcome for women is common. On an abstract level, Hobbes simply maintains that the child is in the father's power if its mother is and vice versa. Either way, authority stems not from any biological or emotional tie but from the power which the dominant partner has to determine the child's destiny. 'Father' is for Hobbes no more a natural term than 'mother': anyone who preserves the child acquires the appropriate title.

If women enter a contract, they may either limit it to 'society of bed only', in which case no parental dominion is relinquished, or extend it to 'society of all things'.[19] What has exercised feminists' minds is the fact that although Hobbes offers no obvious reason why equal women should enter a contract that disadvantages them, this appears to be the usual outcome.[20] In commonwealths, Hobbes informs us, there is no controversy over contractual terms, because civil law determines conjugal relations 'and for the most part, but not always, the sentence is in favour of the father'. The reason is that 'for the most part commonwealths have been erected by the fathers, not by the mothers of families' (XX, p. 197). This implies both that men write civil law in their own favour and that they must have been the dominant force in the state of nature, since it is they who are in a position to create a civil power which they use to institutionalize their prior advantage. His comments regarding sexual equality notwithstanding, Hobbes does seem to accept this latter implication. At best he simply ignores women when speaking of the family, as when he defines its constituents as 'a man and his children' or 'a man and his servants' or 'a man, and his children, and servants together' (XX, p. 200). And at worst he describes it, as we have seen, as positively patriarchal, as when he advises that children be taught

that originally the father of every man was also his sovereign lord, with power over him of life and death; and that the fathers of families, when by instituting a commonwealth, they resigned that absolute power, yet it was never intended, they should lose the honour due unto them

(XXX, p. 300)

But what can we infer about the mother? Why did she originally submit and what becomes of her status in the family? Several possible answers present themselves: she might be treated as a slave, servant or child—all subordinate roles which Hobbes does discuss—or she may remain a deliberate enigma.

Clearly she is not a slave. The role is an uninteresting one for Hobbes because it involves only naked force. Since a state of war endures, the owner keeps the slave in bondage and the latter will rebel at the earliest opportunity. In other words, this remains a natural relationship but bestows no authority; it yields *de facto* power but no *right* of dominion. If there are women slaves, their sex is irrelevant to their situation and they cannot be members of a family, whose relations rest on consent.

The possibility of women being servants is a more plausible one. Brennan and Pateman dismiss it on the grounds that servanthood, like slavery, originates in force.[21] But this is true of all sovereignty by acquisition; it does not preclude legitimate relations of subordination as long as the weaker party consents to subjection in exchange for life. Now, the fact that the sexes have a rough equality in nature would seem to rule out the origin of women's subjugation in force, but this might equally be argued of the master and his servant. Hobbes's point is not, however, that natural strength is impotent, but that the power it yields is insecure. If the woman were temporarily subdued by force and consented to her subordination in exchange for life, then she would have entered a covenant that morally obliged her to service her husband. Indeed, it is only on the basis of such an unequal relationship that a lasting agreement could be made, since equals can never escape the state of war unless it is by instituting a superior authority. It is therefore irrelevant to Hobbes's argument that one partner should have exercised natural force as a means to initiating a contract from which he(/she) gains a greater benefit; it happens in all relationships originating in conquest.

Although both sexes potentially have the 'strength or prudence' to triumph thus, Hobbes does believe the male to be at an advantage: 'men are, naturally fitter than women, for actions of labour and danger' (XIX, p. 195). In other words, despite the ostensibly voluntary nature of women's submission, it remains ultimately founded on superior male strength and thus on a natural advantage men possess. Although there is no necessity that contracts in the state of nature should take this form—and this would be why the Amazons' reputed strength permitted an exception—there seems to be a good chance of it, in which case the husband will enjoy the same rights over his wife as the master does over his servant: 'master also of all he hath: and may exact use thereof; that is to say, of his goods, of his labour, of his servants, and of his children, as often as he shall think fit' (XX, pp. 199f). It is this relationship that subsequently crystallized in matrimonial laws underwritten by civil authority.

The possibility of the woman's status being that of a child seems less likely, although such a position is not very different from that of servants in so far as children's weakness obliges them to exchange obedience for preservation. The suggestion that woman's legal position might be tantamount to that of the child arises from Chapman's contention that the father's absolute power in the Hobbesian family is modelled on that of the Roman *Patria Potestas*.[22] Where marriage was with *manus,* the wife was placed in the position of a daughter in relation to property rights. But Brennan and Pateman are surely right in rejecting this solution, on the grounds that it was too much at variance with seventeenth-century practice and is anyway an unnecessary paradigm, since Hobbes's individualism could readily yield the contractarian family without resort to a Roman model.[23]

This leaves only Brennan and Pateman's own solution, shared by Okin, which is that Hobbes deliberately left the status of wives enigmatic. His reason for doing this, they claim, was to camouflage his capitulation to patriarchalists, since he could subvert women's equal authority in the family only by conceding a natural superiority to men—as when he admits to their 'greater parts of wisdom and courage'.[24] Hobbes's silence does not however rule out the probability that he assumed women's contracts would usually leave them the status of conjugal servant. A natural superiority would not accrue to all men to give them automatic victory, but where it did, Hobbes might plausibly have argued that this was not due to any abstract and irrational principle such as the patriarchalists might use. Instead, he suggests good reasons why women, out of rational self-interest, ought normally to consent to subjugation/protection under a stronger power, just as the mass of citizens willingly transfer their natural rights to the great Leviathan. Yet between the logical individualism and the naturalistic assumptions regarding women, there is a fatal inconsistency and it is this concession which subsequent liberals will exploit to strip the doctrine of its egalitarian implications.

A final implication must be drawn from the conclusion that whatever women's status in the family, it is an inferior one. If the protagonists in the war of all against all are male heads of families, then it is they who have an interest in negotiating peace. Hobbes has been explicit that it is such persons who generally forge commonwealths by acquisition, but he leaves the impression that they must also be the contractors in commonwealths by institution.[25] There is nothing in the original account of individuals to suggest that men are any more inclined to develop the reason necessary for recognizing natural law and thus the importance of the state, than women are. But there is some evidence that Hobbes actually believed it so. In sketching conditions for a ruler's popularity, for example, he writes that he 'needs no more, for his own part, to turn the hearts of his subjects to him, but that they see him able absolutely to govern his own family' (XXX, p. 309). And in establishing credentials for recognizing the laws of nature, he argues that of these 'no man, that pretends but reason enough to govern his private family, ought to be ignorant'.[26] If ruling a family is indeed a sign, or requirement, of political qualification, then the dearth of matriarchs has obvious consequences in excluding women. But in any case, Hobbes has already announced that each family needs one master, who will almost invariably be the male, and critical decisions such as instituting a state would clearly be his should any dispute arise.

In conclusion, then, the *form* of Hobbes's argument that all authority must rest on consent, overturns claims regarding woman's natural inferiority. However, although Hobbes says little overtly about women, he does seem to retain sufficient patriarchal assumptions in this respect to introduce, perhaps in spite of himself, a fatal inconsistency into his work. Once women submit in the family, due to the natural unfitness they frequently evince, then by implication they renounce the opportunity to register political consent. Their acquiescence to the state can then be mediated, even imposed, by their husbands.

Filmer's tracts on patriarchy were first written more or less contemporaneously with *Leviathan* and they mount a challenge to Hobbes's work. However, they gained real popularity only during the 1680s, whence they incited Locke to publish a refutation. Although this project is most evident in his *First Treatise,* it has been convincingly argued that Locke wrote both *Treatises on Government* as a single discourse (between 1679 and 1683) for this purpose. He possibly postponed completion of the *Second Treatise* (which additionally takes issue with Hobbes's absolutism) when Filmer's *Patriarchia* was published in 1680, in order to engage in the more detailed refutation that we find in the *First Treatise.*[27] This latter work is not widely read today since it is regarded as having little more than historical interest. Yet when it comes to early liberal pronouncements on women, it is an important work, showing clearly how the original contentions regarding their position derived from the attack on patriarchalism.

Filmer used biblical sources to sustain his theory, and although Locke's penchant is for rational rather than scriptural discourse, he challenges Filmer in his own terms in the *First Treatise.* Looking at the Creation and Fall, Filmer had argued that the power God gave Adam over Eve and over his children was testimony to his absolute and God-given monarchical power. In attacking this line of argument, Locke reveals his attitude to women. His interpretation of Genesis has further interest in the light of discussion in the previous chapter, and the very necessity that Locke felt to reply to Filmer in these terms, reveals the influence religious thinking still exerted in the seventeenth century.

Looking at relations between the sexes, Locke contends that the whole species was made in God's image by virtue of its intelligence. On this basis it gained dominion over lesser creatures and so the original grant must have been made to Adam and Eve equally. Eve's subsequent subjection to her husband was an 'accidental' consequence of the Fall and does not exclude women from the more general dominion exercised by the race.[28]

Locke goes on to offer two possible interpretations of Eve's malediction. She might represent all women, such that her subjection is passed on to them. But this would yield only *conjugal power* to husbands, not *political power.* The distinction is significant for Locke's rejection of patriarchalism since it denies that Eve's curse can be taken as evidence for husbands' (political) power of life and death over women (and thus *a fortiori,* over anyone else). But this prompts a definition of an alternative conjugal power which it might yield: 'the Power that every husband hath to order the things of private Concernment in his Family, as Proprietor of the Goods and Land there, and to have his Will take place before that of his wife and all things of their common Concernment' (Locke, *Two Treatise* I: 48, 67).

It is quite possible, however, that God's punishment was reserved for Eve alone and that His reference to a general subjection and pain accruing to women were merely prophetic: 'we see that generally the Laws of Mankind and customs of Nations have ordered it so'. This would have been to continue in the vein of woman's merely contingent inferiority, were Locke not to have added that 'there is, I grant, a foundation in Nature for it' (I: 47). Although it is unclear quite what this foundation might be, it is probable that Locke associated it with women's reproductive capacities: their 'natural' weakness which sustains the conventional disadvantages that women suffer.[29]

Formally, Locke's account is radical. If women are not cursed in perpetuity, then they have no duty to honour the prophesy. A woman is free to strike a better bargain for herself 'if the Circumstances either of her Condition or Contract with her Husband' should permit it (I: 47). In other words, his position here is similar to that of Hobbes. Women are naturally the 'weaker sex' (as Locke calls them), but there is no reason why they should not strive for a favourable conjugal contract if, as in the case of queens, they are able. Here then is the novel and revolutionary core of liberalism: every individual is at liberty to compete for autonomy and success through the exertion of will. Yet it is unlikely that many women will succeed because their natural and customary disadvantages remain. Thus emerges the hiatus which prevents the doctrine from fulfilling its radical, universalist promises.

It is in this context that we must read Locke's references to women in the *Second Treatise,* where he again discusses distinctions between conjugal and political power. It is now less obvious that his argument is specifically aimed at a refutation of patriarchalism but it would be a mistake to interpret it as a genuine concern for women's status. Locke's statements here lend credence to the suggestion that he was writing both treatises more or less simultaneously and his claims in the Second bear the same ambivalence regarding the voluntary yet naturalistic basis of women's position, that we found in the First.

Confusion undoubtedly arises from the complex polemic in which Locke is engaged. On the one hand, he wants to contest a husband's absolute (political) power over his wife in order to eliminate this particular piece of ammunition from the patriarchalist arsenal. He thus describes a limited and contractual relationship between spouses. But on the other hand, he does not wish to reduce the family to an institution predicated on pure consent, as Hobbes had done. He intends instead to maintain certain natural bonds there in order to demonstrate—again in opposition to patriarchalism—that since domestic and political relations are of a different ilk, the latter can never be derived from the former. The problem is then to fit women into this complicated nexus of contractual and natural relations, since it is they who are the crucial link in uniting, yet keeping apart, the familial (natural) and juridical (contractual) spheres.

Locke speaks of the relationship forged by parents in entirely functional and contractual terms. '*Conjugal Society* is made up by a voluntary Compact between Man and Woman' (II: 78). Yet the purpose of matrimony is a natural one: procreation. Since it is in order to fulfil obligations to their offspring that the parents stay together, it follows that they might legitimately part once their progeny mature. It is to Locke's credit that he accepts this implication (II: 81), although its corollary is the unsubstantiated assumption that women and children must originally remain with a father because they are dependent upon him.

Besides the access to one another's bodies required for procreation, marital relations involve a common interest in the production of family property (II: 78, 80, 83). It is power over the community of goods which is the main concern of the marriage contract. Like Hobbes, Locke insists that only one person can rule where disagreement is likely (although he finds cooperation rather than a state of war or conquest to be more normal between the sexes) and he couples this with a reiteration of his claim in the *First Treatise* that women are simultaneously naturally inferior and free to make as advantageous a contract as possible. Domestic authority

naturally falls to the Man's share, as the abler and the stronger. But this reaching but to the things of their common Interest and property, leaves the Wife in the full and free possession of what by Contract is her peculiar Right, and gives her Husband no more power over her life, than she has over his.

(II: 82)

In other words, women might keep those possessions which they are perspicacious enough to exclude from common ownership in the contract (although it is unlikely that many would be able to insist upon this, other than a few heiresses) and they retain certain natural rights, such as those to life and their offsprings' honour, regardless of its terms. But over common concerns it is usually the husband who has authority due to his innate superiority.

Although there is no natural reason why paternity should confer absolute power on husbands and fathers then, Locke believes that there are nevertheless sound natural reasons why a man's qualities should give him authority over his wife and children, even if it is limited and rests, in the woman's case, on consent.

Unlike Hobbes and Filmer, Locke distinguishes parent—child relations from the conjugal ties for which they are the primary *raison d'être*. Here the bond is an entirely natural one, although Locke has some difficulty in establishing on what grounds this is so. The topic arises in the *First Treatise,* where he contests Filmer's claim that the very act of begetting gives a father absolute power over his progeny. Now for Hobbes, remember, it was preservation rather than generation that yielded such absolute authority. Locke must associate begetting with some power in order to describe the family as natural, but he must also limit it if he is not to concede the patriarchalist case. He therefore argues that the power of life and death belongs to God alone, and to make this point he needs to challenge the Aristotelian account of generation.

At first Locke seems only to be making Hobbes's point: that even if begetting did yield power, it would be to both parents.

But having acknowledged the mother's nourishing role, he moves on to challenge the father's spritual one:

And it is so hard to imagine the rational Soul should presently Inhabit the yet unformed Embrio, as soon as the Father has done his part in the Act of Generation, that if it must be supposed to derive anything from the Parents, it must certainly owe most to the Mother

(I: 55)

Whatever their respective contributions to the child's substance, it is not the father, but God, who imparts the crucial life and soul into it. Although Locke does not mention Aristotle (or Aquinas), this is obviously the theory which he has in mind, since it was this which Filmer had presented when he argued that God gave man sovereignty over women 'as being the Nobler and Principal Agent of Generation' (I: 55).[30] In Locke's view, begetting is thus a dual task but God is a third party who, in imparting vitality, retains sole right to retract it. Begetting, then, contra Filmer, does not bestow absolute power.

Nevertheless, Locke does want to contend that generation yields parents some natural authority, otherwise he will be back to the utilitarian Hobbesian family where relations are indistinguishable from those in the state. He therefore argues that natural law prescribes parents a right to their offsprings' honour and obedience. The bond of subjection which this entails is likened to the swaddling clothes which constrain yet support the infant during its early weakness (II: 55). The right to infantile obedience is thus complemented by a reciprocal duty. Children also have natural rights—to nourishment, property sufficient to support life and education from their begetters—and the obligations these entail are taught to parents by 'Natural Love and Tenderness' (I: 90, 93, 97, 101; II: 63, 68). Locke's reasoning here follows a similar path to that used more explicitly in the *Second Treatise,* where he establishes that natural law obliges individuals to sustain one another even in the state of nature. As God's workmanship children, like His other creations, must be maintained in a suitable condition of life and general well-being so that they might fulfil the purposes for which He made them. In the case of children it invokes only a more active duty, which falls specifically on parents.

It is the grounding of this parental duty which proves troublesome to Locke. At times he contends, like Hobbes, that it is guardianship rather than begetting which bestows it, such that 'foster-fathers' (sic) may acquire its powers (II: 65; I: 100). But it is difficult to see how the obligations that parenthood incurs can be allocated if they do not arise from actual generation. More commonly, then, Locke admits that 'young ones . . . are to be sustained by those that got them'; that 'the Father . . . is bound to take care of those he hath begot' since 'my children also, being born of me, had a right to be maintained out of my labour or substance' (II: 79, 80, 183). If it is God who bestows life, the natural parent is yet a significant mediator in the divine drama (II: 67). Without such natural relations, which throw women and children into dependence on the fathers who share their rights and obligations, Locke would be left, like Hobbes, with no sound basis for advocating monogamy and the patriarchal family: institutions whose significance will emerge shortly.

To summarize so far, Locke has established a range of powers: conjugal (contractual), parental (natural) and magisterial (political). He does not see authority as all of a piece as had Filmer (all natural) or Hobbes (all contractual), although there is the crucial slippage of category when he posits natural reasons for women's habitual contractual subordination. As one critic points out, these distinctions would render Locke's thought more serviceable than that of Hobbes, to a posterity which wished to differentiate the family from the public arena as an antidote to the latter's individualist and competitive ethic.[31] Locke's own concern, however, is to challenge patriarchalist arguments for absolute monarchy without destablizing either the authority of the state or the husband's domination in the family. He wants to challenge the patriarchal state but not the patriarchal family and this is problematic for him precisely because it was the latter which patriarchalists had used to justify the former. *Prima facie,* women's subjection in the family now resembles that of subjects in the state, in so far as both rest on voluntary consent. But women's submission can be said to rest on enlightened self-interest only if their natural disability is established, whereas civil relations are predicated precisely on the equality of natural persons. It is now necessary to see what political implications follow from women's place in the Lockean family.

Locke's aim in the *Second Treatise* is to show that legitimate rule rests on consent and thus to distinguish political obligation from the natural authority found in the family. Our main questions must be whether women share an interest in the purposes for which Locke says the commonwealth is instituted and to what extent they are active members of the body politic. Because of the significance which Locke attaches to property in discussing the origins and functions of the state, it will be instructive to examine women's relationship to this phenomenon especially carefully. I shall suggest that the terms of the marriage contract are crucial to the outcome. It must be acknowledged at the outset, however, that Locke rarely refers specifically to women in political contexts and any conclusions must rest largely upon inference and conjecture.

Aware that social contracts were not the normal route to statehood, Locke sketched a more credible historical development which is essentially a peaceful equivalent to Hobbes's commonwealth by acquisition. In the state of nature, where families were once autonomous and scattered, ''tis obvious to conceive how easie it was . . . for the *Father of the Family* to become the Prince of it' by sheer inertia (II: 74, 110, 112). It was

almost natural for Children by a tacit, and scarce avoidable consent to make way for the *Father's Authority and Government*. They had been accustomed in their childhood to follow his Direction, and to refer their little differences to him, and when they were Men, who fitter to rule them? . . . where could they have a fitter Umpire than he, by whose care they had every one been sustain'd, and brought up, and who had a tenderness for them all?

(II: 75)

Locke is at pains to show that this is not patriarchalism because it rests on tacit consent. The father recommends himself as ruler on the basis of past performance and by the affection which tempers his power: on prudential rather than natural grounds. No greater security for peace, liberties and fortunes could be found. Yet Locke does seem to have made substantial concessions to patriarchalism here and not least because, as in Hobbes's case, the mother seems once again to have disappeared. Locke has repeatedly told us that she equally deserves her children's honour and obedience in exchange for nurturing them, yet there is no suggestion that queens would emerge 'almost' naturally out of this habitual relationship. Evidently, the wife's subordination in the pre-civil family paves the way for her subsequent political subjection; we must assume that, as Brennan and Pateman put it, 'the marriage contract involves the wife's "consent" to her husband's transmogrification'.[32]

Locke offers a further path by which fathers gain a special authority in civil society. One of the crucial arguments in the refutation of patriarchalism had been that while parents guide their offspring during their pre-rational youth, the latter emerge on maturity as free adults whose consent must be received before further authority can be exercised over them. Yet despite this limitation and despite equal natural rights of both parents over their progeny, 'there is *another Power* ordinarily *in the Father,* whereby he has a tie on the Obedience of the Children' for a much longer period. This is 'the Power Men generally have *to bestow their Estates* on those, who please them best' (II: 72). It is law and custom—that is, the habitual form taken by the marriage contract in civil society—which grant such power to the father. This is important because inheriting is presented by Locke as a form of express consent to government. The right to bequeath therefore allows the father both influence over his sons' political allegiance, since only the favoured inherit (there is no mention of daughters), and the opportunity to write political obligations into the terms of inheritance, since 'that Estate being his Fathers Property, he may dispose or settle it as he pleases' (II: 116). This allows Locke to surmount the practical limitation on paternal power without damaging its moral validity,[33] permitting the father considerable political leverage thanks to the terms of the marriage contract which generally make him sole executor of the family property.

The argument above suggests than men gain political influence thanks to their right to bestow the family property. But it has also been suggested (in line with Marxist thinking) that a major *purpose* of Locke's argument was precisely to provide a theoretical basis for the absolute right of the male to pass his property on to his rightful heirs.[34] Such would be the obvious corollary to a theory which saw the protection of estates as a primary end of government, for what would be the point of such protection unless private acquisitions could be securely bequeathed to the next generation? The 'natural' infirmity of women would then be deliberately compounded by the socio-economic disadvantages imposed upon them by the marriage contract, in order that their resultant dependence might give husbands the required power over their fertility. Certainly Locke presents monogamy as advantageous in encouraging the provision, security and indivisibility of property: 'so their Industry might be encouraged, and their Interest better united, to make Provision, and lay up Goods for their common Issue, which uncertain mixture, or easie and frequent Solutions of Conjugal Society would mightily disturb' (II: 80). He has also offered reasons as to why it should be the husband who administers it. According to this interpretation, his statements concerning women's natural weakness would not then be a dispensable inconsistency in the argument but central to it, since the establishment of monogamous marriage (during reproducing years) and the patriarchal family, are prerequisite to the sustaining of private property via patrilineal inheritance.

Locke has already acknowledged that civil law and custom favour men in matters matrimonial. This suggests that it is they who exercise political control. We have already seen this to be the case where paternal slides into princely authority, but what about civil governments instituted by social contract? Is there anything in Locke's formal account of the passage from state of nature to political association, to suggest that women might not share equal rights in the latter?

The *Second Treatise* begins with a description of the state of nature. As in the Hobbesian state, there are variations but still each is born 'to all the same advantages of Nature, and the use of the same faculties' (II: 4). All are equal in a moral sense because they are God's workmanship and this yields them universal natural rights to life, liberty and the property needed for subsistence. Natural rights are more circumscribed for Locke than for Hobbes because laws of nature preach a general ethic of sociability, even mutual aid. It is less fear of death than the inconvenience of lacking an impartial adjudicator, especially troublesome where property is concerned, that drives actors to consent to civil society.

Locke thus shares Hobbes's sexually egalitarian framework, even if its basis is a moral rather than materialist one. In addition to their moral equivalence, all his individuals are born with at least equal potential for reason (a legacy of Christian notions of the equality of souls) and for autonomy, since they can all shift for themselves. The concept of property occupies a pivotal point in the further development of the argument, because it explains the purpose of the state which such individuals agree to found: 'The great and chief end . . . of mens uniting into Commonwealths, and putting themselves under Government, *is the preservation of their Property*' (II: 124). It has already been suggested that monogamy and father-rule aid this purpose; we must next consider whether it would be a purpose of sufficient attraction for women, for them to consent to the instituting of the state.

At times Locke defines property extremely broadly: the natural rights possessed by everyone to life, liberty and estate yield a property in those things, from whose protection all will surely benefit. However, a woman's estate, as well as a significant portion of her liberty, has been in most cases surrendered in the marriage contract. It is only her life which Locke places specifically under the aegis of political power. Under this broad definition, women will therefore receive limited benefits from the state, although these will be sufficient to oblige them to obedience to it. However, Locke at other times equates property with estate alone, and if it is the protection of property in this narrower sense that is the state's prime concern, its appeal for women is less evident. Having a natural right to their own property, men allow government interference here only with their consent. But women have already consented to forfeit control over their property, in the marriage contract. At best their interests in its protection are indirect and mediated by husbands.

Women's interests in instituting political association thus remain unclear; certainly they are less direct or pronounced than those of their husbands. Such a conclusion conforms well with subsequent liberal assumptions that women's interests lie only in the private realm. While for men the right to emigrate is essential, since this allows that withdrawal of consent without which its grant becomes meaningless,[35] for women retreat into the family offers an other dimension where questions of the state's legitimacy remain essentially irrelevant. It does not much matter whether they consent or not. Men have good reason to consent to the state because they enjoy its protection and services, but for women these are largely provided by the family. It is therefore appropriate that their consent to authority should be expressed via the marriage contract. Of course, the state does intervene here, because it enforces a contract which disadvantages women, but it is inconceivable at this stage that the latter might organize to overturn particular pieces of patriarchal legislation.

We are left, then, with the questions of why women would have consented to the state and whether in fact Locke assumed that they would be party to the original contract at all. After all, they were already members of patriarchal families in the state of nature, and their husbands might well be supposed to have consented on their behalf. Although there is no textual evidence which allows a definitive answer, it does seem likely that women were implicitly excluded from giving express consent in either of the ways that Locke specified (inheriting property and participating in the social contract).[36] Of course, Locke was writing before universal suffrage appeared on the agenda as a means of expressing consent, and thus before women's exclusion from citizenship was made explicit. But his liberalism leaves at least an impression that women were already being excluded from those active expressions which were necessary for political rights and citizenship.

If property offered a central motive for entering civil society and a means of consenting to it, it was also people's relationship to their property which in many ways illustrated and facilitated their capacity for active political participation, for Locke. While women's marital status yields them a relationship to property which seems to bring only a tenuous interest in the state, I shall now suggest that it also appears to rob them of credentials for active political membership (of the 'majority' which sets up a government) and the exercise of political rights.

Locke contends that although God gave the earth to the race in common, he intended it for 'the use of the Industrious and

Rational' who might appropriate it by their labour (II: 34). It is labour which imparts value to nature, by rendering it useful for subsistence. Locke gives enthusiastic sanction to this form of corporeal activity, by which the property a person has in their own body is mixed with the products it works upon, to yield ownership in a very intimate fashion. There is no reason to exclude women from such works of acquisition for they are clearly capable of the acts Locke offers as examples—picking acorns and gathering apples—and would, in the seventeenth century, have dominated some of the value-adding forms of labour he cites: producing bread, bran, cloth, dying-drugs, planting and cutivating (II: 28, 32, 43, 46).[37] From this individualist perspective it is obvious why women would consent to a government which would protect their industry, though not why they would consent to a marriage transferring its products to a husband.

It is, however, *unequal* property that causes sufficient conflict to motivate the institution of government. Money disrupts the initial equilibrium by allowing the more industrious to transcend natural laws against hoarding and thus spoiling, perishables. Henceforth only some persons can accumulate limited resources like land, while others must sell their labour in exchange for their subsistence.

Women do not seem to fall into either of the latter categories because although they are quite capable of shifting for themselves, Locke implies that it is in fact to families that property accrues in the state of nature. In an abundant environment, for example, he asks 'what reason could anyone have there to enlarge his Possessions beyond the use of his Family, and a plentiful supply to its Consumption . . .?' Surely land would remain unworked in so far as it 'was more than would supply the Conveniences of Life to be had there for him and his Family' (II: 48, 36, 38, 74). Women's labour must be subsumed within the family. Now, the servant alienates his labour by means of a contract, and Locke is not averse to including in the master's own labour 'the Turfs my servant has cut', which 'become my property' (II: 28). But here the exchange of labour for a wage makes at least formal sense in terms of mutual self-interest. When women alienate their labour and its products via a (marriage) contract, there is no obvious reciprocity. In other words, Locke's abstract picture of industrious individuals cannot explain why women would alienate their property and so become men's dependants. This was why he had to intrude a natural disability which made it rational for them to make the transfer to a more able partner.

What is significant here is not just that the woman consents to economic dependence for scant return, however, but the political consequences that flow from it. For Locke suggests an equation between consent and reason, with reason having intimate links to property.

For Locke each child is born to, but not in, reason. It must therefore be guided through its nonage until it is able to recognize natural law and achieve self-mastery. Only at this juncture will it become free, capable of acting independently, as a moral agent able to offer informed consent and thus to accept the responsibilities of citizenship. It is with this in mind that temporary parental obligations are imposed, with special emphasis placed on education.

This suggests that although each is born with the same rational potential—Locke's psychology is necessarily egalitarian in describing each mind as a blank slate to be written upon by experience—there is work to be done and hence scope for differential outcome.[38] Now, one prerequisite of mature reason is autonomy and Locke gives this a significant material component. He suggests that children are ready to leave parental guidance when 'they can be able to shift for themselves' or alternatively, when they inherit: 'when he comes to the Estate that made his *Father a Freeman, the son is a* Freeman too' (II: 60, 58). If it follows that those lacking material independence also lack the symbols and preconditions of reason, then women's marriage contracts must exclude them from the ranks of the rational.

According to Locke's theory of property, it is the life, liberty and possessions which are its constituents, that allow a man to perform the duties attached to his station. The use to which he puts his property manifests the direction and industriousness of his chosen life such that property plays both an expressive and an instrumental role: it is simultaneously a route to, and a sign of, one's rationality.[39] This implies not only that one must labour in order to qualify as rational, but also that one must own the property on which it is employed in order to determine its use and so stamp one's personality upon it.

Such a conclusion was drawn by C.B. Macpherson when he asked a question similar to our own, only wondering whether labourers, rather than women, might not be excluded from rationality and hence an active role in the state, due to their lack of estate. His answer, if controversial, is instructive. Looking to works beyond the *Two Treatises*, Macpherson concluded that one reason why Locke found labourers incapable of a rational life, was that they lacked time or opportunity to raise their thoughts above the monotonous round of daily subsistence.[40] Those without land also lost the wherewithal to demonstrate industriousness and rationality. Their reason was considered too rudimentary to grant them political rights: they remained ruled but never rulers.

How might this apply to women? Many would of course be among the ranks of labourers, among whom Locke includes spinsters and dairymaids. But even those married to property owners would only follow their husbands' orders; they would not, according to Locke, be at liberty to impose their own will on the estate and so could exercise no reason there. And in so far as capitalism's increasing separation of home and workplace increased women's toil by subjecting them to a double load of productive and domestic labour, they would most certainly fall into the ranks of those who lacked time and opportunity to develop their reason. Indeed, when Locke elsewhere explains that where 'the hand is used to the plough and the spade, the head is seldom elevated to sublime notions' but must content itself with 'plain propositions, and a short reasoning about things familiar to their minds, and nearly allied to their daily experience', he suggests that this is even more true of 'the other sex'.[41] According to this reading, then, the marriage contract which excludes most women from command over the family property must simultaneously exclude them from the means and signs of substantial rationality.

It is implausible that Locke would have wished to classify women with infants, or with the lunatics, idiots and madmen whom he thought incapable of ever achieving reason (II: 60). Besides, he did find women able to consent to marriage. But the terms of the latter do imply them to be insufficiently rational, motivated or interested, to warrant active participation in affairs of state. Women seem destined to be among the ruled not because they are naturally irrational, but because their status and role in the family are inimical to the development of reason. Yet since these are natural to most women, the irrationality of the majority is not simply contingent. In short, if women for Locke are not naturally irrational, most are naturally destined for a social role which renders them so. Such a position would be adopted by many of Locke's liberal successors, some of whom would use it to plead for better female education in order to overcome the intellectual limitations imposed by domestic life. And even Locke seems to have believed that girls might benefit from an education similar to that given their brothers, since the child's mind is 'only as white paper, or wax, to be fashioned as one pleases'.[42] As in the interpretation of Genesis, then, Locke sustains the notion of woman's natural weakness while implying that some individuals might well escape to better their condition. Again, this mix of radicalism and élitism would be manifest in much subsequent liberal thought.

Several useful commentaries have recently touched upon the difficult question of women's place on Lockean civil society. Brennan and Pateman conclude that Locke found women lacking the rationality required to enter the social contract and that it was only fathers of families who participated, although they offer little to substantiate the claim.[43] Okin reaches a similar, if more tentative conclusion: 'the exclusion of women from political rights is implicitly justified by the assumption that, as head of his family, the father alone can represent its interests in the wider society'.[44] Melissa Butler disagrees. She finds women in Locke's work capable of the rational thought (Lockean psychology and views on education are used to support this), property acquisition (they can labour) and consent (as in marriage) that are a requirement of political membership. She concludes that Locke remained silent on the question of women's political consent only to avoid offending his audience.[45]

Lacking Locke's explicit views on this subjct, it is impossible to reach a definitive conclusion. Yet his critics' positions are not necessarily mutually exclusive. Filmer had seen clearly that the logic of consent theory would drive its exponents along the path to universal political participation. The formal aspects of Hobbes's and Locke's writings testify to this and Butler is right to point out the implications of this radical individualism. However, it is also undoubtedly true that Locke was no more willing to carry this theory through to its logical conclusion than were his contemporaries. This is why he, like Hobbes, clung to assumptions regarding women's natural inferiority that belonged to the thought of a previous age. While it is possible to dispute how far this was intentional, there can be no doubt that women's deference to husbands in both matrimonial and political matters, would be accepted wisdom for liberals well into the nineteenth century.[46] The egalitarian implications of formal contract theory have been consistently undermined by assumptions regarding a natural inequality between the contracting parties. Although agreements are voluntaristic and their outcome is in principle open, women's supposed natural infirmity has provided grounds for assuming it to be in their rational self-interest (whether or not they recognize it) to submit to husbands. There is no accompanying suggestion among liberals, that the economic inequalities of their position might also be an issue in the one-sidedness of the resolution.

In this chapter, I have suggested that a focus on women introduces a hiatus into liberal thought from its inception. The substitution of rational for natural authority flounders when it comes to sexual relationships. To this extent the framework of abstract individuals who consent to authority only on the basis of rational self-interest, is adulterated, its universalism undermined by discrimination on pre-rational grounds. It was such inconsistency that would allow early feminists both to criticize liberalism and to use its own radical premises to do so, whilst at the same time discovering that the doctrine could be put to use by their opponents.

Both Hobbes and Locke disclosed a certain radicalism in at least allowing women the potential for forging advantageous contracts. This is typical of liberal beliefs in abstract freedoms and equal rights. Yet at the same time, neither believed that many women would be successful, due to certain disadvantages they suffered. It is true that these are not natural in quite the same sense as that intended by their predecessors. The term now denotes biological weakness (in strength and function) rather than teleological inferiority (although allusions to feminine reason sometimes stray in this direction).

This implies a certain contingency, allowing the apparently liberal claim that women are free to strive for optimum status. Yet like their liberal successors, these thinkers have no interest in exploring women's plight further, to see whether their weakness might not be rectified or, failing this, compensated for. Their individualism militates against the latter solution, which would demand some stronger sense of collective responsibility. But in any case, since the very purpose of a contractual basis for society was to eliminate relationships based on force, women's physical weaknesses should never have been an issue.

Moreover, it was not self-evident in the seventeenth century that women were weaker than men in any substantial sense. There was still historical evidence of women's economic self-sufficiency, which might have sustained a genuinely egalitarian individualism in an age when ideals of the idle housewife had yet to emerge and when the boundaries between private and public life (whether material, as in the home/work split or theoretical, as in the individual/state opposition) had yet to crystallize.

There was also the experience of the English Civil War. This had seen the efflorescence of all sorts of radical religious sects (such as Quakers and Ranters) whose beliefs and practices included female equality, libertarian sexual habits and an attack on marriage.[47] Women had also been active in radical political movements. In 1649, for example, Leveller women petitioned Parliament when their leaders' lives were in danger. In response to the rough treatment they received, they produced a petition, carried to the House by 1,000 women bearing green ribbons and signed by 10,000 more. Its wording clearly shows that such women did consider politics their concern: 'Have we not an equal interest with the men of this nation in those liberties and securities contained in the *Petition of Right,* and other good laws of the land?'[48]

Although patriarchy was secured with the Restoration in 1660, feminist ideas were not completely suppressed, and by the end of the century Mary Astell was calling for an institute of higher learning for women.[49] The subjection of women, which was buried in the thought of liberalism's founding fathers, was not then sustained out of any historical or theoretical necessity. To some extent it did mirror contemporary marital practices, which were not questioned sufficiently radically due to assumptions which had been inherited, via the Scriptures, from medieval and classical times. But the late seventeenth century was also an age of emerging market relations, when women and men were for the first time being thrown into economic competition with one another. Perhaps it is therefore unsurprising that patriarchal sentiments should have been allowed to slide unhindered into a modern thought which continued to benefit its male proponents.

5   Rousseau and Wollstonecraft:
Female Virtue and Civic Virtue in the Liberal State

If the early liberal theories of Hobbes and Locke had sustained an implicit inconsistency between their egalitarian logic and natural infirmities imputed to women, with Rousseau the distinction is made clear and explicit: civic equality is juxtaposed with a natural order in the family predicated on an irremediable sexual difference which denies to women any directly public role. The suggestion that they might freely compete with men for success, even if success will be rare, is replaced by a claim that this is contrary to nature and upset at society's peril. Rousseau reverts to an Aristotelian conservatism in defining a differential virtue and function for the two sexes and in advising that females be trained for their particular role in a manner quite different from that of males. The potential radicalism of seventeenth-century individualism was thus surrendered to a vision of the sentimental family, which would offer a new rationalization for women's private and subordinate role and which would thrive from the eighteenth century on.

The question remains whether political theorists can continue to read *The Social Contract* as though it were a gender-neutral text and Rousseau's misogyny elsewhere an expendable aberration, or whether in fact the role he gives to women in *Emile* is an essential component of his plan for social regeneration. In order to answer this, I shall look first at Rousseau's account of social corruption and his solutions to it, then at his prescriptions for women, before examining the probable relationship between the two. The second half of the chapter will show how Mary Wollstonecraft prised the political and sexual accounts apart again in order to reconstruct them in a different manner.

Rousseau begins his Second Discourse, *On the Origin of Inequality,* with a distinction between two types of human inequality: natural and moral/political. Only the first sort of inequality exists in the original state of nature, and while it is insufficient to engender any natural authority, Rousseau denies that it would produce either a Hobbesian conflagration or presuppose a Lockean natural law to prevent it. The Rousseauian natural savage is truly pre-social: isolated and self-sufficient, she/he wanders through forests fulfilling pristine needs. Conflicts remain atypical since encounters are themselves sporadic and needs are in broad equilibrium with resources. Natural woman/man suffers neither the scarcity nor conceptualization of difference, that would provoke competition for gain or glory.

Humans are motivated, however, by a faculty of self-improvement and this is brought into play as growing numbers and natural adversity invite new skills. Gradually natural woman/man learns to compare the efficacy of different abilities and to form pride in their cultivation. As advantages of cooperation emerge, they encourage stable communities and greater industry. Objects are compared as dependence upon them grows; persons are compared and sentiments of public esteem, vanity, envy and contempt ensue. Following the invention of metallurgy and agriculture, property also flourishes and with it, the disparity between persons. The strong and ingenious produce more; a division of labour emerges enhancing dependence on others and on the products which have engendered an explosion of desire. It is only now that rivalry and competition become the norm. As Hobbes recognized, this in itself can facilitate no stable order: the strong and rich are attacked by the poor, united by dreams of plunder. In response, civil society is born: the rule of law presents itself as a rational solution. For Rousseau, however, the rationality and benefits of this development are not universal. Rather, it is a cunning device fabricated by the wealthy in order to institutionalize their own advantage. The origin of political association brought 'new fetters on the poor, and gave new powers to the rich', who 'for the advantage of a few ambitious individuals, subjected all mankind to perpetual labour, slavery and wretchedness'.[1] While Rousseau's account of the transition from natural to civil society is structurally similar to that of Hobbes and Locke, then, what it reveals is a process of degeneration. Natural liberty is lost to civic servitude; the natural individual is corrupted by empty values and false needs.

The Social Contract is Rousseau's ideal solution to this state of affairs on a collective level. Here a 'good' agreement facilitates real civil liberty and a moral/legal equality which transcends all natural disadvantage. Instead of a triumph of interest for the rich and powerful, there is to be a universal citizenship which continually and actively gives consent. This is expressed as its General Will.

The General Will is an ideal, and not something necessarily manifest in the will of the majority. At first its expression is rare and imperfect, but this improves as political participation introduces a process of public education. Through its active concern with public affairs and political decision-making, the people gradually learn to discern what is in their collective interest. The public good emerges as something quite distinct from their merely aggregated private interests, because it benefits them as members of a community rather than as particular individuals. The emergence of the General Will is contingent upon a transformation of human nature: the moral and intelligent human must replace the instinct-driven animal who, though innocent, is enslaved by passion. Instead of finding himself tossed by caprice and driven by narrow self-interest, the citizen is to achieve self-mastery: emotion and appetite are to be subdued beneath the control of the enlightened self. It is this self which expresses the General Will.

The General Will that emerges must be general in the sense of being universal (everyone must be consulted) and in remaining abstract (no particular applications of general laws can be endorsed). If either condition is betrayed, particularity reigns. But despite such formal guarantees against particularity, its transcendence ultimately depends upon individuals ceasing to be committed to, or blinded by, selfish perceptions and interests. In sum, the citizen body must develop civic virtue. When it succeeds, each is able both to obey the law and be free, since each is the author of their restraint and since those restraints coincide perfectly with the true desires of the individual as a moral being.

One of the major problems posed by *The Social Contract* is how the corrupt persons of *The Second Discourse* are to undergo the transformation necessary to express the General Will. However, Rousseau breaches the vicious circle via the person of the legislator: appearing from outside the state and deriving no benefit from its arrangements, he understands the nature of its people sufficiently to offer them an appropriate constitution. Living under good laws provides the initial education that will set the people on their way to civic virtue. But Rousseau also offered an alternative solution to this problem. In *Emile* he suggests that individuals might be saved from corruption by the right sort of education. Emile is taught how to become an exemplary man by retaining his natural goodness. Secluded in a rural retreat, he retains his autonomy by learning to restrain his desires to that level where they can be fulfilled within nature's boundaries. His education is a process of learning self-control and temperance in order that he might remain free by avoiding dependence.

Were Rousseau to have written *The Social Contract* alone, the most obvious conclusion would be that women must participate as citizens if the required generality of will is to manifest itself, otherwise the result would be an expression of, among other things, a particularly male interest. Yet in *Emile* we learn that participatory citizenship is to be a specifically male prerogative and that Sophy's education is to be quite at variance with that of her future spouse since it is designed to equip her for a very different role. It is to the account of sexual difference that we must turn next and this takes us back to *The Discourse on Inequality*.

The first stage of Rousseau's state of nature is more sexually neutral than that of his seventeenth-century predecessors because he stresses that its constituents really are individuals rather than father of families. Copulation is brief, spontaneous and indiscriminate—'every woman' Rousseau writes (at once adopting the male standpoint), 'equally answers his purpose'.[2] The father, ignorant as to the identity of his offspring, reveals no affection for it or for its mother. The woman remains self-sufficient, carrying her child with her and nursing it as she goes; even for her, 'the offspring was nothing . . . as soon as it could do without her'.[3] Sexually differentiated but ungendered, these primitive beings nevertheless begin to discover conformities among themselves and to associate more—a development in which sexuality must have played a crucial role since it is the only necessary form of natural encounter.[4] With greater association and industriousness there arrives a 'first revolution, which established and distinguished families, and introduced a kind of property'.[5]

The first expansions of the human heart were the effects of a novel situation, which united husbands and wives, fathers and children, under one roof. The habit of living together soon gave rise to the finest feelings known to humanity, conjugal love and paternal affection. Every family became a little society, the more united because liberty and reciprocal attachment were the only bonds of its union. The sexes, whose manner of life had hitherto been the same, began now to adopt different ways of living. The women became more sedentary, and accustomed themselves to mind the hut and their children, while the men went abroad in search of their common subsistence.[6]

This account of the different stages of natural woman/man's development has important implications since it is evident that neither monogamy and patriarchy, nor a sexual division of labour and gendered identity, were natural to the primordial state. Later developments in these directions are not necessarily unnatural, but they are clearly contingent. Yet almost everything that Rousseau will write subsequently implies that such phenomena are natural in the sense of being both unassailable and an ideal whose attempted negation is dangerous and artificial. The 'law of nature', he will contend in *Emile,* 'bids the woman obey the man'.[7] Instead of the initially autonomous female, we have the 'naturally' dependent wife and child: in the 'monogamous species' among which humans are now classed, 'the male shares the care of the little ones'—a fortuitous occurrence since 'mother and children could ill dispense with the father's affection, and the care which results from it'.[8] The only natural society, Rousseau continues in *The Social Contract,* is the family, where 'the ruler corresponds to the father'.[9] In other words, he has gratuitously taken as his model of what is natural for women, that configuration which emerged at a particular stage of development, namely the patriarchal family, even though this appeared only with a revolutionary change and was succeeded by another.

In his *Discourse on Political Economy,* Rousseau actually explained why he believed that men *ought* to rule families. 'In the family', he writes, 'it is clear, for several reasons which lie in its very nature, that the father ought to command'.[10] In offering his reasons, Rousseau accepts claims by Hobbes and Locke that authority in the family is indivisible. The case of making the father its repository relies on a variation of Locke's 'abler and stronger' theme, which is now more specifically tied to woman's reproductive function: 'however lightly we may regard the disadvantages peculiar to women, yet, as they necessarily occasion intervals of inaction, this is a sufficient reason for excluding them from this extreme authority'.[11] Furthermore, because (due to the sexual division of labour) the father provides for the child, he must know it to be his own and so the woman's conduct must be carefully supervised.

The motivation behind Rousseau's account seems to lie in a desire to repeat the Lockean refutation of patriarchy, and he concludes with the familiar point that children leave familial authority behind when they come of age to become freely consenting citizens.[12] Nevertheless, Locke—despite certain lapses on this point—had tried to distinguish between natural parent–child bonds and a contractual relationship between the parents. Rousseau, on the other hand, extends natural authority relations in the family beyond the parent–child nexus to include the conjugal relationship itself. Domestic and political relations are therefore more sharply distinguished for him because, like Aristotle, he discovers a natural distinction between sexual roles, such that the male–female relationship can never be reduced to that of a contract between two virtually equal and identical individuals. It is because of the clarity of his family–state distinction that Rousseau will be able to condemn political inequality while sanctioning marital hierarchy. The logic of his argument in the *Discourse on Political Economy* does not imply sexual equality, and so he avoids the inconsistency into which the unpalatable implications of his argument had driven Locke. At the same time, however, Rousseau's claim that the patriarchal family is natural is at odds with the history he narrates in *The Second Discourse.*

Returning to this latter work, further implications arise from the assumption that the period of the first revolution is the natural one. The sexual division of labour which is suddenly announced there, is never explained even though its implications are devastating for the formerly self-sufficient female, now forced into dependence on her husband. Rousseau will subsequently pass off the division as a natural one: 'Nature teaches us that they should work together, but that each has its own share of the work'.[13] There is no suggestion that inequality is being introduced, only a mutually beneficial complementarity. Yet when a division of labour segregates *men,* in a second revolution, dependence, servitude and inequality are all condemned as its inevitable corollary.[14] While men are to be taught to limit their needs in order to escape such dependence, women will be simply ascribed the servile qualities appropriate to a dependant, with their education designed to reinforce them.

The evolution of patriarchal families is associated with other simultaneous developments. It is only with stable couplings that men become aware of their paternity: a knowledge which soon seeks guarantees and justifies control over every aspect of women's lives. It is perhaps no accident that Rousseau sees patriarchy and property emerging simultaneously, even if he does not yet make the explicit causal links between inheritance, private property and legitimacy that Engels will. Okin points to a further significant coincidence: woman's economic dependence on man is introduced simultaneously with his sexual dependence on a *particular* woman,[15] the implication being that women must be made dependent in this manner in order that equal power be sustained between the sexes. Finally, it is germane to note that all these developments coincide with the appearance of language, such that meaning is refined within a specifically patriarchal world. Thenceforth two quite different spheres, each with its own values and significance, will develop: the private, familial one where love, romance and womanhood flourish, and its public antithesis where only men are active.

Keeping in mind that the convergence of events in which the family appears marked a significant departure from the originally free and equal individuals who first populated the natural state, it is now necessary to see what characteristics Rousseau nevertheless extricated from it and imputed to the 'natural' woman.

* * *

The account of woman and of the education most appropriate to her, occurs primarily in Chapter 5 of *Emile,* although Rousseau illustrates his ideas further in the novel *Julie ou La Nouvelle Héloise.*[16] 'But for her sex', he declares in the former work, 'a woman is a man'; she has the same organs and faculties as his male norm.[17] However, her sexual function is soon discovered to suffuse a woman's entire existence; it, rather than her humanity, defines her. For while the 'male is only a male now and again, the female is always a female, or at least all her youth; everything reminds her of her sex; the performance of her function requires a special constitution'.[18] Pregnancy, nursing, childbearing, gaining the father's love and credulity sufficiently to integrate him into the family, all conspire to fill her life.

From the sexual act itself, Rousseau concludes that men are strong and active, evincing power and will, while women are weak and passive, lacking resistance. The argument is reminiscent of Aristotle's except that in the eighteenth century it is no longer feasible to support it with his account of generation (although there are in *Emile* post-natal echoes of the Aristotelian belief that the mother nourishes while the father imparts reason: the 'real nurse is the mother and the real teacher is the father'[19]). Nevertheless, Rousseau goes on to make the same sort of teleological deductions, documenting the type of qualities a woman must have in order to fulfil her natural function with virtuosity. Made for man's delight, she must service and charm him since to bear him legitimate children and win his love for them is her proper business.[20] Her duties are to please, attract, counsel and console her mate; to 'make his life pleasant and happy'. In order to cultivate the good reputation that is necessary to persuade her master of her fidelity, she is modest, retiring and devoted. In order to compensate for the man's greater strength she cultivates her own powers, which lie in cunning, beauty, wit and wiles. She rules by gentleness, kindness and tact; by caresses and tears; by modesty, distance and chastity. She simultaneously allures and repels, stimulates her husband's desire only to succumb with reluctance. Although all these qualities require careful nurturing, Rousseau is adamant that they are quite natural:

The obedience and fidelity which she owes to her husband, the tenderness and care due to her children, are such natural and self-evident consequences of her position that she cannot honestly refuse her consent to the inner voice which is her guide, nor fail to discern her duty in her natural inclination.[21]

From the role he ascribes to woman, Rousseau deduces a whole range of 'natural' qualities, from the little girl's preference for dolls as play things to feminine tastes which evince a preference for milk and sweets. All reflect the virtue which is appropriate to the domestic sphere. Woman's right is not to be free and equal but to win love and respect through obedience and fidelity.[22] She has rights only so that she might perform her duties better.

Having sketched Rousseau's vision of socio-political regeneration and juxtaposed it with his account of the ideal woman, it now remains to be seen what relationship might exist between the two. I shall first examine ways in which the treatment of women is simply antithetical to the political schema. It was by exploiting inconsistencies here that feminists like Wollstonecraft were able to attack Rousseau's misogyny while subscribing to his revolutionary political ideal, appealing only for women's inclusion in it. Second, however, I shall suggest that the domestic function Rousseau allotted to women was actually a moral prerequisite for civic virtue in the male state (as it had been a material prerequisite for Aristotle). Wollstonecraft would herself recognize that this contribution needed dealing with before integration could succeed.

Okin argues that Rousseau's views on women 'violate all the major principles of his ethics and social theory'.[23] Examples of such violation abound. Rousseau demands equality and autonomy among male citizens but authority and heteronomy in the family. He sees that men cannot be free while they depend on the economic or arbitrary power of other men yet he deliberately fosters women's dependence on husbands, from provision of their daily bread to choice of their religion and judgement of their virtue.[24] He looks back to the originally free and self-sufficient natural man whose liberty is to be recaptured in civil life, yet the natural woman he idealizes is the dependent being of the patriarchal family. He advises male citizens to suppress their private interests on behalf of the General Will, yet he would imprison women in the particularity of domestic life. He sees in men a limitless drive to self-improvement through development of their rational capacities, yet defines women according to natural functions which yield them moral and psychological qualities of a fixed and limited type. In short, if Rousseau's political thinking is inspired by Locke, his sexual beliefs are closer to Aristotle.

The characteristics ascribed to women rob them of the credentials for citizenship: they lack the right sort of reason, autonomy, judgement, sense of justice and ability to consent. We have already seen that Locke probably doubted women's rational qualifications for active political membership but that this only resulted from a lack of opportunity to develop their faculties. Rousseau returns to more traditional claims regarding innate sexual differences here. Although women do have reason, he writes in *Emile,* it is of a practical nature. Woman lacks the accuracy or attention for success in the sciences; she cannot appreciate genius. For abstract and speculative truths, principles and axioms, generalizations as such, are beyond her grasp.[25] Of course, the education that Rousseau advises makes this a self-fulfilling prognosis, but it is of obvious significance in the political sphere where it is just that reasoning of which he finds women incapable, which is required to discern the General Will.

In order for the General Will to emerge, individuals must not only reason but they must do so independently. Should their thoughts be too influenced by others' beliefs or interests, then the delicate balancing of individual differences will degenerate into clusters of particularity. Yet it is impossible to imagine Rousseau's women making any impartial assessment of the public good, since they have been raised to make no independent judgement: their guide is always the question 'what will others think of me?' Appearance is for them everything. They lack a capacity to penetrate to, or articulate, truth. In any case, confinement in the home surely denies to Sophy and her sisters the breadth of vision which they need to evaluate public issues. The 'genuine mother of a family', Rousseau insists, 'is no woman of the world, she is almost as much of a recluse as the nun in her convent'.[26] She has her sights fixed on the well-being of her particular family, not on the world outside. She is not therefore predisposed to considerations of impersonal justice and Rousseau goes so far as to suggest that this is a natural limitation: 'woman is made to submit to man and to endure even injustice at his hands. You will never bring young lads to this; their feelings rise in revolt against injustice; nature has not fitted them to put up with it'.[27]

Finally, it is evident that women cannot give the sort of consent needed in the polity—or, what comes to the same thing, they are incapable of withdrawing consent and so of making its granting meaningful.[28] In the family, their duty is to arouse their husband's desire only to control it through a natural modesty which men lack. It is left to men to interpret the real message that might be at odds with more overt expressions:

Why do you consult their words when it is not their mouths that speak? Consult their eyes, their colour, their breathing, their timid manner, their slight resistance, that is the language nature gave them for your answer. The lips always say 'no', and rightly so; but the tone is not always the same, and that cannot lie. Has not a woman the same needs as a man, but without the same right to make them known?[29]

She who says 'no' when she means 'yes'; whose real language is that of the body rather than of the mind and who responds to passion by camouflaging rather than transcending it, is hardly a candidate for the General Will.

Thanks to all these lacunae in their reason, autonomy, judgement and consent, women are thus as unsuited to the ideals of citizenship as are the unreconstructed males of the *Second Discourse*.[30] The only difference is that their shortcomings are natural and hence immutable. It might be argued, of course, that it is in their very feminine qualities (whether natural or acquired) that women are uniquely well-equipped for the sort of communitarian politics Rousseau envisaged. Separated from property acquisition, they are rarely avaricious and inspired by self-gain; associated with infantile and virile dependants, they are well-practised in putting the needs of others before their own; lacking strength, they are used to extending persuasion rather than force. And it is indeed because he recognizes such virtues that Rousseau does ultimately find women indispensable to the just state. But the role they yield remains for him indirect and largely implicit. It is next necessary, then, to examine the purpose which sexual differences played in his political philosophy as a whole.

*   *   *

Despite the dichotomies that Rousseau insisted upon between women and men in the ideal state, he was nevertheless unable to sever them completely. It is in the family that new male citizens are reproduced. Moreover, nature, which remains for Rousseau an ideal realm, primitive yet undefiled and authentic, is associated with the family and woman. Indeed, the rural family remains for him something of a Utopian model: the Golden Age in which it is the primary social unit is one where the conflicts and miseries of modernity might be avoided. It is therefore both impossible and inadvisable to insulate the private and public spheres too definitively, as Rousseau is well aware. Accordingly, the plan for woman's education is 'crucial to Rousseau's vision of the good society'.[31] Why is this?

The ideal woman is for Rousseau, as his critics have frequently noted, simultaneously madonna and whore. But this schizoid picture is also applied to women as a whole, dividing them into two classes: those who, like Sophy, remain naturally good and domesticated and those who eschew their natural duties in order to emulate men and take up positions in the public world. It is this division which accounts for the apparent inconsistency with which Rousseau discusses women's influence on men. In his Dedication to the *Second Discourse,* for example, he eulogizes the influence which Geneva's female inhabitants exert, implying that it is they who teach civic virtue to the Republic's male citizens.

Amiable and virtuous daughters of Geneva, it will be always the lot of your sex to govern ours. Happy are we, so long as your chaste influence, solely exercised within the limits of conjugal union, is exerted only for the glory of the state and the happiness of the public. . . . It is your task to perpetuate, by your insinuating influence and your innocent and amiable rule, a respect for the laws of state, and harmony among the citizens.[32]

In the *Letter to M. D'Alembert,* on the other hand, Rousseau condemns the introduction of theatre to Geneva on the grounds that it will encourage the sexes to mingle in public, allowing women's influence to render men weak and effeminate while distracting them from their public duties.

This apparent hiatus is resolved once we recognize that Rousseau refers in the two pieces to his different types of woman. He values Genevan women precisely because their seclusion, which he fears the theatre will destroy, places them in the virtuous category. A note in his *First Discourse* clarifies his position: he is 'far from thinking that the ascendency which women have obtained over men is an evil in itself. It is a present which nature has made for the good of mankind. If better directed, it might be productive of as much good, as it is now of evil'.[33] It is her public profile that corrupts contemporary woman, to render sinister a power that is naturally beneficial. But what is the relationship between sexual segregation and woman's moral mission? To answer this, it is necessary to return to the *Discourse on Inequality* once again.

When we first encounter primitive individuals, they exhibit two tendencies: a diluted self-interest concerned with self-preservation (*amour de soi*) and compassion (*pitié*), which is a sort of prereflective empathy with the suffering of others. It is because these instincts bind one another in a broad equilibrium that the natural state is a peaceful yet progressive one. Development, however, enflames these incipient passions. The mother's tenderness for her offspring is claimed as an early example of the natural virtue of compassion, out of which social virtues like generosity, friendship and eventually civic virtue itself, will emerge. The first step in its enhancement occurs precisely in the reproductive domain, where conjugal love and paternal affection are sparked by cohabitation. But unfortunately self-love is also enhanced as the proliferation of property and produce transform gentle self-regard into an avaricious and aggressive *amour propre*.

The initial psychological equilibrium seems to imply a more sexually 'neutral' human type than had Hobbes's portrayal of insatiable egoists, and there is no sense at this stage of masculine or feminine natures. However, the passions unfold at the same time as the sexual division of labour, and it seems logical to assume that they will now tend to disaggregate along sexual lines. The woman who tends her children will enrich her compassion and it is she who is responsible, according to *Emile,* for inciting paternal affection. And since it is property which is especially associated with the degeneration of *amour de soi* into *amour propre,* while it is men who go 'abroad in search of their common subsistence', we would expect the male half of the species to strengthen its self-regard disproportionately. In other words, beings who were first androgynous in their sentiments now evolve gendered personalities as the dyadic disposition which was originally so well-balanced, splits. Its two halves can no longer bind one another and so one part flourishes in a distorted manner, varying according to sex. It follows that if social beings are to reclaim their natural equilibrium on a moral level, the two qualities must be resynthesized.

One means by which this might be achieved would be for individuals of both sexes to redevelop the quality they lack and this would imply integrated personalities sharing domestic and civic tasks. Rousseau's solution, however, is to fuse members of the two sexes in a marital unity such that the different qualities can again complement and bind one another; they become virtually one person. Thus he describes the woman as the eye and the man the hand; they 'are so dependent on one another that the man teaches the woman what to see while she teaches him what to do'.[34] There is nevertheless a constant danger that one sex will imitate the other and then the balance will be destroyed. This is why Rousseau counsels sexual segregation outside the home, fearing both men who become effeminate when they are consumed with winning a woman's love and women who compete with men in intellectual endeavours.

Ideally, then, Rousseau believes that mutual dependence will limit the excesses of both sexes. The male uses his strength to rule but also his reason, thereby defusing the particularity to which woman's compassion inclines her. But the woman uses the love which that compassion incites, to temper her husband's competitiveness and coldness, reminding him of the sentimental bonds that unite persons. This is why the female's domestic domain evinces an ethic so different from the public world where 'unbridled passions' of rich and poor have 'suppressed the cries of natural compassion and the still feeble voice of justice, and filled men with avarice, ambition and vice'.[35]

Rousseau's preference for female seclusion in the home is thus twofold. First, it prevents women from taking their particular powers into the public realm, where they would be inappropriate. As he writes in the *Letter to M. D'Alembert,* 'Love is the empire of the fair. Here they must give the law, because in the order of nature, resistance belongs to them, and man cannot surmount this resistance, but at the expense of his liberty'.[36] Because women's natural modesty is always better able to control their sexual desire than men's reason can their own, infatuated males are at a woman's mercy. If her powers are unleashed outside of marriage they are destructive because they entice citizens away from the masculine world of generality and abstract reason, infecting it with rampant desires for particular persons and encouraging illicit relationships. But second, women must also be kept out of public in order to safeguard their natural qualities. Those who participate in the public realm of men themselves quickly develop *amour propre* and then not only do they fail in their guardianship of the compassionate side of human nature, but they use their advantages in the sphere of love to dominate men rather than to assuage them. It is because women are associated through their relationship with their young with a natural compassion, that they must be protected by confinement in the domestic world, where they are awarded a crucial role in sustaining the sentiments which are required for civic virtue. Without their compassion, a regenerating social contract would remain inconceivable. This is perhaps why Rousseau places such great store on the strength of the original mother—child bond: 'when mothers deign to nurse their children, then will be a reform in morals; natural feeling will revive in every heart; there will be no lack of citizens for the state; this first step by itself will restore mutual affection'.[37]

To be good citizens, individuals must not only obey the law as a set of formal instructions; they must identify with it because they see in it an expression of the community, of which they are a part. They must therefore empathize with others and it is just this feeling which women teach. Ironically, it is from their mothers that men first learn the sentiments necessary to patriotism, fraternity and discernment of the General Will. Thus Rousseau asks: 'can devotion to the state exist apart from the love of those near and dear to us? Can patriotism thrive except in the soil of that miniature fatherland, the home? Is it not the good son, the good husband, the good father, who makes the good citizen?'[38] As part of a romantic reaction against the Enlightenment, Rousseau believed that sentiment as well as reason must guide justice. Yet we now see that these two attributes tended to be contributed by the different sexes, united through marriage. Without domestic virtue, in short, there could be no civic virtue; the conventional state does ultimately require a foundation in nature and this can only come from the family. Such a conclusion at first seems to contradict Rousseau's denial in Chapter 2 of *The Social Contract,* that the state can originate in the family. However, he is merely reiterating here the Lockean case against patriarchy and this does not conflict with the impression *Emile* conveys, that the natural sentiments engendered in the family during the child's immaturity are a prerequisite to the virtues the citizen will require. It is natural feeling, not natural authority, which allows the family still to underpin the state; if it cannot legitimize it, it can facilitate it.

There are further civic implications of women's domestic confinement for Rousseau. The family provides a place where particularity and passion can be safely expressed because they are defused there. The wife who services her husband encourages such expressions but then safeguards them such that they never cross the domestic threshold to invade that public realm where they would be so threatening. Even within the home, marriage, as Mary O'Brien says, 'purifies the passions of particularity, thus making the private realm truly ethical' and less of a threat to the universality required of citizen-husbands.[39] In a similar vein, Carole Pateman contends that within 'the shelter of domestic life, women impose an order, a social pattern, and thus give meaning to the natural world of birth and death and other physical processes, of dirt and raw materials'.[40] Yet because women mediate for men between nature and society, they are always tainted by the process and represent a constant threat to social order. Finally, Lynda Lange suggests that 'the nature of Rousseau's ideal state makes the refuge of the home a virtual necessity for the citizen. Because the demands of citizenship are so stringent, it would be appalling to imagine everyone called to that status'.[41] Again, then, the domestic realm plays an important role as that arena in which private passions are safely indulged and discharged.

If women were active in the polity, the differentiations without which justice and liberty could not endure for Rousseau, would collapse. Compassion–self-love; particularity–generality; love–law; personal–impersonal;

natural—conventional are all for him oppositions which are simultaneously sustained and harmonized only as long as women and men maintain their diffuse identities in an intimate relationship. The moral complicity of the sexes, who together fuse the originally balanced virtues, is embodied in a family-state dyad. This explains why Rousseau, despite his paranoid denunciation of factions in *The Social Contract,* fails to cite the family as one of those manifestations of particularity that would threaten the state.[42] It is indispensable to it.

In conclusion, I do not think that Rousseau's enchantment with the Ancients can be overemphasized here. In essence, he adopts Aristotle's view that women should be excluded from citizenship but accepts, with him, that they might provide its preconditions. In propounding a rather Aristotelian notion of civic virtue, he grants to women an indispensable moral and emotional mission. As he says of the Greek use of slaves, there 'are some unhappy circumstances in which we can only keep our liberty at others' expense'.[43] Like his predecessor, Rousseau distinguishes between beneficiaries and others according to their supposedly natural functions, on the basis of which he ascribes to them an appropriate type of reason and virtue. He imputes to women the typically Greek virtues of fidelity and modesty. He recognizes, like Plato, that the virtues of family life are needed in the just state even while they threaten it, but he must eschew the Platonic/Spartan attempt to overcome the sexual division of function and to collapse the family into the state, otherwise the necessary tensions will not be sustained. His preferred solution, to seclude women in the home and to segregate the sexes even there, is rather that of Aristotle and of classical Athens.

It was Hegel who would take up the mantle of this sexual conservatism; it is to Mary Wollstonecraft that we must now turn for its radical critique. We can discern in her engagement with Rousseau a further rehearsal of that ancient debate between Plato and Aristotle regarding woman's real nature and public role.

Mary Wollstonecraft's *A Vindication of the Rights of Woman* (1792) was by no means the first feminist appeal to be published, for the question of women's place in society had been in the air since the English Civil War.[44] But it was probably the first sustained argument in English for women's rights. In this book Wollstonecraft combined natural rights arguments inherited from Locke with utilitarian claims concerning the social benefits of sexual equality. This involved her in a direct confrontation with Rousseau's image of natural sexual difference, yet the ideal which the utility of women's improved status was to serve often came close to Rousseau's own vision of citizenship.

As a young woman, Wollstonecraft had set up a school in Stoke Newington, where she was befriended by a group of radical dissenters who 'worshipped reason and Locke'.[45] It was through these acquaintances that she met Thomas Paine and her future husband, William Godwin. Tomalin suggests that Paine, engaged in writing his *Rights of Man,* may have suggested to Mary that she write a book on women's rights.[46] However, her first *Vindication* was a defence *Of the Rights of Men,* written in opposition to Burke's conservative *Reflections on the Revolution in France* (1790).[47] Always committed to the revolutionary attack on privilege, it is not surprising that Wollstonecraft should have discerned a parallel between aristocratic and patriarchal abuses which alerted her to inconsistencies in the liberal position.

Wollstonecraft was fully aware of the radical implications of natural rights theories: if all individuals are born free and equal bearers of such rights, then it is 'both inconsistent and unjust' to exclude women from their enjoyment: reason itself demands 'JUSTICE for one half of the human race' (Wollstonecraft, *A Vindication of the Rights of Woman,* pp. 11, 13).[48] She thus demands that women share in the 'rights of man' in being accorded civil and even political, rights. But she realizes, too, that the argument must be applied to relations in the family: the '*divine* right of husbands, like the divine right of kings, may, it is hoped, in this enlightened age, be contested without danger' (p. 46).

In order to establish her rights claim, Wollstonecraft needed to refute Rousseau's description of women as possessing reason and virtue that naturally differed from men's. For the Lockean tradition associated both virtue and rights with the capacity for moral and rational agency, and if women could be shown defective here, their sex might legitimately be used as a criterion for excluding them from equal rights with men.

Accordingly, Wollstonecraft issues her challenge: 'if women are to be excluded, without having a voice, from a participation of the natural rights of mankind, prove first, to ward off the charge of injustice and inconsistency, that they want reason' (pp. 11f). It is such a contention that she sets out to refute.

In order to overturn Rousseau's depiction of the natural woman, Wollstonecraft makes use of the argument that Rousseau had himself launched against Hobbes: that in deducing the essential being stripped of its acquired characteristics, he had not gone far enough. The 'crude inferences' he makes are in fact drawn from the eighteenth-century Frenchwoman, raised from infancy only to please men (p. 90). While she shares Rousseau's distaste for the females who ignore their motherly duties, Wollstonecraft equally condemns those who emulate Sophy. The behaviour prescribed for the latter is not natural because it is insincere and it is not moral because it rests on falsehood. She sees both types of woman as the creation of poor education and patriarchal culture, which encourage development of the senses at the expense of reason and wrongly identify ignorance with innocence. Femininity as described by Rousseau is, in short, an artificial construct; resocialize women in the same manner as men and their essential humanity will reveal itself.

It is interesting that in this criticism Wollstonecraft never makes the point, explored above, that Rousseau's assumptions about the patriarchal family and sexual division of labour are equally unnatural since women were first presented as self-sufficient. Rather she herself accepts these institutions, neither questioning their inevitability nor, therefore, attempting to justify them. The thrust of her argument is rather that Rousseau's prescriptions for Sophy are antithetical to the duties he gives her. The woman trained only for love is unlikely to remain a faithful wife, since she has learnt none of that autonomy which must underlie a woman's domestic duty. While she challenges the idea of a gendered rationality, then, she accepts the differential roles in which it is to be exercised. In fact, the structure of her argument is similar to that of Socrates in the *Meno,* where, as we saw in Chapter 2, he contends that an identical virtue is required for managing both household and state even though the association of these domains with

women and men, respectively, goes unchallenged. Like
Socrates, too, Wollstonecraft leaves open the question of
whether women might actually evince the same degree of virtue
as men, arguing only that under current conditions of their
distorted natures it is impossible to know.

The intuition and practicality which Rousseau praised as
women's particular mode of thought is, Wollstonecraft
contends, no natural deficiency in reason but the result of an
unmethodical education reinforced by disorderly experience.
As a result, women are arrested at the level of chaotic and
infantile associations rather than learning the power of
deduction and generalization instilled in men. Only the latter
kind of reasoning process will free them from habitual,
piecemeal thinking to permit reliable judgement and rational
autonomy (pp. 26, 56, 60). For such powers are indispensable
to virtue, whose appearance depends upon the sort of self-
mastery and reflection that a capacity for abstract thought can
alone yield. Lacking these abilities, women must rely on men's
judgements while their obedience can reproduce only
servitude. Wollstonecraft cites chastity, modesty and public
spiritedness as the social virtues (pp. 134ff, 153), but these are
for her far broader and more sexually neutral than the marital
fidelities and subterfuges of which Rousseau had spoken. They
require a far-sightedness, a perception of universal order and
justice and of one's place in it; a constancy that is impossible
for women stifled by trivia and devotion to appearances, to
acquire. Such virtue is 'one eternal standard', the foundation
of civic virtue and beyond sexual divisibility (p. 31):

I still insist that not only the virtue but the *knowledge* of the two sexes should
be the same in nature, if not in degree, and that women, considered not only
as moral but as rational creatures, ought to endeavour to acquire human
virtues (or perfections) by the *same* means as men, instead of being educated
like a fanciful kind of *half* being—one of Rousseau's wild chimeras.

(p. 44)

In asserting that the female half of the species should be
treated first as human rather than as sexed beings,
Wollstonecraft draws on a well-established series of dualisms:
reason–passion, mind–body, freedom–slavery,
civilisation–barbarism. While these had traditionally been
used to associate women with the lower, appetitive and thus

subordinate half of the equation, however, she invokes them precisely to eliminate their sexual connotations. For her it is essential that every individual subordinate their passions to rational control. The ideal conventionally equated with men defines the humanity of both sexes, and it is as appropriate in the family as in the public realm.

Love, Wollstonecraft is convinced, is a poor basis for marriage precisely because it rests on passions that are hard to control, fickle and evanescent. The woman who relies on so ephemeral a base must ultimately turn elsewhere or grow bitter. More enduring are respect and friendship, facilitating a cool, calm partnership that allows a couple to perform their respective duties without distraction (p. 32). The ideal conjugal relationship is of the type one would expect from the sort of contractual foundation liberals like Locke had described.

In order to fulfil the duties of life, and to be able to pursue with vigour the various employments which form the moral character, a master and mistress of a family ought not to continue to love each other with passion. I mean to say that they ought not to indulge those emotions which disturb the order of society, and engross the thoughts that should be otherwise employed.

(p. 35)

She goes so far as to suggest that 'an unhappy marriage is often very advantageous to a family' and 'a neglected wife is in general, the best mother' (p. 35).

So far, then, we have seen that Wollstonecraft offered a natural rights argument for sexual equality and that to do this she attacked Rousseau's image of woman as both unnatural and unvirtuous, replacing it with the moral agent who cultivated abstract reasoning powers in order to exercise autonomy through self-control and to recognize justice. The woman who realized these qualities would nevertheless continue to exercise them most often in the domestic sphere where, indeed, they were a prerequisite to an efficient performance of duty.

Now, the feminist case which bases its plea for equality on a natural rights argument inherits all the weaknesses of that form of argument, most notably that it is unconvincing to ethical sceptics and that unless the dispossessed have power to enforce their claims, it must rely upon a commitment by the powerful to the realization of justice even at the expense of their own advantages. Lacking any women's movement to fight for her demands, Wollstonecraft therefore tries to show men that women's liberation from the Rousseauian ideal would actually benefit them. In other words, she supplements her rights argument with an appeal to social utility. Ironically, she moves closer to Rousseau here in so far as she recognizes the significance of domestic virtue (albeit of a very different kind) for good citizenship.

'Make women rational creatures and free citizens, and they will quickly become good wives and mothers' (p. 197). Here is the first part of Wollstonecraft's equation: without the protection of civil rights and a rational education, women cannot perform their domestic duties properly. The second part announces that if they fail here, then social decay must follow.

Contending for the rights of woman, my main argument is built on this simple principle, that if she be not prepared by education to become the companion of man, she will stop the progress of knowledge and virtue. . . . And how can woman be expected to co-operate unless she knows why she ought to be virtuous? unless freedom strengthens her reason till she comprehends her real good.

(p.10)

It is an argument that J.S. Mill will take over in its entirety. If women are to be exemplary partners and to raise good citizens, then they must themselves be educated according to male ideals; if one were to put it in a Rousseauian way, it would be to assert that women must develop those skills needed to recognize the General Will, if they are to habituate their children and husbands to the practice. In Wollstonecraft's words, 'love of mankind, from which an orderly train of virtues spring, can only be produced by considering the moral and civil interest of mankind; but the education and situation of woman at present shuts her out from such investigations' (p. 10). To confine females as Rousseau wished, 'immured in their families groping in the dark' (p. 11), is to advance a dangerous particularity, not to defuse it or to protect women from the corruption of public life. Wollstonecraft sees that the family which remains entirely privatized does pose a threat since the women who are imprisoned there will inevitably use cunning and trickery to disturb more rational plans they cannot appreciate. And if they educate their children in so narrow a fashion, this too must inevitably seep into the polity. In short, the civic qualities that women guard do not spring from natural compassion but from a commitment to universal justice, which they acquire only after the sort of rational education whose necessity Rousseau had recognized for men.

The only way to eliminate that fear which Rousseau had of women is therefore to cultivate their reason so that they will identify with universal aims and perform the civil task given them, in an enlightened manner. 'Let women share the rights, and she will emulate the virtues, of man'. For 'the private duty of any member of society must be very improperly performed when not connected with the general good' (pp. 203, 215). It is not a matter, then, of taking women out of the home and into social production or political work, but of rendering the domestic sphere one in which public virtues are practised. Wollstonecraft's vision is explicit: she looks forward to a time when all are active citizens with the man employed in the departments of civil life and 'his wife, also an active citizen . . . equally intent to manage her family, educate her children, and assist her neighbours' (p. 160). The utilitarian message is thus clear: it is not merely women who suffer from their degradation but all members of the community. Ironically, the sort of civic ideal that Rousseau held and that Wollstonecraft shares, called for a 'revolution in female manners' (pp. 51, 213). The domestic duties which she envisages have nothing to do with the alternating allurement and coyness of a Sophy; indeed, they have little to do with sexuality or the servicing of men at all: 'woman was not created merely to gratify the appetite of man, or to be the upper servant who provides his meals and takes care of his linen' (p. 45). In Puritan style, Wollstonecraft presents a woman's reproductive work as a vocation which requires an ascetic dedication to duty that is not clouded by passion or self-indulgence. To fulfil it she must be educated as a rational being just like any citizen who pursues her or his callling. Such industry will in turn help develop the sort of reason Locke had denied her.

What must be kept in mind in reading the *Vindication of the Rights of Woman* is the relative novelty of the very recognition that women were an oppressed group. Neither Locke nor

Rousseau had ever suggested that this might be the case. In a political landscape where the terrain sculptured by structures of patriarchy had yet to be mapped out, Wollstonecraft was an early and courageous explorer.

The most oppressive element in women's lives is for her the lack of control which they exercise over themselves. Like Rousseau, she identifies dependence as anathema to freedom and finds it most profoundly manifested in an individual's enslavement to passion. However, lest women themselves be blamed for their own victimization, she also stresses that their inflamed senses are the result of that type of education and cult of femininity of which Rousseau was a prime exponent. The villains of the *Vindication* are particularly those men who enhance and prey upon women's resulting over-sensibility. Outside of marriage, the 'foundation of almost every social virtue', they are the tyrants of the sexual realm. It is to escape their enticements that women need self-discipline; it is independence from the desires they evoke that will set women free. Male sensuality oppresses women, reducing them to a sex class.[49] The virtues praised in 1792 do not oppose the domestic and social realms or allot them a differential ethic; rather, they pit the libertine, that harbinger of private passion, against both home and community, seen equally as domains where public acts require civic virtue.

Wollstonecraft is convinced that sexual inequality operates primarily on a psychological level. We have already seen that she identified slavery first as a state of mind, and it is this quality that allows woman to be simultaneously slave and tyrant. 'Whilst they are kept in ignorance they become in the same proportion the slaves of pleasure as they are slaves of man' (p. 192). Such a state is the antithesis of rational self-determination, engendered by 'the mistaken notions that enslave my sex' (p. 41). However, she recognizes that these artificial denizens do indeed wield the sort of powers that Rousseau had credited them with: the enslaved woman is also a petty tyrant who must be eliminated:

taught slavishly to submit to their parents, they are prepared for the slavery of marriage. I may be told that a number of women are not slaves in the marriage state. True, but they become tyrants; for it is not rational freedom, but a lawless kind of power, resembling the authority exercised by the

favourites of absolute monarchs, which they obtain by debasing means.
(pp. 171f, and cf. pp. 6, 68, 207f)

This is not a means for balancing male authority, as Rousseau had claimed, but an exercise of unmerited power which degrades the bearer and society in general. Lacking control over her own desire or the ability to organize her affairs with dignity, the capricious wife exercises an arbitrary and unregulated sway over those around her, just as the aristocrats in pre-revolutionary France had stultified and corrupted the state. In the same way, such women share the vices of the rich. Lacking the moral fibre that comes from a performance of duty, hard work and reason, their idleness is translated into petty displays of power, whimsical projects and tantrums. Such analogies must have appealed to Mary's Jacobin sympathies.

To sum up Wollstonecraft's analysis of women's oppression, this remained rudimentary, as we would expect of an early attempt to locate it. She engages in a swingeing criticism of eighteenth-century womanhood, which she views as an artificial construct, crafted by a male culture with erroneous ideas of the natural woman. Although she never really explores why men should promote such ideas, at times she does seem peculiarly modern in describing their manifestation in everyday life. She deplores the fact that 'many men stare insultingly at every female they meet'. She despises the latter's reduction to 'alluring objects', 'insignificant objects of desire'; she condemns men's 'indecent allusions' and 'obscene witticisms' at women's expense, as well as the way in which an effort to appear agreeable to men dictates women's own behaviour and dress (pp. 4, 6, 137, 207). She thus recognizes that women's disabilities do not lie solely in their exclusion from rights but also in a patriarchal culture requiring transformation on the most intimate levels. It is finally necessary to elicit and evaluate the solutions she offered.

Wollstonecraft's agenda for women's emancipation is a typically liberal one: education; civil rights; an opportunity to compete for access to occupations; political rights. Of these, education is perhaps the most important, and it was an educational tract that the *Vindication* won popularity when it first appeared.[50] In this capacity it was inevitably compared with that other great educational work of the eighteenth century, *Emile*.

A rational education for women is crucial to Wollstonecraft's enterprise on a number of levels. First, it is needed to transform female identity away from its false parody of humanity. Second, it is a right; as rational beings, all persons deserve the opportunity to develop their faculties in order to achieve self-determination, autonomy and virtue. And third, a proper education is essential if orderly thought processes are to emerge. These are necessary for women's self-respect but also for their role as citizens. A sound education for both sexes thus serves public utility but it is first of all associated with liberty for women.

Wollstonecraft's idea of liberty is always of that positive variety which associates freedom with self-mastery and an identification between self and community. Like Rousseau, she accepts that each being has a higher self which is morally and intellectually superior to, and thus freer than, the isolated appetitive self which pursues only its immediate self-interest. She thus diverges from the British liberal tradition which tended to see rights in terms of a negative liberty; a right to be left alone in pursuit of unspecified interests of which each individual was the best judge. This is why she has no need to present the family as a private haven where the state is absent and public concerns have no place. It is in order to free themselves from the demands of the lower self, so that duties in which the public has a legitimate concern can be undertaken, that women need the sort of education Rousseau had prescribed for Emile.

Civil rights in the family are associated by Wollstonecraft with the duties that women are to perform there. If women are to be good mothers, they require the protection of the law against despotic husbands. She implies that the transfer of a wife's property is especially pernicious since it renders her entirely dependent on her spouse's goodwill. The association of rights with duties is tied to a model of the bourgeois family. The middle class is, Wollstonecraft says, the rank 'in which talents thrive best'; the class with the most 'virtue and abilities' (pp. 63, 84). It is here that the calling of a reproductive vocation is most likely to be harkened to, for it is middle-class women who 'appear to be in the most natural state' (p. 5). It is the indolent ladies of the upper classes who best exhibit the artificial female values of vanity, over-refinement, sickly health and feeble minds. Wollstonecraft applauds Adam Smith's condemnation of the rich, whose frivolous accomplishments undermine the knowledge and industry found among the productive middle ranks (p. 64). The same applies to women. The aim of the bourgeois wife should be to emulate not the aristocratic parasite but her husband. As Barbara Taylor puts it, 'If the model for genteel femininity was the life of the idle rich, the model for feminine freedom, it seems, was the life of the self-made businessman'.[51]

Wollstonecraft's experience and aspirations focus almost exclusively on middle-class women. After all, Rousseau's model could hardly penetrate the working-class family, where women's economic contribution remained as vital as it had been in feudal times.[52] She does praise the labouring poor for doing their duty, claiming that she has seen much virtue among them since idleness is of necessity absent. But the vocational pursuits that are to re-educate and free women are clearly not those of industrial toil, and if bourgeois women are to practise the former, it seems that it can be only at the expense of their proletarian counterparts.

To render the poor virtuous they must be employed, and women in the middle rank of life, did they not ape the fashions of the nobility, without catching their ease, might employ them, while they themselves managed their families, instructed their children, and exercised their own minds. Gardening, experimental philosophy, and literature, would afford them subjects to think of and matter for conversation, that in some degree would exercise their understandings.

(p. 83)

The model is that of the bourgeois, Protestant family and since women's civic contribution is, according to this model, that of unpaid reproductive labour, it is simply inapplicable to families that cannot be sustained by a single (male) breadwinner. It is this vision which is spelt out in sentimental detail:

I have then viewed with pleasure a woman nursing her children, and discharging the duties of her station with perhaps merely a servant-maid to take off her hands the servile part of the household business. I have seen her present herself and children, with only the luxury of cleanliness, to receive her husband, who, returning weary in the evening, found smiling babes and a clean hearth.

(p. 156)

Despite allusions to women's need for material self-sufficiency, Wollstonecraft does not seem to realize that the sexual division of labour which she advocates must reproduce the patriarchal family, since cultural equivalence cannot cancel out economic dependence.

But what of unmarried women? They had been virtually ignored by the liberal tradition thus far, and Wollstonecraft's pleas on their behalf yield some more radical applications of the doctrine. 'I cannot help lamenting', she writes, 'that women of a superior cast have not a road open by which they can pursue more extensive plans of usefulness and independence' (p. 161). Here, then, is the Lockean claim that women are free as individuals to struggle for the best possible arrangement for themselves. Although she expects most to choose marriage, it must be freely chosen; only access to respectable occupations can prevent its being simply an alternative to prostitution or jobs of the most humiliating and menial kind.[53] For those 'honest, independent women' who cannot or will not marry, she calls for opportunities to work as, for example, physicians or shop and farm managers. She goes on to suggest that women might even have representatives in government, although it was not until the next century that suffrage would be seriously demanded, and Wollstonecraft's views on governmental corruption prevent this from being an especially urgent appeal (p. 161). Nevertheless, these were the undeveloped but radical demands that would be taken up by the women's movement in the second half of the nineteenth century and that allowed suffragists in the 1920s still to look back on the 1792 work as a seminal text regarding the premises of their movement.[54]

In conclusion, Mary Wollstonecraft's vision of sexual equality remained a liberal one. It stressed the cultural and psychological foundations of women's oppression and sought to overcome these via an equality of education and rights predicated on a single model of suprasexual humanity. It is true that equal but different roles were to be embodied in a division of labour which placed women in the family and men in the commercial world, but both realms were perceived as public ones where significant civic duties were performed in a spirit of civic virtue and under the protection of civil rights.

Any theory of women's emancipation had to deal with the fact that children needed reproducing and rearing. Wollstonecraft suggested two possible ways of doing this, both typically liberal. The first was keeping women at home, supported by husbands and unremunerated. Traditionally, this division had been backed up by theories of natural difference and function, but Wollstonecraft eschewed such justification. Her claim that household duties required the same qualities as other acts of citizenship then begs the question of why roles should not be interchangeable between the sexes, but this was not raised. An alternative suggestion was that a minority of talented women might choose either not to reproduce or if they did, to purchase domestic services from others. The radical individualism of this second proposition remains problematic from a feminist perspective, however. Wollstonecraft implied that only women's services would be bought for such tasks and we must assume that this would have occurred both at a minimal wage and without precluding its recipients from performing their own domestic labour when they returned home. Indeed, even the first proposal implies that the duties associated with reproduction are performed best if domestic drudgery is relinquished to hired servants. In other words, Wollstonecraft's proposals would have emancipated only middle-class women, because they relied upon an army of wage-labourers to supplement their domestic performance. This conclusion is perhaps a disappointing one in so far as she must have been aware of the far more radical solutions being developed by Godwin. He advocated the elimination of marriage and single-unit families with their replacement by communal arrangements.[55]

It was left to the Utopian Socialists to take up this suggestion. It should be remembered, nevertheless, that Wollstonecraft did support the Jacobin cause; she was a critic of commercial society and of disparities in wealth as well as in rights. Her appeal on behalf of women was made in the context of a belief that all people should be freed from arbitrary power and exploitation.[56] It was this belief that allowed her to attack Rousseau's treatment of women while supporting his vision of an egalitarian community.

6 J.S. Mill: Political Economist, Utilitarian and Feminist

John Stuart Mill (1806–73) has gained a reputation as the most significant liberal thinker to apply the doctrine's premises explicitly to women.[1] In his *Autobiography,* he refers to his 'strong convictions' on complete sexual equality in all legal, political, social and domestic relations (the exclusion of the economic is significant), reminiscing that these convictions 'were among the earliest results of the application of my mind to political subjects'.[2] The outcome was one text—*The Subjection of Women* (1869)—devoted exclusively to the topic of women's emancipation, and references to sexual equality scattered throughout his other works. The *Subjection* has rightly been the subject of substantial commentary,[3] but in this chapter I shall argue that it forms an integral part of Mill's liberal vision: it can no more be discussed in isolation than it can be dismissed as an esoteric or marginal concern. Mill's support for female emancipation was but one part of a broader project for social regeneration, yet perhaps the most significant one. Only by encompassing all of Mill's writing can we do justice to his views on women.

Accordingly, I will show how Mill's advocacy of sexual equality fitted into his more general pursuit of social utility, demonstrating that his arguments concerning women were analogous to, and related to, those concerning workers and the disenfranchised generally. Within this framework, it will then be possible to address the more specific treatment of women, examining the explanations which he gave for their subjection, the areas in which he believed change to be most vital, the adequacy of his solutions and the theoretical grounds on which he demanded their emancipation.

Mill's liberalism was an economic as well as a political creed, however, and it is instructive to begin by situating him within a tradition of political economy. The discipline is significant because it flourished in an age when political thinkers had grown accustomed to separating the private realm of the family from the public spheres of production and government, so that they rarely discussed women's economic activity. Classical economists were nevertheless obliged to surmount this dichotomy on two key topics: reproduction and wages. In both areas they recognized certain familial and sexual arrangements as conducive to economic well-being. Although these were usually unfavourable to women, Mill's commitment to the latter's emancipation was at least partially inspired by the gains for economic utility which he glimpsed there.

Liberal pronouncements on free and equal individuals were well attuned to the needs of a market economy with its model of anonymous persons freely exchanging equivalents without concern for any natural difference or status. All the leading Utilitarians were political economists who associated limitations on government with both civil liberty and *laissez-faire*. Reproduction was treated by them in an unsentimental manner, as one of the constituents of a healthy economy. The focus was on the physical supply of the labour force and on the level of wages needed to guarantee its effective replacement. Such concerns had already been evident in Adam Smith's *Wealth of Nations* (1776).

Smith recognized that the worker must receive a wage adequate for both his own subsistence and that of dependants since 'otherwise it would be impossible for him to bring up a family, and the race of such workmen could not last beyond the first generation'.[4] Citing evidence that the wife would be able to earn her own subsistence and calculating that half a couple's offspring would die, he concluded that the man must additionally earn enough to support four children—the equivalent of one male subsistence wage. This 'advantage' allows the father to claim greater remuneration. Smith went on to acknowledge that poverty is unfavourable to childbearing though not necessarily to fertility. In the 'inferior ranks' it is infant mortality which limits numbers and higher wages will therefore encourage survival.

Two significant assumptions emerge from these speculations. First, it is accepted that the male is the breadwinner and that he, rather than the wife, should be paid a family-wage. Not only is her lower earning capacity (which is never explained) to remain uncompensated, but it is actually to be increased relative to the man whose dependants she and her child must become. This representation of the family economic unit is then quite different from that seventeenth-century model where husband and wife made equally important contributions to the domestic economy with the wife only subsequently relinquishing control over her share. It reflects the differential effects of capitalism on the two sexes. Second, the whole area of reproduction is removed from that realm in which individuals act as moral agents: it is the hidden hand which regulates the supply of labourers. Where demand for labour increases, so do wages and chances of child vitality; where labour is superfluous, falling wages will restrict the number of children who reach working age: 'It is in this manner that the demand for men, like that of any other commodity, necessarily regulates the production of men; quickens it when it goes on too slowly and stops it when it advances too fast'.[5] Lest we baulk at these impersonal imperatives, we are assured that to complain 'is to lament over the necessary effect and cause of the greatest prosperity'.[6] This calculus of reproduction could hardly be further from Aristotelian or Christian accounts with their elaborate symbolism of natural and moral status. Women's disability and heteronomy are still taken for granted, but they now take a more appropriate pragmatic and economic form where previously they were clothed in the language of disability and sin.

Before moving on to Mill's response to demographic problems, one further aspect of Smith's work must be mentioned. This is his distinction between productive and unproductive labour. Smith harangues against unproductive labourers—those who produce services rather than vendible goods; use rather than exchange values—whom he perceives as parasites and a drain on funds that would be better invested.[7] Although he does not mention women among those 'frivolous' persons whose professions are unproductive, the derogation of activities which yield nothing to the market could only promote the idea that a domestic labour productive only of use-values, was actually unproductive and unimportant, a separate sphere to be ignored by the bourgeois science of production. As Marx would write, in 'political economy *labor* occurs only in the form of *wage-earning activity*'.[8] Women would count, then, only in so far as they produced commodities, and when they reproduced, it would be at the behest of the market. The analysis is almost too ruthlessly egalitarian; it desexualizes productive and reproductive activity into components of the market but excludes women *qua* women from consideration, while taking for granted the structural disadvantages they suffer.

Smith's speculations on population were systematized at the turn of the century by Thomas Malthus, whose *Essay on Population* was still largely accepted by Mill in his *Principles of Political Economy* (1848). Mill acknowledges that population has a tendency to grow much faster than food production, with its corollary that wages must fall as labour is oversupplied. Demographic control is therefore essential, and one solution he offers is women's emancipation. Mill was an early exponent of contraception but since this was neither available nor its advocacy permissable, he advises as alternatives 'provident habits of conduct' and 'the opening of industrial occupations freely to both sexes'.[9] The latter facilitates a utility which goes unmentioned in the later *Subjection:* ' a great diminution of the evil of over-population'. If childbearing ceases to be women's main role, then population will be stabilized and the sexual instinct weakened:

It is by devoting one-half of the human species to that exclusive function, by making it fill the entire life of one sex, and interweave itself with almost all the objects of the other, that the animal instinct in question is nursed into the disproportionate preponderance which it has hitherto exercised in human life.[10]

Women who work rather than marry serve a valuable Malthusian function in suppressing both reproduction and passion.

The question is taken up again in the essay 'On Liberty' (1859). Mill's aim here is to establish 'one very simple principle', namely 'that the sole end for which mankind are warranted, individually or collectively, in interfering with the liberty of action of any of their number, is self-protection'.[11] In attempting to draw a line between those self-regarding acts which concern only the agent and 'other-regarding' acts whose effects on others' interests justify social interference, we might have expected Mill to make a neat division between a private familial realm and a public one. But he eschews this option, citing at least two instances in which intervention in domestic affairs is desirable. First, he berates the state for failing to control the way in which domestic power is abused: the removal of husbands' despotism over wives is equated with the simple expedient of giving women equal rights and legal protection. However, it is in the case of children that Mill finds a special failure of public diligence. The state must enforce an obligation on parents to educate their children as future citizens, or a 'moral crime' is perpetrated against both child and society.[12] But it is the state's interest in reproduction that most concerns Mill. It is no longer provident habits and working women which are to limit population, but the law itself.

To produce children under Malthusian penalties is for Mill no private act but 'a serious offence against all who live by the remuneration of their labour'. Accordingly, he denies that laws forbidding marriage, in those cases where there is inadequate proof that a family could be supported, are a violation of liberty.[13] Reproduction falls into his category of other-regarding acts and so warrants public sanction. The family thus provides an extreme and perhaps surprising example of the extent to which Mill was willing to accept public intervention despite his reputation as a proponent of negative liberty. On the question of reproduction at least, he seems to have been ready to suggest measures that would indiscriminately promote or hinder women's interests, in the name of public prosperity.

In the last section I suggested that Mill's treatment of women needs to be seen in the context of a wider concern with social utility, at least on the question of reproduction. His interest there was mainly an economic one and we saw that political economy did treat its reproducing units in a cavalier fashion. In this section I intend to look more generally at Mill's utilitarian and liberal vision, to show how women's emancipation fitted in as perhaps its most vital component.

Bentham's classic utilitarian model of individuals who are each a bundle of appetites striving to maximize their pleasure and minimize their pain is not dissimilar to the Hobbesian paradigm and it manifests the same fundamental egalitarianism in its logic. For Bentham all pleasures are of equal value and all persons have an equal capacity to pursue them. It is possible to argue, as it was in Hobbes's case, that the resulting picture is peculiarly masculine—his egoistic individuals do not readily conform, for example, to an image of self-sacrificing and nurturing family life—but Bentham at least suggests a universal psychology which avoids the Rousseauian distinctions of the gendered mind (much as Hobbes had escaped its Aristotelian formulation). His assertion that the greatest happiness of the greatest number should be the criterion of all individual and public acts formally implies that the female half of the race be included in the felicific calculus.[14]

J.S. Mill's main quarrel with Benthamite utilitarianism is its indifference to the quality of pleasure. For him intellectual and moral pleasures are more rewarding and enduring than the immediate gratifications of selfish and sensual delight and are therefore to be encouraged. When Mill affirms his commitment to utility as the ultimate ground for appeal on all ethical questions, he explains that 'it must be utility in the largest sense, grounded in the permanent interests of a man as a progressive being'.[15]

Despite the generic 'man' used here, it is evident that Mill's refined notion of utility must encompass both sexes in his vision of 'progressive being'. But individuals cannot develop their faculties in isolation: formal instruction is not sufficient and individuals must be placed within a vibrant culture where stimulating discourse and an active concern for public affairs will feed the intellectual capacities. It is this goal which underlies Mill's belief that liberty of expression is essential and it is especially significant for women, whose expressive powers have been so effectively stifled. He is concerned, then, both that women fail to develop if they are excluded from such involvement and that society as a whole is impoverished if it denies itself their contribution. In order to appreciate the way in which Mill developed this argument, it is helpful to see how he applied it to the three radical causes which he took up:

socialism, democracy and feminism (all of which are of course relevant to women and not just the last).

Given Mill's liberal reputation it is surprising to discover that he was for a while a self-proclaimed socialist. He supported the Chartists and probably found a striking resemblance between their demands and those of early feminists, for the vote. However, Mill's concern for the working class extended beyond their enfranchisement. In his *Principles* he accepts classical economists' account of production and thus supports competition and private property in liberal fashion. But he also envisages a more equitable distribution of wealth via restrictions on inheritance, extensions of peasant proprietorship, universal education and more equal opportunities. More significantly, he points to the utility of actively involving workers in the economy rather than leaving them as passive wage-earners, advocating profit-sharing and cooperatives to achieve this.[16] His socialism inclined towards a syndicalist version of small, competing associations, and the prime value he ascribed to these was directly related to his utilitarian interest in 'man' as a progressive being.

Labouring under self-imposed rules and thereby developing a business sense and an interest in the wider operations of the economy, will, Mill believes, enhance self-respect and dignity; it will encourage precisely that moral and communal spirit which he associates with the maximization of happiness. In short, his socialist suggestions are motivated primarily by liberal values: responsibility, autonomy and reason will thrive through participation. He speaks of the 'civilising and improving influences of association' as well as a 'moral revolution' arising from 'the conversion of each being's daily occupation into a school of social sympathies and the practical intelligence'.[17] Mill explicitly includes the right of both sexes to govern these associations, as a requirement for advancing social utility, but he makes it clear that his primary interest lies with that social utility rather than with the working class as such: 'The prospect of the future depends on the degree in which they can be made rational beings'.[18] Nevertheless, the chapter in the *Principles* 'On the Probable Futurity of the Labouring Classes', makes abundantly clear the parallels that Mill saw between sex and class oppression and the need in both cases to abandon paternalistic protection in favour of responsible self-government.

Mill's concern with extending the suffrage and with participatory democracy is motivated by an identical logic. Both Bentham and James Mill had viewed the franchise as a defensive check on rulers' sinister interests and the latter had gone on to exclude women from the vote for reasons which will become apparent in the next chapter. The younger Mill profoundly disagreed with his father regarding both the purpose and extent of enfranchisement. He eulogizes the benefits of public involvement: democracy, like workers' co-operatives, will encourage a higher moral culture by promoting an interest in public affairs. And he finds this argument especially applicable to the question of female suffrage, since it is women who most languish in privacy and thereby threaten public integrity. When he presents their case before Parliament, he is eager to show that in stimulating woman's faculties, the vote will widen and liberalize her sympathies as well as taming her power: 'I want to make her influence work by manly interchange of opinion, and not by cajolery'.[19]

Mill's argument that participation and practice are the route to a moral education is also applied to the family, but here the case is more fundamental and presented by him as the *conditio sine qua non* for improvement in all other areas of life. When he speaks about 'sympathetic association' as the sole route to a just and equitable society, or claims that the 'only school of genuine moral sentiment is society between equals', [20] he has in mind domestic as well as productive relations. The family is the most important institution for inculcating progressive social and political values:

Citizenship, in free countries, is partly a school of society in equality; but citizenship plays only a small place in modern life, and does not come near the daily habits or inmost sentiments. The family, justly constituted, would be the real school of the virtues of freedom . . . it should be a school of sympathy in equality, of living together in love, without power on one side or obedience on the other. . . . The moral training of mankind will never be adapted to the conditions of the life for which all other human progress is a preparation, until they practise in the the family the same moral rule which is adapted to the normal constitution of human society.[21]

The importance of equitable family relations is underlined in 'On Liberty', where Mill defines them as 'a case, in its direct influence on human happiness, more important than all others taken together'.[22]

Mill's point in all three examples is that values can neither be taught like pieces of knowledge, nor imposed: they must be learnt by a participation which renders them habitual. The experiences of the child and the relationship it sees between its parents is an education—in justice or despotism. But marriage itself, when it is not egalitarian, poisons the sentiments of its practitioners and destroys any propensity in them for civic sympathy. Mill, perhaps under the influence of Robert Owen, blames all the evils of selfishness and self-worship on the state of nineteenth-century marriage.[23] Social justice cannot survive in a sea of domestic despotism since the latter will have 'a perverting influence of such magnitude that it is hardly possible with our present experience to raise our imaginations to the conception of so great a change for the better as would be made by its removal'.[24] There is no doubt as to the social disutility that contemporary marital arrangements bring, then, because they corrupt all members of society. But their indirect evil, via their effects on women, is especially pernicious.

Exclusion of women from the public sphere represented a total antithesis to the enlightened culture of free expression which Mill sought. In the list of utilities which he presents in favour of female emancipation in the *Subjection,* the concern is invariably with the contributions that free women would make to a culture from which all would benefit, just as everyone suffers from the ills their exclusion brings.

Giving women use of their potential in occupations of their choice would double the mental faculties at humanity's service as well as stimulating men's own intellects by the additional competition (the argument here parallels the more general plea on behalf of liberty in the essay of that title).[25] Women's power over their husbands would also be more responsible if they had an interest in its social ramifications, whereas currently, it may be 'not only unenlightened, but employed on the morally wrong side'.[26] As long as woman is imprisoned in the private sphere, she 'neither knows nor cares which is the right side in politics, but she knows what will bring in money or invitations, give her husband a title, her son a place, or her daughter a good marriage'.[27] Her ignorance even makes her a menace in economic terms: at a time when the most obvious channel open to active women was that of philanthropy, Mill contends that charity is misplaced unless it helps the poor to help themselves, since it upsets the equilibrium of market forces.[28]

The list of narrow-minded woman's threats to society continues. In *On Liberty* Mill had condemned the stifling of novelty by the mediocrity of public opinion. Now it is unreconstructed woman herself whom he associates with the despotism of custom: the 'wife is the auxiliary of the common public opinion'.[29] The exceptional man will be ground down by the wife who fears risk and jealously guards her family's reputation, thereby inhibiting the social regeneration which Mill anticipates: 'With such an influence in every house . . . is it any wonder that people in general are kept down in that mediocrity of respectability which is becoming a marked characteristic of modern times?'[30] In other words, unless women are forced into the public arena wherein participation will enlighten them to more lofty interests, they will encourage the mass levelling which Mill identified as the modern syndrome *par excellence*.

As long as the family is organized along hierarchical lines, then, children will be schooled in tyranny, and public virtue will be undermined by the self-love encouraged in men and the narrow-mindedness enforced in women. As in the case of the working class and the disenfranchised, it is public engagement and free association which are to engender social responsibility and the transcendence of narrow self-interest. Familial education, like a political or economic one, lies in the practising of social virtues; Mill's discussions of women, workers and voters are all components of one strategy for achieving a liberal society and they use structurally identical arguments. The domestic realm is nevertheless the lynchpin in so far as it is at home that the moral sentiments are first generated and in women's seclusion that their greatest threat is nurtured. Once we see this, it is highly misleading to believe that Mill's politics can be appreciated without giving a central place to his views on women.

During Mill's lifetime, feminism developed from an idea in the minds of scattered individuals to a well-organised movement. Mill was involved in this development in a practical as well as a theoretical capacity. As MP for Westminster, he spoke to the

House on behalf of (single) women's suffrage. He also gave evidence to a Royal Commission on the Contagious Diseases Act, which he claimed offensive to his principles of liberty, and contributed towards scholarships which would assist women's entry into the universities.[31] The areas on which his published writings concentrated were those of marriage, employment and the vote—all subject to agitation by the fledgling women's movement which was aided by the theoretical arguments that Mill presented on its behalf.

We have already seen why Mill found marital arrangements inimical to society as a whole, but it is also obvious from the *Subjection* that he believed them to be the source of the greatest humiliation suffered by women. Julia Annas argues that Mill was concerned with marital relations only in so far as 'they reflect profound social and economic inequalities between the sexes'.[32] Yet Mill himself seems more predisposed to reverse this claim and presents marriage as the source of all other limitations: the men who benefit from their powerful position at home fear that were women given alternatives to marital inequality, they would seize them and so such options must remain closed.[33] Although Mill's analysis of the causes of women's oppression is a theoretical advance, then, it is typical of the limits of liberal analysis that he should find them in a legal relationship and throw his energies into pursuing change here.

To demonstrate the inequities of marriage, Mill draws on the familiar nineteenth-century litany of legal horrors: the wife lacks rights over children, her property, even her own body; she is the subject of domestic violence and sexual abuse. In sum, there 'remain no legal slaves, except the mistress of every house'.[34] Women's legal and conceptual condition had worsened quite considerably since the seventeenth century when Hobbes and Locke equated wives with free servants. Worse still, however, the wife is under constant surveillance; even her mind is enslaved since men desire control over women's sentiments as well as their obedience.[35] The result is that woman's very nature is distorted. Like Wollstonecraft, then, Mill challenges the idea that woman is naturally equipped for private seclusion; instead, false attributes of self-sacrifice and submission are enforced, and those qualities of moral agency so admired by liberals are correspondingly crushed.

Mill's attack on marital conventions is perhaps the most progressive aspect of his thought. But when he tries to work out its implications, his radicalism often falters. The discussion of marriage invoked related considerations centring on questions of property. For woman's status within the family, like her freedom to choose whether to marry at all, is contingent upon her access to material independence. It is nevertheless where economic relationships appear on the agenda that Mill is least adequate in addressing women's problems. He supports a rather Lockean form of marriage contract: while favouring a community of goods, he believes that as long as the law insists on recognizing only personal ownership, each should retain what they would have had had they not married. Where a family relies on its earnings, he prefers that the man should earn the income and the wife supervise its domestic expenditure.[36] It is to introduce such arrangements that he believes woman must have the vote, but the solution he presents is clearly inadequate.

First of all, Mill replicates Locke's shortcomings: the right to retain one's own property ignores the fact that women earn and inherit substantially less than men. Second, then, the situation only reinforces the wife's economic dependence on her husband, a fact which will render the legal changes which Mill advocates a merely formal improvement for the majority. We have already seen that political economy accepted the idea of the family wage with its implications of the male breadwinner and female dependant. And despite Mill's enthusiasm for free association, he still foresees a practical authority in marriage yielded according to the 'comparative qualifications' which are to facilitate not legal but 'voluntary adjustment'. Since the criteria for these qualifications involve age, the bringing of material support, mental superiority and 'superior decision of character', it is difficult not to conclude that custom, if not law, will yet reinforce patriarchy.[37]

Third, it follows that Mill's claims never amount to an attack on the sexual division of labour which underlies much inequality. Indeed, when it comes to the question of equality in this context, Mill inverts his argument to speak of duties rather than rights: if the woman supervises the household economy as well as bearing and raising children, then she performs at least her fair share of the domestic tasks. He fails to ask whether she also reaps her fair share of the benefits.

To be fair to Mill, he does recognize that if woman is *obliged* to earn, this makes her susceptible to exploitation by her husband and subject to double toil. But this obscures the issue, which is surely one of opportunities rather than obligations. Nor does Mill consider that husbands would lack power and incentive to exploit genuinely equal women, or that women's economic contribution to the household might engender an equivalent obligation on men to share the housework.

Apart from a few women with exceptional faculties, Mill in any case finds marital duties incompatible with social production. His case for their access to jobs rests on the rather weak assertion that the '*power* of earning is essential to the dignity of a woman, if she has not independent property'.[38] His main concern in calling for occupational opportunities for women is that they should have the choice of whether to marry in the first place. Here their earning power must be adequate to offer an alternative and to provide the security for those who do wed, to know that they can survive should their husbands mistreat them or die (in the former case, Mill is willing to sanction separation).[39] But as far as married women are concerned, he thinks less that they *should* be materially independent than that they should know they *could* be if it proved necessary. This, then, is the basis of his plea for access to 'respectable' employment and equal opportunites in the competition for all kinds of work.

It was left to Harriet Taylor, Mill's more radical partner, to assert the benefits of female independence within marriage: 'a woman who contributes materially to the support of the family, cannot be treated in the same contemptuously tyrannical manner as one who, however she may toil as a domestic drudge, is dependent on the man for subsistence'.[40] Taylor's concern to show how these benefits outweigh the problem of a flood of new competitors onto the oversubscribed labour market (where they would have the same effects as their prolific progeny in depressing wages), perhaps explains why Mill, the more orthodox political economist, was reluctant to go so far. Taylor, more faithful to the Mills' socialism, looks ahead to an age when rewards are no longer determined by the market.[41] J.S. Mill's commitment to liberal economics, like his liberal emphasis on formal rights, therefore severely limits his feminism. Ultimately, his concern for women's employment is less economic than psychological: the experience will enhance their sense of autonomy and responsibility, as long as they do not need to put such values into practice. Yet Mill's psychology is also problematic here, since despite his avowed commitment to the malleability of human nature, he does intermittently lapse into suggestions that women are on the whole naturally predisposed for domestic life; that they are innately practical and intuitive rather than speculative.[42]

The details of emancipation which Mill supplies in the *Subjection* offer further cause for disappointment because the abstract argument he had presented in 'On Liberty' had suggested that far more radical proposals might be forthcoming. Here he had spoken of liberating individuals from the despotic hand of custom; the importance 'of framing the plan of our life to suit our own character'.[43] This, together with the promotion of 'different experiments in living' seems to imply a more thorough attack on traditional roles than he subsequently ventured. Perhaps the reason, as Mill's critics like to suggest, was his fear of further alienating his audience. The Utopian Socialists were advocating far more imaginative 'experiments' in domestic relations than Mill and being roundly condemned for it. But it is also tempting to explain Mill's caution by his élitism. The liberty which he most valued was that of the exceptional genius or eccentric, whose innovations were being sacrificed to a stifling public opinion. Similarly, he appears to have sincerely believed marriage and domesticity to be the right choice for the majority of women. When he puts the case for their enfranchisement, he acknowledges that the 'ordinary occupations of most women are, and are likely to remain, principally domestic'.[44] His main concern is that the talented few—like Harriet Taylor—should be free to escape and shine. When he eventually married Harriet, he signed a statement formally repudiating the legal implications of the act.[45] But perhaps he feared that genuine and widespread female independence would after all unleash an explosion of passion, sweeping away those 'provident habits of conduct' required to control reproduction and his own lofty ideals of the enlightened individual.

*   *   *

The weakness of Mill's solution to women's oppression arises in large part from the analysis which he offers of its causes. This relies less on empirical investigation than on deductions from his philosophy of history. Although he offers examples, such as marriage, of women's subjection, he never really accounts for the phenomenon beyond allusions to a sort of historical inertia.

Mill perceives history as undulating through cycles of crisis and consensus, but overall he shares the nineteenth century's optimism in its progress. He equates that progress with a transition from barbarism to civilization. This means that relations of subordination which were originally based on force, have now been replaced by rational, liberal relations resting on consent and legitimized by appeals to social expedience. It was indeed this faith which underlay the reformism of the Utilitarians. But Mill perceives sexual relations as something of an anomaly, the result of uneven development. 'The disabilities . . . to which women are subject from the mere fact of their birth, are the solitary examples of the kind in modern legislation'.[46] Women's dependence is not based on social utility but is 'the primitive state of slavery lasting on'; it has no other source than 'the law of the strongest'. 'It has not lost the taint of its brutal origin'.[47] Once the inconsistency has been exposed and sexual arrangements subjected to rational scrutiny, then Mill is optimistic that they will fall into line. Only then will marital relations mirror the free and sympathetic association which he saw emerging in civil and economic affairs.

At times Mill shrouds such a development in an air of inevitability: 'We are entering into an order of things in which justice will . . . be the primary virtue; grounded . . . on sympathetic association'; as modern life 'progressively improves, command and obedience become exceptional facts in life, equal association its general rule'.[48] But when it came to actual campaigning, he could not underestimate the difficulty of such a shift. The strategy which he adopted was then the most appropriate to his analysis: publicization and discussion of women's case in articles, public speeches and Parliament, were the route to public enlightenment

And there are so many causes tending to make the feelings connected with this subject the most intense and most deeply-rooted of all those which gather round and protect old institutions and customs, that we may not wonder to find them as yet less undermined and loosened than any of the rest by the progress of the great modern spiritual and social transition.[49]

He does not appear to have recognized that there might be structural reasons for women's continued and reinforced subjugation, predicated on contemporary interests which might be perfectly rational and useful to their practitioners. He does not see that capitalism might benefit from women's domestic role nor that men may have continuing reasons for oppressing women beyond their own bad principles and barbaric legacy. He acknowledges only that 'from the very earliest twilight, every woman (owing to the value attached to her by men, combined with her inferiority of muscular strength) was found in a state of bondage to some man'.[50] In so far as Mill explains the origin of patriarchy, he finds it rooted in men's greater strength and love of power: 'Whatever gratification of pride there is in the possession of power, and whatever personal interest in its exercise, is in this case . . . common to the whole male sex'.[51] Despite such seeming universality of a gendered consciousness, however, Mill goes on to assert that a more intellectual culture now negates the advantage of strength, while he attributes men's continued urge for power only to the unhealthy lessons taught by the inequities of marriage. Here, he has faith that such men will be persuaded of the moral harm they are inflicting upon themselves. In sum, the subordination of women, which is embodied in the law, relies for Mill only on a tradition that has yet to be reformed according to rational principles.

The suffrage issue had brought out into the open the whole panoply of prejudice against women as well as highly confused notions concerning sexual corruption which were entangled in the distinction between private and public spheres. Women's particularity was perceived as a threat to public enlightenment (and we have seen how Mill turned this contention to their advantage), yet politics was itself perceived as a threat to the female virtue exercised in the home, due to its Machiavellian/Hobbesian ethos. It is the same conundrum that Rousseau and Wollstonecraft had clashed over in a different context, with public interests being viewed as distractions from female duty, on the one hand, and the prerequisite for their civic virtue, on the other. Even the suffragists jumped into the fray when they tried to claim that women would purify politics, ignoring the fact that they could do so only with a virtue which was, as Wollstonecraft and Mill recognized, a product of their oppression.

Mill's attempt to subject discussions about women to rational debate marked a real advance, even if the accompanying assumption that this alone might suffice to eliminate their subjection was naïve. The terms of the discourse which he set for the debate were of course those of social utility. We have already seen how women fitted into the broader picture of Mill's utilitarianism, but before concluding this chapter, it is necessary to assess the adequacy of the utilitarian argument for sexual equality.

In positing their ideals of justice and equality, liberals tended to have recourse to one of two types of argument: natural rights and utilitarianism. In the previous chapter we saw an example of the former, with its attendant difficulty in convincing sceptics that such claims were intellectually grounded or practically desirable. For while the demise of teleological arguments meant the liberation of persons from categories with fixed qualities ascribed to them, no compelling counter-argument had emerged to prove that they were self-evidently equal. Utilitarianism was in large part an attempt to surmount this difficulty by demanding that all arrangements be justified according to their capacity to increase aggregate pleasure, but its application to questions of sexual equality reveals similar strengths and weaknesses to those it experienced elsewhere.

Surmising that women were in a powerless position to enforce their claims, Mill believed that they must persuade men of those claims' desirability. His utilitarian arguments in both the *Subjection* and the *Representation of the People Bill* (1867) accordingly dwell on the increase in the sum of happiness which will emerge from women's greater participation in it. One problem with such an approach from a feminist perspective, is that it meant Mill rarely focused on benefits to women: the thrust of his argument is more often (as in the case of population control) designed to appeal to men's interests. Only at the very end of the *Subjection,* for example, does he mention 'the unspeakable gain in private happiness to the liberated half of the species; the difference to them between a life of subjection to the will of others, and a life of rational freedom'.[52] This subterfuge is made necessary by his individualistic approach to political change. Only when women have the jobs and votes he campaigns for, does Mill envisage them exercising power on their own behalf. It is therefore men (like himself) who must mediate women's demands, and so their support must be won. (Although Mill was not alive to witness the militant disruption and civil disobedience to which suffragettes would eventually be driven, it is unlikely that he would have approved.)

A second and related problem, and one suffered by utilitarianism generally, is that it embarks upon the slippery slope of expediency. In advertising the social benefits of sexual equality, it invited counter-arguments regarding its dysfunction. These were not slow in coming (women would corrupt and be corrupted; they were already too powerful, they were too dependent to think for themselves). The case for female emancipation thus threatened to rely on the outcome of a cost–benefit analysis (a calculation intrinsic to utilitarianism, although one whose crudeness Mill's appeal to 'man' as a 'progressive being' was designed to circumvent). At this point the moral thrust of the natural rights position disappears and the implication that compromises might be prudent, creeps in. For rights are now means to general well-being rather than absolute ends intrinsic to every individual. Perhaps this is why Mill sometimes lapses in the *Subjection,* as his critics have pointed out, into contentions that sound suspiciously like appeals to natural rights.[53] But let us look at this charge more carefully, since it is important regarding the grounds on which sexual equality is demanded.

Mill's opening paragraph in the *Subjection* does indeed seem to appeal to both types of argument: women's subordination is 'wrong in itself' but also 'one of the chief hindrances to human improvement'. Perfect equality before the law is a matter of 'justice and expediency'.[54] Can these be reconciled?

While rejecting the argument for natural rights, Mill believes that it is those who wish to discriminate against certain categories of person, who must prove that their exclusions enhance social utility. Justice demands equal treatment of all persons unless acceptable grounds are offered for discrimination. He rejects many of the sexual differences which are cited in this context, since they are frequently artificial ones, the result of 'forced repression in some directions, unnatural stimulation in others'.[55] And where they are irreducible, they are generally irrelevant to questions of civil and political right. In his essay *Utilitarianism,* Mill more explicitly demonstrates the relationship between appeals to justice and social utility.[56]

In listing aspects of justice here, Mill makes the point that it is 'inconsistent with justice to be partial; to show favour or preference to one person over another, in matters to which favour and preference do not properly apply'.[57] Justice is therefore closely allied to equality: it demands equal protection of everyone's rights. All this sounds like a natural rights argument, but Mill goes on to reveal its utilitarian rationale. General utility demands the punishment of those who inflict harm on society since all have a vital interest in security. If transgressors go unpunished, pain follows. But each also needs to know that their rights—claims which society has agreed to guarantee—will be equally protected, otherwise insecurity and hence disutility, again follow. In short, injustice means disutility because arbitrary treatment means general insecurity, while the greatest happiness principle presupposes that each person's pleasure (hence security and rights) counts for the same. All inexpedient inequalities are therefore unjust, but all injustice is also inexpedient. Here Mill returns to his theme of progress in history: social improvement occurs as the disutility of unwarranted privilege is increasingly recognized and so it will be 'with the aristocracies of colour, race and sex'.[58]

Although this discussion apparently resolves any conflict between rights and utilitarian appeals, it does not seem to apply very well to women, and this is perhaps why the clarification is absent from the *Subjection.* For the insecurity which Mill presents as the greatest evil of injustice arises from the fear of arbitrary treatment. Quite apart from the fact that Mill's opponents believed that they had good grounds for discriminating against women, there was clearly no danger of men suffering women's fate and so there was no reason for them to feel insecure. For there was no likelihood of judges or legislators or men in general falling into that proscribed category of women, who did not even qualify for citizenship.

Ryan criticizes Mill's emphasis on security because he omits the notions of merit and desert which we usually associate with the idea of justice.[59] This is perhaps especially unfortunate in women's case, since Mill might have made a stronger argument for the justice (*qua* utility) of their emancipation on some such basis. Given such lacunae, it is not surprising that when Mill mentions justice in the context of women, he sometimes lapses into moral claims over and above the arguments he presents on grounds of utility. For while the latter are persuasive, they are not as compelling as Mill's commitment to the cause demanded. The concern for a rich and progressive culture (i.e. utility in its broadest sense) makes a more convincing utilitarian case for sexual equality, but this relies on a plea for liberty rather than for justice—a claim perhaps less appropriate to the legal reforms being demanded. It is not then entirely clear from Mill's discussion, whether a purely utilitarian case can be convincingly made for the justice of sexual equality.

In this chapter, I have intimated that despite his undoubtedly sincere commitments to women's emancipation, Mill's vision of what that would entail is quite restricted. Some of the criticisms that I have levelled at his feminism are simply more specific applications of a general critique which socialists have made of liberalism: its focus on abstract freedoms and formal rights, characteristically expressed in legal form, ignores the underlying causes of oppression. In women's case, these causes might reside in sexual (male) as well as in economic (capitalist) interests, but in either case, liberals were unwilling to identify and therefore to rectify, these more profound structures of subjugation. The result as far as Mill is concerned, is a tendency to underestimate the tenacity of sexual domination and to overestimate the changes which suffrage and a handful of legal changes, will bring.

Within these liberal constraints, Mill nevertheless introduces a further limitation. I have stressed the relationship between his commitment to sexual equality and his broader utilitarian project. The latter is predicated on a vision of enlightened individuals who pursue only life's 'higher' pleasures, and it is into this ethereal culture that he wishes to introduce women. His image of the emancipated woman is of a rational, talented being who suppresses her passion in pursuit of cultural interests and the development of her faculties—an aspiration more or less shared with Wollstonecraft. Yet this vision remains a peculiarly bourgeois and élitist one (which almost certainly takes for granted the availability of domestic servants), while the suppression of the flesh which it implies, only continues that distaste for the body and hence for reproductive activities (reflected in Mill's pronouncements on population) which had traditionally granted to things female an aura of baseness. Beneath the surface one suspects that there lurks Platonic and Christian opinion that the truly equal woman is she who eliminates all traces of femaleness. The liberal goal is therefore less one of androgyny than of a generalized androcentrism. In all these capacities the Utopian Socialists, with whose work Mill was quite familiar, were well in advance of him despite their slightly earlier appearance. It is to them that we must now turn.

7 Socialism: Utopian and Feminist

By the mid-nineteenth century, liberalism was triumphant yet already approaching a crisis of confidence. Its demands for freedom and the removal of arbitrary authority had been economic as much as political, designed to challenge royal and religious intrusions in the market. They had borne fruit in a flourishing industrialized, capitalist economy. The corollary was, however, a burgeoning working class concentrated in the new urban centres under conditions of immense deprivation. Periodic crises fuelling unemployment drove many below the breadline. The plight of proletarian women was especially dire since they earned less and had to perform domestic and childbearing roles as well as working long hours under appalling conditions. For many, prostitution was the only option: they sold their bodies on the market in a far more total and degrading manner than men ever sold their labour power. Observers predicted the demise of the working-class family itself. Some liberals responded by considering a more positive role for government to help relieve the suffering. Others, including J.S. Mill, hoped that a more co-operative spirit might emerge. He was inspired in this by a new social theory which had become popular in Britain and France during the 1820s and 1830s. This was socialism, subsequently designated Utopian Socialism to distinguish it from its Marxist successor.

Early socialists realized that the formal rights demanded by liberalism were insufficient to relieve the daily miseries of women and the working class; they looked instead to a reorganization of the whole socio-economic fabric. Although their descriptions of class relations remained rudimentary, they were complemented by an integrated critique of sexual relations. Lacking any scientific analysis of capitalism, they were more like liberals in their emphasis on cultural, moral and psychological factors, although unlike liberals, they recognized the latter's material ramifications. They condemned capitalism primarily on the grounds of its competitive ethic and looked instead to an economy founded on benevolence and co-operation. Selfishness, rather than exploitation, was identified as the real evil. They associated liberalism with an aggressive individualism and centralized state, rejecting both in favour of communities based on small-scale production and voluntary association. The influence of William Godwin, husband of Mary Wollstonecraft and author of the anarchistic *Enquiry Concerning Political Justice* (1793), was apparent in this vision. The French Utopians moved on to contempt for the suffrage issue, but the British socialists continued to promote votes for women and the working class as an interim and educational venture.

The question of women's place in the new arrangements was no marginal matter. It is true that no comprehensive account of the relationship between their oppression and private property had yet been developed, but Utopian Socialists both offered a more thorough account of women's subjection than liberals had managed and made their emancipation an integral part of their solutions. All the theorists to be examined in this chapter presented virulent attacks on marriage, not simply because it denied women civil rights but also because of the personal misery and social degeneration it caused. Socialists recognized that women were often mere commodities bought on the marriage market and were not therefore so different from prostitutes. The latter they perceived as an economic rather than a moral problem. Their main concern, however, was with the values that marriage and the nuclear family promoted, which they charged with contaminating the public realm.

All the early socialists were eager that sympathetic, organic relations should replace competitive, contractual ones. Marital arrangements militated against this. An enlightened and compassionate society required rational, honest relationships—the antithesis of the duplicities practised in matrimony. These early nineteenth-century thinkers perceived marriage as an artificial institution sustained by Church and state. Since it is unnatural for love and desire to be confined in so rigid a structure, misery, boredom, deception and adultery are the inevitable outcome, infecting the whole of society. In the communities aspired to, amorous relations would mirror economic ones in voluntary, open, reciprocal associations. While Mill would take up some of this attack on marriage, he did not perceive it as an instrument of control nor condemn the family itself. He wished to reform family relations, whereas for the socialists the family, like capitalism, Church and religion, must disappear.

Socialists condemned the family on economic as well as on moral grounds. They equated housework with both drudgery and inefficiency. If, together with childrearing, it were collectivized and performed by public employees who were remunerated accordingly, it would gain in status while eluding the sexual division of labour and the isolation that made it so unpleasant. There would be substantially less repetitive, hence wasteful labour and women's talents would no longer be lost to the community. This is well illustrated, for example, by the Irish socialist William Thompson, who writes of domestic activities:

From more than five-sixths of this species of labour, the proposed arrangements free married women, and allow them to co-operate almost as effectively as the men, in contributing, by productive labour, to the common happiness. From purchasing and preparing solid and liquid food, fire-making to heat and light apartments, with all the attendant operations, and retail bargainings, they are relieved by the common kitchen, and lighting and heating apparatus managed by a few for the use of all. From the care of children over two or three years of age, they are relieved by common dormitories, and places of useful training within their view. We may set down the value of this capital arrangement very fairly as one-third added to the means of human happiness, as far as dependent on articles of wealth.[1]

Furthermore, it was anticipated that specialists would be more likely to educate children in co-operative values. Parents' very love for their own offspring rendered them the worst teachers. Of course, many women would still perform such tasks, but they would have the choice and they would no longer be dependent on husbands: both emotionally and economically, the whole community would sustain them. Localized industry and agriculture, plus more communal living arrangements, also meant that the split between home and work, initiated by capitalism and so detrimental to women, could be healed. Criteria of what counted as a contribution to the collective would be broadened such that activities other than those producing exchange value could be rewarded. Women's reproductive activities would be valued and they would have equal opportunities to develop their other capacities.

Although Marx and Engels designated these early socialists utopian, because they considered their work pre-scientific, the latter judgement was not shared by the Utopians themselves. On the one hand, they sought a scientific account of human nature such that it might be nurtured in a felicitous manner. On the other, they tended to place their faith in a technology that would free people from toil while fulfilling their needs. Both ideas were relevant to women: the former implies a belief in the plasticity and educability of the mind as well as stressing the political importance of suitable childrearing practices; the latter was a belief enthusiastically applied by the Utopians to domestic labour.

The Co-operative Movement, as British socialism came to be known, produced two outstanding theoreticians: William Thompson and Robert Owen. Together with his friend Anna Wheeler, Thompson presented his *Appeal on Behalf of Women* in 1825. A decade later, Owen delivered ten lectures 'On the Marriages of the Priesthood of the Old Immoral World'. Together these texts offered what a recent author has described as 'the intellectual founding documents of Socialist Feminism'.[2] I shall look at their theoretical implications in more detail in the first part of this chapter. A discussion of French utopianism as it related to feminism, will follow.

These early versions of socialism had much in common, and this is not surprising given the personal and intellectual associations between the two movements. It was Anna Wheeler who was the real point of contact between Thompson and Owen, on the one hand, and Fourier and the Saint-Simonians, on the other. Well schooled in French rationalism, Wheeler had joined a Saint-Simonian circle as early as 1818, wherein she was proclaimed 'Goddess of Reason'.[3] She brought Saint-Simonian ideas back to England, where she translated them for the co-operative press and also introduced

Fourier to Owen, although their relationship soured when Fourier accused the Owenites of plagiarism. There were also close contacts between the Utopians and progressive liberals. Thompson and Wheeler were both friends of Bentham; Thompson publicly debated with J.S. Mill, with whom he forged a friendship.[4] But while Mill was impressed by Owen's attack on marriage, Saint-Simon's theory of history and the French socialists' economic ideas, it was Fourier's esoteric pronouncements on women that would catch the imagination of subsequent generations of socialists, from Marx and Engels to Bebel and Kollontai.

Historically, *The Appeal* appeared almost mid-way between Wollstonecraft's *Vindication* and Mill's *Subjection*. Indeed, it both prefigures much of the argument regarding women that is popularly associated with Mill and goes beyond it in significant ways. *The Appeal* is a pertinent work for us because while it marks an early argument for women's equality, it also uses a utilitarian framework to suggest that such equality can truly be realized only with co-operation. It nicely bridges the gap between liberalism and socialism. A further, and rather ironic relationship, is Anna Wheeler's contribution to the argument since, as in Harriet Taylor's collaboration with Mill, she provided many of the ideas without being attributed authorship and the extent of her responsibility for the final text is equally difficult to establish. For brevity's sake I refer to the book below as Thompson's own, but his insistence on Wheeler's inspiration must be kept in mind.

Throughout *The Appeal,* the greatest happiness principle remains the pre-eminent criterion for evaluating all socio-economic and political phenomena. It is used, however, to criticize capitalism (referred to as competition), which is identified with attitudes inimical to women's emancipation, and to advocate socialism (a term also absent but denoted by references to Mutual Co-operation or Voluntary Association). Utilitarianism is thus used to advance from a demand for individual rights to a vision of a co-operative system which will transform the entire social structure.

The book is divided into three parts. The first, and longest, offers a refutation of James Mill's case against female enfranchisement. The second part moves towards a broader definition of utility to emphasize the educational advantages of political participation. In the final section (as in the introductory 'Letter to Mrs Wheeler'), and that which is of most interest to us here, *The Appeal* sweeps towards its conclusion that socialism alone is able to facilitate the maximum happiness of both sexes.

The book opens with an attack on James Mill's 'Article on Government' (1820). Here, the elder Mill had argued that since human nature inclines each to pursue their own pleasure at others' expense, institutionalized checks such as the franchise must be introduced to prevent rulers from abusing their power. He had gone on, however, to argue for women's exclusion on the ground that their interests were included in those of husbands and fathers.[5] It is this claim that Thompson attacks.

Thompson claims that there are no good utilitarian grounds for sexual discrimination and that the diminution of aggregate happiness which results from it, offends against the central goal of the doctrine: 'Women are one half of the human race, and as much entitled to happiness on their own account, for their own sakes, as men'.[6] More specifically, however, Mill's case for exclusion must presuppose either that men benevolently safeguard women's particular interests or that there is some sort of natural coincidence between the interests of the sexes. The first view is inconsistent with Mill's own view of human nature, the second empirically incorrect. The very basis of Mill's argument for male rights is that men have a boundless appetite for power and will enslave opponents unless prevented. As Thompson points out, this has been especially true of their behaviour towards women. He goes on to illustrate significant differences between the interests of the sexes, much as the younger Mill will when he fights for female enfranchisement almost half a century later.

Were *The Appeal* to have stopped here, it would have marked an early and significant statement on behalf of women's suffrage, notable if we compare it with Wollstonecraft's cryptic plea just thirty years prior. However, Thompson goes on to argue that even had James Mill been correct regarding a coincidence of interest, he would still have lacked utilitarian grounds for denying women political rights. His claim rests on an expanded notion of utility, which anticipates that of the younger Mill (Thompson already distinguishes 'higher enjoyments' in a most un-Benthamite way). This suggests the necessity of moving from a negative position—rights are needed for self-protection—towards a more positive one which recognizes the political sphere as an arena for the self-development that is requisite to a full enjoyment of civil rights. Women especially need the educational experiences offered by the public realm, owing to the 'casualties of gestation' which confine them, thereby inclining them to 'mere local and personal sympathies'.[7] This emphasis on civic education is again typically liberal, but *The Appeal* connects it with broader proposals that lead Thompson out of the liberal orbit altogether. It is necessary to look at his view of human nature, especially in its gendered capacity, to appreciate this extended utility and its fusion with socialism and feminism.

Thompson does not believe that the aggressive human nature defined by James Mill is universal, nor that the utilitarian premise of pleasure-pursuit/pain-aversion necessarily implies a selfish society. Only where force, competition and ignorance reign is selfishness the norm, but under such conditions, James Mill's puny checks could never be adequate. Instead, it is necessary to eliminate institutionalized power altogether and to back this up with a culture of enlightened utilitarianism that would render association voluntary. Then Bentham's felicific calculus would truly become 'moral knowledge', a 'social science of human happiness'.[8]

For Thompson such a culture is but the outcome of utilitarian logic, since it seems obvious that rational beings must take the effects of their actions on others into account, recognizing themselves to be caught in a web of relationships. Such computation will incorporate others' reactions to our acts such that the pleasure of another's approval or the gratitude received as a result of our benevolence—'the cheap and delightful pleasures of sympathy'[9]—will greatly enhance the happiness available to us. Education is the key to this 'real and comprehensive knowledge, physical and moral'.[10] The distinction between selfish and benevolent recognitions of utility therefore calls for no denial of self-interest but hinges on the difference between ignorant and rational calculations of that interest. Only the latter can negate the 'unhallowed lust of domination'[11] that motivates man in a world driven by force. Those who suffer most under such a system are women, whom men subordinate for the sheer pleasure of command as well as for the fulfilment of appetite, parcelling them out for 'sexual delight' and moulding their minds accordingly. Not only will they therefore have most to gain from a more enlightened culture, but Thompson also suggests that they have a special talent for it owing to their propensity for sympathy with others. In other words, women's nature is different from that described by James Mill and anticipates a higher social stage.

In a world where force reigns, two factors are held responsible by Thompson for women's subordination: their muscular weakness and the childbearing that periodically indisposes them. Neither can any longer offer a *rational* justification for male dominance in public life since the importance of strength is declining with the evolution of machinery and a more intellectual culture. Nor is pregnancy any more a physical handicap than the weaknesses of the male body: men are equally distracted by the diseases and excesses which their imprudence, intemperance and vice summon. Women's weakness is in fact a real advantage in legislative matters since, unable to govern by force, they must favour persuasion as their means, peace as their end. Such legislators could afford to invoke no dissent from unjust policies: 'the sympathies of women for the whole race . . . must, from the fact of their inferior physical strength, have been much more active than those of men, and much more inclined to promote impartially the happiness of all'.[12] In other words, although women's physical disadvantages render them a prey to male strength and domination in primitive cultures where such factors predominate, they equally equip them to be exemplary utilitarians and co-operators by encouraging them to make the calculations necessary for that 'moral knowledge' requisite to socialism. Such qualities are further enhanced by the characteristics they develop in their social roles: caring, nurturing, patience, perseverance, passive courage and fortitude. If legislating were to be the domain of but one sex, Thompson concludes, it would be better done by the nurse than the warrior.

The essence of the nineteenth-century stereotype of woman clearly remains in this sketch, but it is revalorized and we see

here something of the glorification of femininity to which
Utopians were intermittently prone, especially in so far as
female qualities were equated with a future, more perfect state.
The conclusion of Thompson's argument for women's rights is
therefore not merely that justice requires them but that certain
feminine qualities predispose women to sympathy with others.
Released from their narrow application in the family, these
characteristics prefigure a new social order where benevolence
rather than selfishness will be recognized as conducive to
maximum happiness. It is on this basis that the liberal gives way
to the Utopian Socialist in the final section of the book.
Economic, rather than legal, conditions consequently provide
the focus here.

Thompson recognizes that civil and political rights are
inadequate to bring women equality with men as long as a
competitive economy persists: 'their rights might be equal, but
not their happiness, because unequal powers under free
competition must produce unequal effects'.[13] Under
capitalism the weakness and childbearing that still allow men
to dominate women are especially discriminatory in the labour
market. As long as happiness is identified with wealth, and
reward with competitive production, the 'natural bar' which
disadvantages women in systems rewarding strength and
endurance, must operate. Rights do not change this since they
offer no compensation (nor can they, according to the non-
interventionist tenets of political economy).

Thompson sees real equality for women very much in terms
of compensation for their natural disadvantages. He thus
moves from a procedural to a social conception of justice. His
ideal society is modelled on an unlimited liability insurance
company. Under conditions of political economy, the
marriage contract, with its dubious rewards, is the only
recompense which women receive for the reproduction that
bars them from fairly competing for wages. Even were the
marital situation improved, women would remain vulnerable
to a husband's death or profligacy, while the law could never
offer adequate protection against domestic injustice nor
against the sense of superiority accruing to man the
breadwinner.[14] Much more clearly than J.S. Mill, Thompson
sees that women's economic dependence on men must be
broken, as must the exclusive bond between labour and wages.

He and Anna Wheeler look forward to a future where

> anxious individual competition shall give place to mutual co-operation and joint possession; where individuals in large numbers, male and female, forming voluntary associations, shall become a *mutual guarantee* to each other for the supply of all useful wants, and form an *unsalaried and uninsolvent insurance company against all insurable casualties;* where perfect freedom of opinion and perfect equality will reign amongst the co-operators; and where children of all will be equally educated and provided for by the whole[15]

Under such conditions, any talent that added to the common stock of happiness would be valued. Women would not need to labour as hard as men for their rewards since their reproductive contribution would be recognized. The text is full of references to the compensations that will be proffered—'every possible aid of medical skill and kindness is afforded impartially to all, to compensate for the bitterness of those hours when the organization of woman imposes on her superfluous sufferings'[16]—but Thompson does not appear to have any rigid sexual division of labour in mind. He argues that women, children and society would all benefit from a system where mothers are publicly active and children of like ages educated together by enlightened superintendents—of either sex.[17] He is especially eager to eliminate the dependencies of marriage. Women will henceforth rely on the whole association, which will support and educate everybody's offspring. With men no wealthier than women, prostitution will disappear and women will lack motives for bestowing love or sexual favour on any but the most deserving. No longer tied by relations of force or need, the sexes, like socio-economic actors in general, will recognize 'the mutual dependence of each on the other to elicit the highest degree of happiness'.[18]

The Appeal was not Thompson's only work. In 1824 he had presented *An Inquiry into the Principles of the Distribution of Wealth*. Although more specifically devoted to the virtues of a co-operative economy, the details given showed women's emancipation to be an integral part of community life. His discussion of population should also be mentioned because of its relevance to women and to Mill's references to the subject.

Thompson rejected Malthus's argument that poverty was a necessary check on demographic explosion, although he was fully cognizant of the latter problem, especially in his native Ireland. Recognizing that increase was greatest precisely among the lower ranks of society, he demanded that a rational education and planning be introduced: a policy which he believed the wealthy opposed precisely because of their hunger for cheap labour. His advocacy of birth control was revolutionary in the early nineteenth century, as was his belief that sexual pleasure might be severed from the fear of unwanted pregnancy.[19] The way he associated political economy, Malthusianism and the position of women had further radical implications, however. Political economists, as we have seen, reified the category of women in discussing reproduction and disregarded the experiences underlying population's vicissitudes. Thompson's demonstration that demography is a *social relation,* predicated on marital conventions, religion and class interests which could all be challenged, in some ways anticipated an analogous process of demystification that would be undertaken by Marx in relation to Capital and Labour.[20] He attempted to restore to women responsibility for their own fertility, rather than presenting it as a consequence of impersonal market forces.

In Thompson's work, some of the themes that would animate a whole socialist tradition—and especially Utopian Socialism—in its treatment of women, are already apparent. He begins to challenge the sexual division of labour and the nuclear family, recognizing both that these structures belie political and legal gains in female equality and that the attitudes they promote are antithetical to socialism. He advocates social responsibility for childcare as a means both to free women from incarceration in the home and to educate the young in social responsibility. Perhaps most significantly, he finds a fatal contradiction between sexual equality and capitalism owing to the latter's competitive ethos and practices.

Like other Utopians, too, Thompson alludes to a superior feminine morality which might serve as a force in social regeneration: 'O woman, from your auspicious hands may the new destiny of the species proceed!'[21] Although his model for free and equal sexual relations is that of a co-operative economy rather than a system of protective rights, the political message for women in *The Appeal* is ultimately more liberal than socialist in so far as it is quite literally an appeal, an exhortation to women to awake and exert their wills. Yet it is also quite clear that specific blame for women's oppression lies with men. No inertia of custom nor logic of economic structures can exonerate them. In this sense Thompson's work is more explicitly feminist than that of his mentor, Robert Owen.

The first practical socialism in Britain developed through the Co-operative Movement associated with Robert Owen. Although Owen himself appears a somewhat authoritarian and paternalistic figure, his message of a New Moral World composed of democratic, egalitarian communities, sparked the imagination of many people alienated by the atomism and inequality of the early nineteenth century. Small socialist societies and even a few communities emerged in response to articles and public lectures delivered by followers like Frances Wright and Frances Morrison. Their attack on religion and property incited bitter opposition, but the condemnation of marriage brought derision even within their own ranks. Nevertheless, the demise of the marital system was perceived as fundamental to socialism, as was the elimination of all hierarchy, including the sexual one. It is for this reason that Owenism retains a special place in the history of socialist feminism.

Owen's lectures 'On the Marriages of the Priesthood of the Old Immoral World' (1835) represent his clearest statement on the subject. Not impressively feminist in content, they are nevertheless important for their condemnation of sexual and familial arrangements. It is true that Owen singles out women as particularly injured by the current marital system—which imposes 'injustice, cruelty, and misery, especially to the female'[22]—but he is eager to show that it also corrupts husband, children, society and human nature. Its public, as well as private, evils are thus manifold. He asks not simply for justice and consistency in the treatment of women, but finds in the arrangements which oppress them an obstacle to co-operation in all other areas of life.

Owen argues that marriage imposes an artificial restraint on natural feeling, forcing couples into self-denial, delusion and mutual ignorance. Such a relationship is 'the greatest of the practical sources of vice and misery'; the cause of 'the most extended calamities known to the human race'.[23] For its vices and deceptions cannot be confined to the domestic sphere; they leak into public life, preventing their protagonists from ever achieving honesty or rationality there. The religious mysteries perpetuated to legitimize marriage similarly pervade society at the expense of reason.

The family which is a corollary of marriage is also a disaster, though again because it is inherently anti-social rather than because it is patriarchal. It is wasteful because it is so labour intensive; harmful because parents are in a position to pass only their own ignorance and selfishness onto offspring. Competing with one another, families advance themselves and their children at others' expense such that it is the mean, egoistic values that are assimilated. No organization, Owen concludes, could be better designed to produce 'division and disunion in society'.[24] The narrow, private interests that would undermine public virtue, which liberals like Wollstonecraft associated with women and used as an argument for their education, are thus associated by Owen with the family as such: it is the privacy of the institution as a whole that threatens social solidarity, and its chief function, the rearing of new citizens, must therefore be made a public responsibility. Kinship values are to be displaced onto 'the great family of mankind'.[25] Moreover, nuclear families help to perpetuate a system of competitive inequality beyond the mere teaching of antisocial values. Large families in the poorer ranks are hastened into poverty, while at the other end of the scale, wealth marries wealth. Selfishness and emnity are thus reinforced while the child remains ignorant of the skills and knowledge needed for a joyful life or a valuable contribution to the community.

The ten lectures are suffused with a thorough-going rationalism: were people open and truthful, mindful of the chains of cause and effect dictating every outcome, Owen is confident that suspicion and immorality would disappear. The key to social happiness or misery lies in this scientific approach to human nature, with the resultant knowledge embodied in social institutions. Only those who are educated for reason can make free choices; a result clearly precluded by the single-unit family but facilitated by a public education undertaken by enlightened co-operators. Once socialists equated a co-operative society with changes in human nature, the organization of the family thus became a crucial part of their political theory.

Nevertheless, Owen finds no opposition between reason and nature and to be natural is the goal of the New Moral Order since 'nature can do no wrong'.[26] This does not mean that socialists seek a pristine or pre-rational state, but they do anticipate one organized according to those natural laws which the new science of society recognizes. Marriage is an illustration in point. Born of an earlier age when unnatural chastity was exhorted, it must now give way to the natural relationship between the sexes which can be understood and institutionalized. Owen's goal for such relations is that mutual transparency reign, for when all illusions have been stripped away he sees only goodwill remaining. At this juncture, humanity will be regenerated, 'raised to a life of intelligence and happiness, that is, to the innocency of paradise, united with the intelligence of all past experience'.[27] Owen answers his critics' claims that general promiscuity will ensue without the safeguards of marriage, by espousing faith in a natural chastity: if permitted to associate freely, the sexes would form bonds founded on mutual affection; a couple would blend into one harmonious whole which naturally regulated encounters.[28] It is the artificial unions imposed by the priesthood which destroy so spontaneous and healthy a balance. For Owen, it is thus affection rather than lust which is natural, and he believes, as many in the socialist tradition would, that this will tend towards permanent, monogamous relationships. Prostitution and adultery will accordingly disappear alongside those lifelong couplings sponsored by considerations of finance and social propriety.

Owen combines his attack on marriage with one on the competitive economic system. The relationship is not particularly clear in the lectures but its very existence is significant, given the tendency of succeeding socialists to reduce social antagonisms to class conflict and change to an economic transition of which women's emancipation would be a by-product. The whole question of marriage was obviously the most controversial and unpopular on which Owen spoke. At times he seems to see in it the most fundamental cause of social decay, as in the following passage on matrimony:

And when the priesthood had introduced these lamentable results throughout human society, it became necessary that the whole arrangements of public and private affairs should be made in accordance with these weaknesses and errors; and, in consequence, a combination of vicious thoughts, feelings, and actions has been engendered, and, from age to age, multiplied to such an extent that, at this moment, the human race, viewed from the eye of sober reason, has obtained to a condition of absurdity and folly that we shall seek for, in vain, among any other tribes of animals.[29]

He argues that the Owenite communities can never work while composed of married couples and that change here is the *conditio sine qua non* of all other social improvements. Nevertheless, it is notable that the above quotation blames the system on the priesthood, and there are many passages in the lectures which present marriage as a device invented by such persons to keep the race in slavish superstition, hence subservient to their own purposes as well as to the unnatural and artificial laws of governments and the wealthy,[30] all of whose authority would be challenged by 'right reason'. At other times, then, the marriage system is seen as one component in an oppressive and irrational trinity, composed also of religion and private property. The triad is bound together in its perpetuation of ignorance such that 'when one shall be destroyed the others shall perish also'. Women's emancipation might be the catalyst for fundamental social change; it cannot occur in isolation but nor can it be postponed in favour of change elsewhere in the system. There is thus a correspondence between marriage, religion and property in that all share a common culture promoting vice, antagonism and ignorance. But there is also complicity: religion sustains marriage while the single-family unit nurtures the selfish motivation required by a competitive economy. Owenites expected their communities to deal with all problems simultaneously by virtue of their rational organization. Theirs was not a revolutionary socialism and so it was unnecessary to prioritize areas for strategic attack.

There are two further relevant aspects of the co-operators' treatment of women which can be summarized in conclusion, although Owen does not discuss them in his Lectures. These relate to a glorification of the feminine and practical aspects of communal living. Such points are discussed in more detail in Barbara Taylor's excellent *Eve and the New Jerusalem.*

Like the French Socialists, the Owenites' commitment to sexual equality was tempered by a belief in women's moral superiority; we already encountered something of this in Thompson's thought. Degraded under existing conditions, femininity would be a source of regeneration, once liberated. The sympathy and compassion evinced by women seemed intrinsically socialist, especially compared with the competition and more brutal physical recreations associated with masculinity. Yet it was the aim of socialists to abolish the conditions producing such sexual peculiarities, and this tension remained unresolved, except in so far as both sexes were encouraged towards a more feminine ideal through the familialization of society as a whole.

On a more practical note, the co-operators experimented with a real communalization of living arrangements. Theirs was no statist solution to inequality and welfare. Owen advocated communities of 2,000, sharing one covered area wherein educational, recreational, productive and domestic activities would be undertaken. Communal eating, cooking, childcare, and so on, were to be practised. All sorts of scientific gadgets, as well as help from children, were envisaged to lighten the burden further. Unfortunately, none of the Owenite communities survived for long; the interstices of capitalist society proved too narrow to accommodate these experiments in autonomy. The women who joined seem to have had an especially hard time since mere survival often meant compromising on the more visionary aspects of sexual politics.[31] Shared housework might have been a reality, but it remained a predominantly female task and one performed under conditions of hardship and chaos hardly conducive to the fulfilment of its emancipatory promises. Perhaps the lament in an editorial of the movement's newspaper, *The New Moral World,* was therefore unsurprising:

We have the feeling that the wives and other female connexions of the Socialists are inimical to our cause. They are attached to their own notions of comfort and privacy and cannot easily admit that residence in community without individual property, individual staircases and individual washtubs can be consistent with human happiness.[32]

Owenism never exerted mass appeal among the working class, and its ideas on women were particularly unpopular there. By the 1830s the ideal of domesticated womanhood was gaining popularity in the proletarian family. Women with children were anxious to strengthen, rather than weaken, the obligations of husbands on whom they were dependent. Competition for jobs and wages was also a source of friction between the sexes. Although some trade unions had female branches, men were generally eager to keep women out of the labour market. As far as rights were concerned, proletarian males had been active on behalf of parliamentary reform since the turn of the century. The Chartist movement, which began to flourish in the late 1830s, originally supported votes for women but soon withdrew this lest its unpopularity harm their own cause. Many women were active in Chartist organizations, but usually on behalf of male enfranchisement.[33] When a specifically feminist movement emerged in the 1850s, it would be a predominantly bourgeois affair and so futher alienate socialists from a feminism whose very title came to be associated with liberalism. In any case, Chartists, trade unionists and proletarian reformers never shared the Utopians' ideal of communalized family life, nor did they offer theoretical statements of socialist feminism. As Owenism slipped into decline in the mid-1840s, the attempt to integrate socialism with feminism thus disappeared with it. Henceforth the focus of struggle would be that of labour and capital, and in so far as women counted, it would be as contributors to production.

Although there are sufficient theoretical connections between British and French Utopian Socialists for them to share a common designation, the French variety is of far grander and more exotic design. The thinkers who concern us here are Saint-Simon, the Saint-Simonians under the leadership of Prosper Enfantin and Charles Fourier. When they described an egalitarian role for women and ascribed superior status to the feminine, it was as an integral part of totalizing theories sometimes reaching cosmic dimensions.

Contrary to the Owenites, these thinkers sustained a faith in private property and inequality as a stimulus to creative rivalry and difference, although they were equally critical of the

competitive individualism spawned by capitalism. The titles of
their major works are perhaps symptomatic of more profound
differences, however. For while Owen wrote of *The New
Moral World,* Fourier looked to *The New Amorous World.*
While Owen sought to replace the deceptions of marriage with
a freely accepted monogamy he believed natural, Enfantin
espoused free love and Fourier vaunted the naturalness of an
unrestrained sensuality expressed in polygamous, bisexual
encounters. Frank Manuel expresses the distinction more
broadly: 'Both systems were expansive in contrast with Owen's
rather barrackslike monastic communism which created
equality by decreasing consumption'.[34] The French Utopians
were eager to rehabilitate the flesh; to release the senses and
passions crushed by an overemphasis on reason and intellect.
The erotic and aesthetic are retrieved in their work as criticial
dimensions of liberation, and it is in this context that a re-
evaluation of the feminine, long associated by Western
thought with such aspects of existence, occurs. Women might
play a full part in contributing to the efficiency of the co-
operative Utopia, then, but in the French version Utopia itself
pulsates with a feminine heart. This esteem accorded the
feminine is in many ways a more interesting and enduring
contribution to socialist feminism than the sometimes prosaic
and ambivalent statements concerning sexual equality.

Saint-Simon himself said little about women beyond calls for
fully egalitarian opportunities in the highly productive future
he anticipated, where capacities would be fully rewarded and
needs fulfilled. On his deathbed, however, he reputedly
described the basic social unit as the couple rather than the
individual. Towards the end of his life he had also given special
status to artists, poets and religious leaders who were to usher
in the humanism of a new organic age. These latter conceptions
formed the basis for quite a different emphasis in the doctrines
of subsequent Saint-Simonians under the aegis of Enfantin.

The artists *et alia* whom Saint-Simon promoted to élite
status, were identified as a particular psychological type with a
propensity for sentiment and sympathy. They were
complemented by the more rational beings who promoted
science and the intellect as well as by more physical types who
excelled in industry. While modern culture impoverished

human beings to the extent that it left little space for the former qualities, the women who exemplified them best were also suppressed. From here it was easy for the Saint-Simonians to associate social regeneration with the emancipation of women and the flourishing of feminine virtues. In Enfantin's hands, these virtues encompassed love of both an emotional and a carnal ilk. Such a position in turn harmonized nicely with the critique of marriage as an unhealthy institution which in limiting sexuality to the conjugal pair, bred an ugly progeny of adultery and prostitution. Thus 'the emancipation of women became the symbol of the liberation of bodily desires'.[35] And conversely, women's oppression became an index of the subordination of the flesh, now to be overturned. Although the association of women with instinct, emotion and materiality is a highly traditional one and one from which their liberators have frequently sought to divorce them, Enfantin thus used the association as a basis for demanding women's liberation and for revalorizing the feminine. As a critic remarks, he 'made these alleged feminine characteristics, which were usually considered as sinful or ornamental, the foundation of his system for the reorganization of society'.[36]

Saint-Simon's remark about couples was also readily assimilated with these views. While credence was given to an androgynous God, His ruling representatives on earth remained sexually differentiated as the Mother and Father. They were to reconcile feminine and masculine qualities such as body and mind or beauty and knowledge, but it was the Mother who was to introduce the cardinal virtues required for the new age: love, peace, productivity, sensuality.[37] Unfortunately, the female Messiah was never located and Father Enfantin reigned alone, but the vacant seat of the ruling dyad did point to the need for women as a whole to rise up in fulfilment of their moral mission. The vision remains a socialist one since the new morality was seen as the prerequisite for a benevolent economy without competition, inheritance or monopoly. But it was unthinkable unless thoroughly feminized.

Of all the Utopian Socialists, it was however Fourier who would bequeath most to future socialist thought on women.[38] At first sight this seems strange since, of the thinkers reviewed in this chapter, his thought is the most bizarre. It comprises a vast system, refined across many drafts beginning with the 1808 *Theory of Four Movements,* in which every part's significance lies in its relation to a whole that is structured in terms of analogies. This means that strictly speaking, Fourier's statements concerning women make sense only in the context of the much larger totality where planets copulate and seas turn to lemonade. In reality, his work provided a rich source of imaginative insight and aphorisms which would be plundered for incorporation in theories of quite a different spirit. Thus Marx and Engels would be impressed by Fourier's critique of marriage—their claim that it is boring is surely a legacy of Fourier—and symbolic equation between woman's liberation and social progress, although they would never advocate homosexuality, polygamy or a feminization of history as he did. For a century, virtually all socialists would accept the need for collectivized housework and child-care—advocated by the Utopians but described most fully by Fourier—as an essential component of female emancipation, although they would continue to define such work as necessary drudgery, never as passionate fulfilment or play. And not until Alexandra Kollontai wrote in the twentieth century, would the tradition retrieve Fourier's crucial association between women's equality and sexual freedom, such that society itself might be founded on libidinal relations.

Just as Newton had described the laws of material attraction, Fourier sets out to disclose those of passionate attraction. Humans, he claims, are motivated by a dozen passions. Since these are pre-reflective and immutable, society must be reorganized to accommodate them. The passions demand sensual and affective gratification; when stifled they do not die but surface in distorted form. There are 810 different types of individual, he continues, manifesting different permutations of the passions. Where a proper distribution of individuals occurs, equilibrium will reign. The happy future era which Fourier refers to as Harmony, will accordingly find itself composed of communities (Phalanxes) which contain just two examples of each type. The contrast between this situation and Civilization—one of several eras preceding it, languishing in ignorance of passionate attraction and thus most unhappily organized—provides the framework for the attack on commercial, patriarchal society and the description of the Phalansterian alternative.

Fourier dislikes just about everything found in Civilization. He condemns its greed, corruption, competitiveness; he rejects the work ethic which enforces self-denial. He finds even the materially rich, poor in sensuous and emotional fulfilment. Boredom is one of the greatest evils of such a culture. This is nowhere more apparent than in marriage, which crushes the passion for a love which seeks far more expansive expression. Although this affects both sexes, Fourier associates the Fall from a primitive Eden with masculine despotism. And he condemns the exclusive couple itself as antisocial:

Theirs is the most banal sort of amorous relationship, a relationship of which everyone is capable. If, however, two lovers remain sufficiently susceptible to amorous intrigue to maintain sentimental ties apart from their own relationship, they will be making a greater contribution to social harmony than a pair of unsociable republicans who love no one else and are courteous and passionate only towards one another.[39]

As he says elsewhere, if 'love is to be a source of generosity, we must base our speculations on the collective exercise of love'.[40] What he anticipates is a society with space for many different expressions of amorous and erotic attachment. Individuals may choose monogamy, just as they may choose to remain virgins in the Vestelate or practice homosexuality (Fourier is especially keen on lesbianism) or polygamy/polyandry. But he doubts that anyone would choose one partner for very long, and in his more fluid system there is no need for deception or seduction. A multiplicity of sentimental friendships will also evolve, spreading trust and cushioning lovers against disappointment or jealousy. Thus the whole community will be bound by overlapping ties of affection with varying degrees of erotic import.

Now, Enfantin had also called for free love but as Gail Malmgreen points out, this in itself could not free women while their economic dependence and responsibility for housework remained.[41] How, then, was Harmony to overcome these limitations? Fourier described arrangements in the Phalanx in great detail, but I shall concentrate here on four related areas that especially concerned its womenfolk: domestic labour, children, the sexual division of labour generally and sexual relationships.

Because Harmony is a society without repression, work must become an activity that is freely chosen as a source of gratification. Fourier's solution is that nobody need spend more than an hour or two on any task while individuals will be matched to those jobs for which they have passionate attraction. He estimates that the efficiency of collective housework would require only one-quarter of its current workforce and that fortuitously, this corresponds to the proportion who would select it. Interestingly, though, when he describes the new arrangement it is with the master–servant, rather than husband–wife relationship that he compares it.[42]

Like other types of labour, the domestic variety will be undertaken by a series—'pages and pagesses'—within which different tasks are assigned. The work itself is to be ennobled and at the same time, each will serve only those for whom they feel affection. The pagess who is a chambermaid, for example (and Fourier does tend to use female examples in describing such work, although he insists that both sexes will perform it and that each task must in any case have at least one eighth of the minority sex), will clean only the apartments of her favourites and in her next job she might find herself commanding them. Fourier contends that both poor and rich will enjoy such services since it is the community which pays. The group of chambermaids thus constitutes a free and honourable society, motivated by love of its work and of those it serves, performing efficiently because collectively and rewarded by the Phalanx. Thus

one of the charms of Harmony is to have a friend eagerly serve you in the most trifling domestic chores. This friend, moreover, is very capable because domestic services in Harmony are minutely subdivided and only experienced associates are assigned to each task.[43]

Kitchens will be communal: Fourier describes trap doors in (common) dining rooms so that tables can be set below and raised up at eating times.[44] Eating is an exceptionally important pastime in Harmony, and indeed so much of the education, production and gratification in the Phalanx involves growing, preparing, tasting and consuming food, that one commentator is moved to describe it as the basis of the whole economy. It is food, rather than money, which circulates; there are even gastronomic battles as in the World War of the Meat Pies.[45] It is no longer easy in this case to draw a distinction between domestic and productive labour.

Child-care is similarly to be a function of the community, although this occurs primarily because of the importance of education, which is responsible for developing physical and intellectual capacities as well as for stimulating appetite. Like adults, children are not repressed or schooled, but incited through pleasurable practice. No sexual differentiation is made during the early stages when Imps and Impesses learn to co-operate and blossom, though subsequently sexual distinctions will be recognized as a means of encouraging the diversity and rivalry Fourier found so stimulating. Nursemen and nursemaids with a vocation for child-care, will tend the infants until they begin work/play at about 2 years old in miniature workshops (their first 'job' being pea-sorting).[46] Universality is achieved through this shared education (particularly via participation in the opera), which has the further advantage of neutralizing a paternal influence that 'can only serve to retard and pervert the child'.[47] Any discipline seems to come from peers, leaving fathers (sic) free to satisfy their real desire, which is to spoil the child.

From the ages of 4 to 15, children are divided into Little Hords and Little Bands. The distinction is important because it demonstrates the conflict Fourier experienced between the real sexual equality he advocated and his own preconceptions about sexual roles and natures. The Little Hords perform unpleasant tasks like tending the dung heap and killing reptiles; they exploit children's love of filth. The Little Bands perform more refined tasks, but it is obvious that Fourier's real sympathy lies with the players in dirt (in whom he discovers the seeds of civic virtue!).[48] Although there are no male or female natures as such, Fourier does associate the Hordes with a boyish love of grossness and the Bands with girls' love of finery. Of the one-third of all girls choosing the Hords, it is those with boyish inclinations.[49]

It does appear, then, that despite freely chosen tasks, there will be a tendency for one sex to be more passionately attracted to certain roles than the other. On the other hand, Fourier does display a refreshingly flexible conception of sexual boundary; he does not perceive the male–female antithesis as one of the core structures of Being or as immutable. Thus children are referred to as a third sex of neuters and he speculates on the advantages of a further sex of powerful hermaphrodites, to give men a taste of their own domineering medicine. We have already encountered his views on bisexuality. Such fluidity suggests that any sexual stereotyping is an aberration at odds with the spirit of the enterprise.

Nevertheless, it is an essential claim for Harmony that it provides everyone with a minimum of material and erotic satisfaction, and the latter raises more serious questions concerning the role of women. For in order to guarantee sexual fulfilment to even the most unappealing, Fourier develops a complex series of amorous rituals and penances which extend to sexual enticements for difficult work. Although men and women are in principle both involved in such practices, it is predominantly the women who feature in Fourier's examples as prizes and bait. The extension of sexuality from a source of individual gratification to an instrument of social utility, no matter how enjoyable it is claimed to be for its practitioners, clearly raises serious questions regarding the nature of Harmony's libidinous foundations.

Like their British counterparts, the French socialists went substantially beyond liberal egalitarianism in their demands for sexual equality. I have suggested, however, that it is the feminization of society which they imply, that is the more interesting development.

In some ways, of course, this position remained problematic. The insistence on feminine qualities seems to imply natural sexual distinctions, such as those between a masculine rationalism and self-discipline and a feminine aesthetic and playfulness, which enemies of female equality had long used to counsel separate spheres (and Fourier was much influenced by Rousseau). On the other hand, recognition of the *experiential* bases of feminine virtue led the Saint-Simonians to advise women's isolation from the corrupt contemporary world lest their regenerating qualities be damaged—an argument also used by conservative critics of their entry into the public realm. Finally, the very idea of superior qualities inhering in one sex (and as we saw, there is also something of this in the British Utopians) fits awkwardly with egalitarianism. Simply re-evaluating sexual differences is thus a two-edged sword.

Despite these caveats, however, there is a real sensitivity among the French Utopian Socialists to a problem that haunted all professions of sexual equality, namely that if men are so competitive and the public sphere so corrupt, do women really want to assimilate such qualities and practices? Instead the Saint-Simonians and Fourier held up the prospect of communities based on principles long identified with the feminine; to this extent they saw women, rather than conforming with a world that was not of their making, remaking that world in their own image. Female and human emancipation became co-terminous. According to such a version of socialism, the woman question could not be marginalized since it was central to the new morality; economic change alone would not suffice.

Philosophically, too, the Utopians performed an important service in their new evaluation of the feminine. Although the expediences of free love and erotic enticement are problematic for women in their communities, the whole emphasis on passionate fulfilment turned traditional deprecations of the female upside down. It is significant, too, that in so far as they associated women with the flesh, it was in terms of gratification rather than motherhood. Suppression of the senses was no longer the prerequisite for a rational, progressive culture but a recipe for unnatural aggression and self-denial. Whether emphasis was placed on a benevolent morality or on the greatest happiness, it could have nothing to do with those qualities political thought had for so long praised in the male of the species and used to legitimize his exclusive access to public activity. The very reconceptualization of nature as exemplary and as a realm to be engaged in and enjoyed, rather than suppressed and dominated, had important implications for images of gender, too. For it is arguable that no amount of formal, or even economic, equality would truly liberate women, as long as these deep-seated symbolic equations remained unchallenged.

8 Hegel, Marx and Engels:
Familial and Productive Determinants of Woman's Role

To an extent the differences between Hegel and Marx/Engels on the question of women mirror those between Aristotle and Plato or even Rousseau and Mill. Hegel accords women a significant but inferior role in a predetermined totality; he does not perceive them as oppressed, but he does deduce from his system their lesser rationality, such that differences between the sexes remain fundamental and immutable. He is thus deeply conservative on this question. Marxism, on the other hand, looks forward to sexual equality and the full participation of women in public affairs. It finds no significant difference between the sexes in this context and offers a comprehensive explanation for women's exclusion from public life thus far. Nevertheless, Hegel was highly influential in the development of the Marxian dialectic, and elements of his views on women are not wholly absent from it.

Hegel's works together constitute a massive system recounting the emergence of reason. In Hegel himself (so he believes) Absolute Knowledge is finally achieved and the history of its becoming can thus be retold. This history is necessary and teleological: its inner purpose always drives it towards self-consciousness of freedom, whence the natural and objective world will become wholly transparent before the omniscient subject. The dualism between subject and object, or mind and nature, which pertains at the beginning of history, is only apparent since the objective world is but spirit in self-estrangement and nature is pervaded by a purpose awaiting rational disclosure. Through a dialectical interplay, contradictions between the world and our understanding of it gradually engender more universal knowledge and integral truths, until the totality emerges as fully rational. Alienation is eliminated and history ends, reconciled as spirit.

This process is recounted by Hegel at a high level of abstraction in his *Phenomenology of Mind* (1807). In the *Philosophy of Right* (1821), aspects of this history are retold from the perspective of objective spirit, which culminates in the state, the embodiment of ethical life. The emergence of an ethical community is necessary at a certain stage of spirit's evolution because particular self-consciousnesses cannot develop far in isolation. They require the concrete substance of social life, and it is at this juncture that the family appears in both works.

For Hegel, the state appears as a synthesis of two less developed moments of ethical life: family and civil society. Both are necessary to his goal of restoring to individuals a sense of community under the conditions of modern life. The family yields the sentiment that binds individuals into an organic unity. Here, concern for others' welfare appears as natural and spontaneous; each member experiences him or herself as subsumed within the unity of a greater whole. It is civil society which facilitates the expressions of concrete personality lacking in the family because it is here that labour and fulfilment of need occur. But over time, recognition of mutual dependence emerges even here—via exchange and the division of labour; class and corporate solidarities; the need for just property laws—to reveal universality underlying the egoism of the bourgeois world. The state which transcends it does much more than provide the necessary framework for its transactions and is not for Hegel simply a contractual edifice. Instead of an aggregate of persons formally related by coercive laws, individuals freely accede to membership since they recognize in the laws an expression of their own rationality. But the state is for Hegel a cultural and social, as well as a legal, association: its relationships resemble those in the family or *polis* in the sense of belonging they imply, except that membership is self-conscious rather than natural or habitual. It is the moment in which particular and universal are reconciled.

In the Hegelian state, we thus find something of that civic

virtue and community spirit with which Plato, Aristotle and Rousseau had concerned themselves. Now, in its previous expressions, as we have seen, such aspirations were accompanied by perceptions of the family as a threat to universal association due to its jealousy and particularity. The family was equated with a natural realm inimical to justice or public law. Moreover, women were especially identified with these subversive qualities. They were therefore to be either safely locked away in domesticity, where they performed a natural function, or else detached from the natural and familial realm and catapulted willy-nilly into the universality of the state.

Hegel tries to move beyond these alternatives (anathema to one whose goal was to reach a final synthesis in which both identity and difference were dialectically preserved) by integrating the family into ethical life without marginalizing or destroying it. Family life is for him an indispensable moment of ethical life because it manifests a certain type of human relationship (particular altruism) wherein we learn to be members of a union which transcends the individual, even if the circle of blood relatives which it embraces limits it. Yet ultimately, the solution fails because it remains a purely ideal one: actual family life is transcended in the final ethical synthesis and the women identified with it are left behind. Similarly, any anticipation that the synthesis of reason and nature might result in a perception of women as natural beings who enter the realm of knowledge (albeit late in history) and find liberation in their accession to spirit—that is, an adoption of the Platonic resolution—is disappointed. Hegel arrests women's development, and they never, for him, reach the point of true spirit. There is no sexual synthesis, only sexual complementarity (in marriage). Ultimately, then, it is the Aristotelian solution that Hegel adopts, granting to women (like family life in general) a significant but lesser role, which denies them credentials for true reason and thus, too, for political life. Let us look at this in more detail.

Hegel's treatment of women occurs in the context of his discussion of the family.[1] The qualities he ascribes to them are intimately related to its own contribution in the unfolding of reason. He describes the family as 'a *natural* ethical community'; '*immediate* ethical existence'; 'ethical mind in its natural or immediate phase'.[2] It remains natural because the bonds that unite its members are predicated on feeling (they are 'immediate' not mediated, reflective or self-conscious), which is intuitive and implicit. But it is also ethical because these relations of love have a universal and spiritual quality; they do not rely on brute force or unmediated egoism. Reason is therefore present, albeit in immature form.

The significance and contours of familial relations are best exemplified in Hegel's account of marriage in the *Philosophy of Right*. The concern of marriage is reproduction and the 'life-process' of the race. To this extent it is outside of history, allied with the pre-rational and the natural.[3] However, the purpose of Hegelian teleology is to render the real, rational; and so these processes must be taken into history and understood. Marriage achieves this by reclaiming reproduction from the alien realm of the merely organic: it transforms the 'natural sexual union' into ' a union on the level of mind, into self-conscious love'.[4] (In the *Phenomenology* an analogous argument associates the family with the retrieval of death, which is integrated into human history and given meaning via the funeral rites performed by family members.)[5]

Hegel condemns those who have portrayed marriage in merely sexual, contractual or emotional terms, for recognizing respectively only the crude, utilitarian or contingent aspects of the relationship. To be ethical, the association must transcend carnality, self-interest and caprice; it must become rational and universal.[6] Individual motives and circumstances remain entirely contingent and thus irrelevant; the objective (ethical) aspect of marriage lies in the act of renunciation by which the self is subsumed within a greater unity (prefiguring that more general community which will define the state). 'From this point of view, their union is self-restriction, but in fact it is their liberation, because in it they attain their substantive self-consciousness'.[7] Passion and sensuality are but a fleeting and barely significant aspect of the marital relationship whose ends are pre-eminently spiritual. Indeed, it is precisely this which distinguishes marriage from prostitution, which remains on the level of desire.[8] And it is for this reason that divorce is to be made difficult: evanescent whims must not be allowed to destroy this ethical order whose sentiments are so important to the health of the community. It follows, of course, that monogamy is to be encouraged, since it alone reflects total immersion of the self in one spiritual union.

It is apparent, then, that Hegel sees two important purposes being served by the husband–wife relationship: it rescues reproduction and sexuality from nature by rendering them rational, and it initiates that unity which is prerequisite to the state. The family remains a natural community because duties are to blood-relatives, and their feelings for one another arise from this (relations are never contractual, as they are in the Hobbesian family and the emphasis is on duties, not rights), but it is more than a merely biological unit and plays a significant role in the emergence of mind. As Gould notes, this idealist account mystifies the family because it ignores the extent to which it is mediated by economic relations and can never be simply a domain of love.[9] Material needs are satisfied for Hegel in civil society, a realm in which men alone are active, but he does not see that its divisions affect domestic relations.[10] He does see, however, that relations in the family are quite different from the universal egoism which prevails in civil society. The altruism practised in the domestic realm is explicitly counterposed to the aggressive world of men. Hegel thus sustains the ideology of the sentimental family, but he at least resists the liberal tendency to reduce human nature and its meaningful expressions to Hobbesian form.

Hegel believes, too, that the family has a quite different significance for each sex. He describes an intellectual and ethical distinction which gives to the female and male different ontological purposes in the unfolding of reason. In man, mind is severed: it both experiences and self-consciously reflects upon that experience. This capacity for conceptual thinking grants the male access to universality and real freedom. It is therefore men who make history since it is they who engage in politics and learning; it is they who labour and struggle to change the world in their own image in order to achieve recognition and self-consciousness there. In relation to the world Hegel says, they are powerful and active. Manhood itself is described not as a biological given but as the successful outcome of a struggle which emulates reason's own development; it is 'attained only by the stress of thought and much technical exertion'.[11]

Women, on the other hand, remain passive and subjective because they are not reflective and self-conscious. Their feelings and experiences remain unified; they love and intuit in that manner most appropriate to family life. They can be educated (though 'who knows how?' It seems to be by 'breathing in ideas, by living rather than by acquiring knowledge'), but they lack the universal faculty that would allow them access to the Ideal—to science, philosophy and art. In their vague sense of unity they are more like plants than animals (men); they have only ideas, taste and elegance, that is, particular, contingent knowledge. Unable to step outside of experience, they remain trapped within it.[12]

It is therefore appropriate, for Hegel, that woman should be confined to the family with its immature rationality and primitive ethical status. Even if her function is teleological rather than merely biological, she is arrested at the level of particularity and immediacy. True, she rises above the natural aspects of her reproductive function into the ethical world, but because she lacks the universal faculty, she is excluded from its highest expressions in public life. Only the male enters into all the human relationships which characterize the three moments of ethical life, and so he alone achieves that combination of feeling and reason, individuality and universality, which defines the whole human being. Women's exclusion from civil society denies them access to the very moment wherein personal autonomy is gained. In the family, such expressions of individualism are quite out of place.

Hegel presents woman's descent into contingency and pre-ethical existence as a constant threat. Her husband can enjoy his relationships with particular family members because he has access to universality in the external world. But lacking this safeguard, women must always fight against immersion in particular relations since the love which they bear for children and husbands offers but a precarious route to the ethical. They must struggle for commitment to marriage and motherhood as such, rather than sinking into the love of this or that man or child.

Without the marital bond offered to woman in union with a man, she is thus excluded from ethical existence (we might recall the Christian thinkers here). This is untrue of the man who is also ethical in his public transactions in civil society and state. In surrendering her body outside of marriage, Hegel concludes, a girl loses her honour because she loses her ethical lifeline. 'A girl is destined for the marriage tie and for that only';[13] a promiscuous man can regain his honour *qua* citizen.

Finally, and in case we are left with any doubts, Hegel spells out the implications of the above for women's relationship to the state. In the *Philosophy of Right* he warns, 'when women hold the helm of government, the state is at once in jeopardy, because women regulate their actions not by the demands of universality but by arbitrary inclinations and opinions'.[14] In other words, they import into political relations a morality and sense of justice that is appropriate to the domestic domain; they cannot be impartial because they lack the conceptual skills to achieve abstraction and detachment. Since the incapacity is ontological, Hegel cannot adopt a liberal solution and advise that public participation will broaden appreciation, although he is aware of the dangers that women pose when they remain imprisoned in the particularity of the family. Human law finds universal expression only in the state, he says, and it must therefore break in on family happiness if history is to advance:

Womankind—the everlasting irony of the life of the community—changes by intrigue the universal purpose of government into a private end, transforms its universal activity into a work of this or that specific individual, and perverts the universal property of the state into a possession and ornament for the family.[15]

It is difficult to see how Hegel hoped to overcome this threat, since the dialectical process culminating in the state depends upon men who leave the family on maturity to enter civil society where they develop an intelligence beyond mere feeling. It is true that the state requires the ethical relations expressed in the family, but women are never themselves dialectically transformed into more rational beings. Girls who leave the parental home only become wives in new families.[16] Hegel's solution to sexual relations is thus quite undialectical; certainly it is quite different from the master–slave interchange, where it is the slave who develops his self-consciousness through work (he completely ignores the incidence of domestic labour in which women might develop their sense of efficacy and identity).

For Hegel, then, there is little point in educating women since their role and nature are necessary rather than contingent. It is their place in his teleology which defines them rather than biology *per se,* although it is the latter which underlines that place. Like Aristotle, Hegel attributes to women an imperfect and immature rationality which excludes them from political acts, by drawing on a whole philosophy. He shares his predecessor's conservatism on this question because his definition of the category 'woman' makes the very notion of her liberation nonsensical. History leaves her behind before it reaches its zenith. For ultimately it is man who is freedom/spirit and woman who represents the necessity/nature which is to be conceptually appropriated. Her repetitive reproductive cycle is to be rendered rational by the work of (male) self-consciousness, in which historical agency is located. Does anything of this remain in Marx?

In a brief account of Marx and Engels in *Woman's Estate,* Juliet Mitchell draws a distinction between two phases in the presentation of women. 'Their solutions', she concludes, 'retain this overly economistic stress, or enter the realm of dislocated speculation'.[17] The first criticism refers to a reductionist tendency found in the later writings, where women are subsumed beneath a historical account of the family to become mere preconditions for private property. Mitchell's second criticism refers to Marx's early works, where women were presented as symbols of historical advance. The distinction is a useful one, and I shall begin by discussing the early approach in this light. However, it will then be suggested that an element of its Hegelianism continued to haunt even the later writings on women.

Fourier had found in women's status an index of emancipation in general. Marx takes up the equation in both the *1844 Manuscripts* and *The Holy Family* (1854), and it is on this that his symbolic usage of the category of women, rests. In the former work it occurs in the context of a discussion about the relations between nature, alienation, labour and private property.

Implicit in Marx's account here is the Hegelian schema: an originally unified man and nature must be severed to allow development through conflict. At the end of this historical process they will be reconciled: the species will fulfil its natural potential and material needs by humanizing nature; by organizing it according to the purposes of the race such that it reflects the creative powers of its immediate producers and abundance replaces scarcity. Since the alienation of the species from nature can occur only with the elimination of private property, it is communism which 'is the *genuine* resolution of the conflict between man and nature and between man and man . . . the riddle of history solved'.[18]

Marx sees relations between the sexes as symbolic of this process: 'the relation of man to woman is *the most natural* relation of human being to human being. It reveals the extent to which man's *natural* behaviour has become *human* . . . the extent to which his *human nature* has come to be nature to him'.[19] The original harmony between man and nature (under conditions of primitive communism), their antagonism throughout history (a history of private property and class struggle) and their final reconciliation under true communism, all find expression in man's relationship to woman. It is the sexual relationship, rather than woman herself, which is identified with nature, and it is the extent to which this 'animal function' (as Marx calls it) has been humanized (in Hegelian terms, rendered ethical), that progress is indicated. 'From this relationship one can judge man's whole level of development'.[20] Yet the implication is that men make history and express their progress in the way they treat their female partners, the passive indicators and beneficiaries of male advance in humanizing nature. Hegel's resolution is thus evident here. It is clarified by subsequent statements.

In both *The German Ideology* and *Capital,* Marx will speak of a natural and spontaneous division of labour within the family; one 'based on a purely physiological foundation' whose origins lie in the division of labour first encountered in the sexual act.[21] From the natural relationship between the sexes a social one evolves and this is itself the first property relationship, 'the nucleus, the first form of which lies in the family, where wife and children are the slaves of the husband'.[22] The natural relation of man to woman thus gives to the husband the power to dispose of his wife's labour power. Marx does not explain how this comes about but in yielding the man the power to exploit his wife's labour, it produces something like a class relationship within the family and thereby allows a materialist account of woman's oppression there.

It is this process which defines the man as maker of history and humanizer of nature. It is true that the woman is not ontologically precluded from sharing man's mission, as she was for Hegel, but she is at an (unspecified) natural disadvantage which leads to her exclusion until history's final stages have been reached. For her enslavement takes her out of that realm of social production that drives the dialectic forward. The question this prompts is whether emancipation in the form Marx envisages it, is a neutral state, inherent in the species as such, or whether it is a contingent outcome designed to fulfil specifically (Promethean) male desires. At the very least, progress towards communism is at woman's expense: the first stage of humanization of the man–woman relationship results in her enslavement, and this is rectified only towards the end of history when man has all but completed his mission. As Engels would later write of monogamy, it 'was a great historical advance' but also a 'relative regression, in which the well-being and development of the one group' was 'attained by the misery and degradation of the other'.[23]

The role of women as passive indicators of historical development is illustrated when the young Marx uses their degradation to demonstrate the dehumanizing aspects of private property. This occurs where he condemns crude communism as a corrupt form of the real thing. In this state, bourgeois values are generalized rather than eliminated: an obsession with possessing leads only to the levelling of private property and the universalizing of wage-slavery. To illustrate the inauthenticity of such a resolution, Marx likens it to a transition from bourgeois marriage—'certainly a form of exclusive private property'—to 'universal prostitution'.[24] Implication: crude communism differs from the free association of producers as general prostitution does from free association between the sexes. Where envy and lust are the norm, the degradation of women discloses the dehumanization of the whole society: the 'secret of this approach has its *unambiguous,* decisive, plain and undisguised expression in the relation of man to woman'.[25]

Here, woman is more than *symbolic* of the historical level:

she quite literally *reflects* it because as property herself she is treated as it is. Again, it is man's treatment *of* her, rather than any dialectical relationship *with* her, that is significant. Where property (the historical form taken by nature) is jealously possessed, violently claimed and universally desired, then woman suffers its fate. Communism liberates her because it abolishes the property relationship and restores the species to a proper reciprocity with nature. Man's reconciliation with a humanized nature must include demystification and free exchange within the sexual relationship, because the transparent relations that socialists define as healthy 'sex-love' are only examples of the more general transparency of a natural world transformed in the image of the species. In all this Marx's Hegelian roots are evident, and this is especially true of the role ascribed to woman. It is true that her passive status as property accurately reflected bourgeois reality, but beyond this she can represent progress by her status only because she is not the historical equivalent of man. Her reproductive and domestic acts make no contribution of historical significance.

In conclusion, it is evident that in his early writings Marx did indeed see women representing an abstract category rather than as actors who might seek emancipation on their own terms. Since the *1884 Manuscripts* were a sketch for a more concrete rendition of Hegel's odyssey in the *Phenomenology,* this is perhaps unsurprising. Women reflect rather than initiate change, but there is as yet no attempt to explain why this comes about or systematically to explain their oppression. All that is offered is a reference to nature and a sketch of sexual relations as an analogue of class relations, the main difference being that there is no dialectic between the man and woman that would bring advance there. Under capitalism woman still retains the status of property, and it is its history which she shares. Her emancipation will emerge only as a logical corollary of its abolition, and even then it seems to be largely symbolic. The later reductionism is therefore apparent already: there is no possibility that women might instigate general change, as there had been for Utopian Socialism, because they are excluded from the crucial processes of productive labour wherein history is made. Marx suggests that the reasons are natural ones, but although he thinks they can be overturned when nature has been humanized, he fails to question the link between woman's nature and her servitude. Later it will become apparent that this flaw continued to blemish even the subsequent historical materialist analyses of women.

Finally, some more general points are in order, which point to more sexually progressive implications in the young Marx. Much of Marxism's inadequacy in terms of the solutions it did eventually offer to women's oppression, would arise from its equating their emancipation with nothing more than a sexually undifferentiated access to social production. The *1844 Manuscripts* do, however, make clear that this solution has nothing to do with equal drudgery or subordination of the individual to social requirements (this would be only crude communism). For Marx, labour is a privileged form of activity which allows free expression, the transformation of nature according to aesthetic as well as utilitarian criteria. In reshaping nature, the producer develops him or herself, and it is this process which capitalism corrupts. Marxism thus recognizes that if the liberal goal of developing one's faculties is to be realized, individuals must be given full access to the means of self-expression. To this extent the integration of women into the category of workers is an enlightened and fundamental aspect of their liberation in which Marx goes considerably beyond Hegel.

Furthermore, because Marxism pays homage to material rather than ideal forces behind historical progress, it does not believe that advance is won through the suppression of the flesh. It is true that it looks to labour rather than reproduction as a privileged mode of practice, but it is able to avoid the layers of symbolic condemnation which philosophers from Plato to Hegel invoked in their discussions of women. Marx insists that communism will mean the appearance of passionate, sensuous persons, able to enjoy their environment in a manner that was denied them when possession was the culmination of desire. Despite a certain sexual prudishness, the early Marx, at least, shared something of the Utopians' regard for the efflorescence of the senses, and in the ideological realm this could only bode well for acceptance of a more female norm. Moreover, Marx saw in communism not a simple domination of nature but a 'metabolic' relationship in which humanity would be naturalized as well as nature being humanized. Final reconciliation remains dialectical and not a resolution into mind alone, since humanity is a part of nature and not something alien to it.[26] In so far as symbolic relations remain between nature and the female (whether in bourgeois science or Hegelian idealism), Marx does therefore imply a more dialectical relationship between nature/mind and female/male. There is no suggestion that the female principle is to be suppressed in the name of historical advance, even if women are themselves agents of (virtually) none of its developments. In this sense Marx is closer to Locke than to Hegel.

Although Marx and Engels did not have a great deal to say about women, they did develop a method for analysing the origin and dynamics of oppression. Historical materialism appeared as a comprehensive approach for the first time in *The German Ideology* (1845–6), and it is the application of this mode of analysis to women, which will be the focus of the rest of this chapter.

Marxism accepted the Hegelian account of history as dialectical: a meaningful process which moves towards completion, or synthesis, by virtue of an internal dynamic driven by contradictions. Like Hegel, its exponents have therefore aimed at a total explanation wherein each component of the historical drama—such as women—must be appreciated as an integral part of a larger process and not as an autonomous phenomenon.

Where Marx and Engels differed from Hegel was in their location of historical momentum. They claimed to 'invert' the Hegelian dialectic by perceiving history as the development of human productive power rather than as the evolution of mind.[27] It was now the species' attempt to control nature in order to fulfil material needs, that gave to history its logic. The conflicts engendered by this process arise from contradictions within the economic infrastructure, between the forces of production (knowledge, tools, raw materials, labour power, etc.), which tend to increasing efficiency, and the social relations which develop at each stage and give to their beneficiaries an interest in arresting development. For each mode of production which yields a surplus also gives rise to class conflict; to exploiters and exploited. Its social relations find reflection/correspondence in an ideological superstructure. But eventually productive forces must burst out of the social relations which increasingly stifle them and then a new set of class relations will appear, at first progressive in accommodating the new productive forces but finally themselves inhibiting further development. Where the tensions between dynamic forces and inertial relations becomes particularly acute, revolution will ensue.

With capitalism the productive forces are fully developed: all that remains is to sweep away its class relations whereby the private ownership of the means of production suppresses their most rational and efficient use. Under communism, production will be planned by freely associated producers and the resulting abundance used to satisfy universal need. The proletarian revolution will therefore be the last, and if history evolves further, it will no longer follow the rhythms of violence and decay. It will, in a rather Hegelian sense, become rational. For the mature Marx and for Engels, a scientific analysis of the objective structural contradictions fermenting within capitalism become the primary concern.

A general applicability of the Marxist approach to women is at once apparent. In attempting to offer a 'scientific' account of oppression, rooted in material processes, Marxism suggested that subjugation and its forms are social, historical and alterable rather than natural, transhistorical and immutable. In opposition to liberal analyses, it showed that oppression does not endure merely because of custom and inertia but results from ongoing material interests. It thus invited the oppressed to discover the material nature of their subordination, to recognize that they were exploited not as individuals but as classes. It followed that liberation could never transpire through acts of personal endeavour, the goodwill of oppressors or an extension of rights; only united action that transformed those structures which reproduce exploitation could succeed, and this ruled out piecemeal reform. This historical, materialist and dialectical approach would later be co-opted even by feminists like Firestone who did not classify themselves as Marxist,[28] due to its potency in disclosing the bases of oppression. Marx and Engels themselves offered only a rudimentary application of this method to women, largely confined to Engels's *Origin of the*

Family, Private Property and the State. However, it is already clear that a method developed to explain class relations cannot be simply imposed upon sexual ones.

Two general difficulties at once arise. First, women are not a class—a term which implies economic position—in the same way as the proletariat or bourgeoisie are. They might occupy a place in the economy which puts them in a variety of classes and they have been in any case more commonly categorized according to their husbands' class. It is not therefore immediately obvious where their class loyalties might lie nor whether they suffer a particular form of exploitation, economic or otherwise, by virtue of their sex. Marx and Engels themselves had little to say about the differential effects of capitalism on the two sexes and even less about those daily humiliations which are 'only' ideological. A theory which analysed progress and conflict in terms of production could not be applied to reproductive relations in other than a highly formal or reductive way.

Thus, second, there arises the problem of reductionism. In so far as women's interests are deduced exclusively from class membership, they are reduced to economic actors: proletarian or bourgeois. It then becomes impossible to locate a basis for solidarity between women of different classes or to pinpoint any specifically female oppression or strategy. There was a tendency for all the early Marxists to envisage women's liberation as a by-product of the revolution that would make them free producers on the same basis as men. In sum, Marxism is relevant to women both because of its general analysis of the dynamics of oppression and because women undoubtedly suffer material forms of oppression which take a particular form under different modes of production but are especially acute under capitalism. It is problematic for them because it cannot account for a specifically sexual form of oppression except in so far as it is functional to private property and production. This is already apparent in Marx and Engels's own later work, and it is now necessary to look at this in more detail.

In offering a materialist account of history, it was necessary to establish what was included in its material foundation. Since the species requires material replacement, reproduction might be quite logically included in the infrastructure, and this would have important implications for the family and for the significance of a women's movement. For if reproductive relations were as determining as economic ones, it would follow that an upheaval there might instigate a thorough social transformation. If on the other hand reproductive relations merely reflect the needs of more fundamental productive ones, then they will lack the potential to initiate change but will be unavoidably transformed should a new mode of production be established. Although some feminists have seized upon allusions by Marx and Engels to the effect that reproductive relations are co-determining,[29] it is the alternative interpretation which textual evidence supports, with its attendant problems of reductionism.

The German Ideology begins with the 'existence of living human individuals' who must both produce and reproduce. Although both functions are fundamental to species-preservation, however, the (familial) social relations which structure reproduction quickly lose a capacity to determine progress: the development of new needs engenders more significant relationships than those pertaining in the family.[30] The latter become subordinate to the new productive relations, losing their determining power at the first, tribal, stage of history. In The German Ideology it is the ensuing historical era which is discussed, and it was not until Engels' Origin of the Family, Private Property and the State appeared in 1884 that a materialist account was offered of the earlier, pre-historical period. This was possible only on the basis of new anthropological evidence supplied by Morgan's Ancient Society (1877).

Engels prefaces the Origin with the statement that 'according to the materialist conception, the determining factor in history is, in the last resort, the production and reproduction of material life'.[31] 'The social institutions under which men of a definite historical epoch and of a definite country live are conditioned by both kinds of production: by the stage of development of labour, on the one hand, and of the family, on the other'.[32]

However, it is obvious from the continuation of the text that the relative power of the two sets of relations to determine others, varies over time. Engels goes on to reiterate what he and

*   *   *

Marx had written forty years earlier: 'The less the development of labour, and the more limited its volume of production and, therefore, the wealth of society, the more preponderatingly does the social order appear to be dominated by the ties of sex'.[33] Kinship plays a decisive role at the stages of savagery and barbarism,[34] although even here it is its productive arrangements which are most significant. Once we pass into civilization (roughly beginning with Heroic Greece) and history, a new set of relationships are determining:

> The old society based on sex groups bursts asunder in the collision of the newly-developed social classes; in its place a new society appears, constituted in a state, the lower units of which are no longer sex groups but territorial groups, a system in which the family system is entirely dominated by the property system, and in which the class antagonisms and class struggles, which make up the content of all hitherto *written* history, now freely develop.[35]

It is just this collision which we encountered in the first chapter, in ancient Greece, and Engels's fascination with the *Oresteia* at this point in the text is not therefore surprising. As far as the issue of material determinants is concerned, it seems clear that once non-familial relations come to the fore, reproductive structures lose any power they once had to shape history.

The German Ideology had begun its account of historical development by taking for granted male dominance, suggesting this to be simply the outcome of natural sexual difference. One purpose of the *Origin* is to offer instead a materialist account of the origins of patriarchy. In showing that the family had a history and underwent change, Engels performed an important service in challenging the generally held view that it was simply natural and universal, hence immutable. More specifically, if the causes of female oppression could be located, this would suggest the most appropriate strategies and priorities for overturning it. The task which Engels sets himself in the *Origin* is thus a most significant one, although, as we will see, it is not very successfully executed. In the following account of his work I shall consider first the explanation of sexual oppression which Engels gives and then the vision of emancipation that follows from it.

Engels accepts Morgan's three major epochs of savagery, barbarism and civilization. Each is categorized by a different level of subsistence and technology: the first era culminates in the stone age; the second is a transitional period when iron ore is smelted, animals domesticated and forests cleared. The appearance of civilization witnesses the invention of the alphabet, hence literary records and history proper. It is the age of Homer and Hesiod, when industry and art begin to enrich a production that had formerly remained close to nature. Corresponding to each phase is a typical reproductive relationship. Compulsory monogamy, the oppression of women, sexual conflict and a family form designed as functional for another set of relations, mark only the final stage. An explanation of this outcome is required.

Engels speculates that humanity's emergence from animality must have been manifested by a primal horde since such an advance would have required a degree of cooperation precluding sexual jealousy. From this original promiscuity, an increasingly shrinking 'family' would have emerged. In the consanguine family, intergenerational incest taboos occurred; in the punaluan family there were additional prohibitions against sibling intercourse. Such forms of group marriage existed in a period of primitive communism, marked domestically by communistic households increasingly organized to exclude those with whom sex was not permitted. While tribes were endogomous, the gentes into which they were subdivided therefore practised strict exogamy.

The force which Engels finds responsible for these changes is a natural one: the incest taboo. He does not explain it but merely says, 'We see, then, how the impulse towards the prevention of inbreeding asserts itself time and again, but in a groping, spontaneous way, without clear consciousness or purpose'.[36] All he can claim is a Darwinian natural selection whereby those tribes proscribing inbreeding develop more rapidly.[37] The more restricted marriages which the incest taboo encourages will be nevertheless crucial to the eventual defeat of woman. By the barbaric age, prohibitions have become sufficiently broad to encourage more enduring coupling and to introduce the pairing family. Thus it is neither 'sex-love' nor economic imperatives which motivate these transitions within the prehistorical 'family'. 'Natural selection had completed its work by constantly reducing the circle of community marriage'.[38] Only subsequently will social factors intervene.

As long as group marriage persists, fatherhood remains uncertain and so descent can be traced only through the female line. Accordingly, if incest taboos are to be upheld then each gens must be organized so that only females remain within the communal household while sons leave to found new ones and husbands are imported from elsewhere. The first social distinction between the sexes works in women's favour and is predicated on their identity with their natural child. This is the age of mother-right.

Engels is eager at this point to establish a material basis for women's power. While maternity yields status, it is more significant that matriliny also brings material power since men are always in transit between different gentes while the women in a household belong to a single gens. Men are continually moved on and it is women who have power over the common stores. This gives them supremacy since the means of subsistence are concentrated in the domestic realm. Although there is no *necessary* relationship between mother-right and the type of work women perform (e.g. they might have used their position as the most stable element in the gens to submit men to domestic drudgery and have themselves gone out in root and fruit collecting parties), and although Engels insists that women's social status and the sexual division of labour arise from quite different causes, further developments make no sense unless such a link is in fact assumed. It must be mother-right that yields women both material power and status, because the permanent position in the household which it brings grants them power over the common stores and hence responsibility for the domestic economy. In other words, reproductive relations actually determine social ones, and it is precisely this source of power which will bring women's defeat. As Engels will acknowledge:

The very cause that had formerly made the woman supreme in the house, namely, her being confined to domestic work, now assured supremacy in the house to the man: the woman's work lost its significance compared with the man's work in obtaining a livelihood; the latter was everything, the former an insignificant contribution.[39]

Engels's difficulty perhaps arises because of his reliance on Bachofen's evidence for a primitive matriarchy. Because

Bachofen offered religious rather than materialist reasons for this, he was able to give greater significance to the sheer esteem which mother-right yielded. Engels's search for a material basis of female power must supplement this explanation, and he is forced to associate matriliny with a sexual division of labour: a crucial link in his argument but one which he fails to make convincingly.

It is women themselves who play the crucial part, Engels continues, in promoting the conditions of their decline. Apparently they long for chastity, for permanent marriages in order to escape the sexual relations which become degrading and oppressive once they lose their 'naïve, primitive jungle character'. Men, he adds, would never dream of renouncing such pleasures.[40] With monogamy, however, paternity can be authenticated and this is crucial in sealing women's fate.

The trend towards stable pairs, promoted by natural and psychological factors, coincides with advances in production. Agriculture and the domestication of animals bring new wealth; the emergence of a surplus sees the introduction of slavery. It is to the man that this new wealth accrues, since as the partner who operated outside the home to produce food and tools, he owns the herds and slaves. As his status rises, so does his desire to pass on wealth to his own children. A silent prehistoric revolution ensues whereby father-right is subsituted for mother-right. It is now the man and his children who remain in the gens and the wife he imports must be strictly controlled to guarantee the legitimacy of his heirs.

The common household under the aegis of the patriarch quickly succumbs to the monogamian family with the institution of private property. The Athenian family is its first expression, the first form of the family to be determined by economic imperatives. If reproductive relations (notably mother-right) could previously *determine* who had material power, father-right now *reflects* and *serves* the material hegemony of the father and we enter the period of history proper, where productive relations alone are in the last instance determining. Class and sex conflict have emerged simultaneously, twin offspring of private property; the commencement of history as a history of class struggle coincides with 'the world-historical defeat of the female sex'. For it is female fidelity which is the guarantor and prerequisite of private property; the woman is reduced to domestic slave and breeding instrument (it is at this point that the family with its master–slave relations appeared in the *German Ideology*; it is the period of the first revolution in Rousseau's schema). The history of civilization will be a thoroughly patriarchal affair, dominated by the power of wealth rather than generation. This is why women can be presented as passive, symbolic ciphers of a history they cease to shape. Engels thus provides an explanation for sexual relations which he and Marx had previously presented as merely natural. But how adequate is this account of female subjection?

To begin with, all sorts of assumptions mediate between the emergence of private property and the subordination of women. Engels does not account, for example, for the male obsession with passing property on to legitimate heirs, nor, even if we accept this desire, does he explain how men gained the power to accomplish the transition to father-right or to maintain exclusive rights over the newly discovered wealth, especially since they began from a weaker position and a society where communal property was the norm. And if the endurance of private property demands that it pass to one's children rather than back to the common stock, why should this not occur through the female line?

But more fundamentally, of course, Engels has offered no explanation for the division of labour that associates men with this new wealth in the first place. We have already seen he and Marx speaking of a natural division within the family, and when it comes to the crucial analysis in the *Origin* Engels has not moved beyond this position. For while it is a biological distinction which first gives women status in so far as they alone have assurance of parentage, there is no natural reason why this should yield a division of labour with men alone working outside the home, especially under the conditions of the communistic household where child-care could be readily shared. Yet ultimately it is to this unexplained social division of labour that Engels attributes woman's defeat. There is no suggestion that the allocation of sexual function changes; it is only turned 'topsy-turvy simply because the division of labour outside the family had changed'.[41] The new wealth provided by herds therefore only alters the relative rewards and significance of primordial differentiation; it does not initiate it. In essence,

Engels's position is little different from that of Rousseau in *The Second Discourse*.

Although Engels's account of women's subordination concludes with the emergence of private property as the decisive step, it therefore relies on premises that are alien to historical materialism: biological materialism, psychology and naturalism. It is natural selection that narrows the family into a form appropriate to monogamy and a quasi-moral repugnance against sex, attributed to women, which lays down its structures. But more problematically, since Engels relies on a naturalistic explanation which assumes the very allocation of function it needs to explain, the crucial link between women's oppression and private property is never shown to be more than contingent. As Lise Vogel concludes, both Marx and Engels 'come perilously close to a position that holds biology to be destiny. A quite damaging spectre of 'the natural' haunts their work, from the earliest writings to the most mature'.[42] If some factor more fundamental than private property is responsible for women's subjugation, it is unlikely that its abolition will be sufficient to emancipate them.

I have suggested that the Marxist method is a fertile one for feminists but that Marx and Engels failed to apply it adequately when it comes to women. So far, this criticism has been directed specifically against Engels's explanation for women's original defeat. But what of the means by which their oppression is sustained and the conditions for their liberation?

The moment of defeat for women arrives, as we saw, once monogamy becomes compulsory. To safeguard private property, the male polices his wife's fertility. He also uses his superior position to exploit her labour power, hence the resemblance of marriage to a class relationship: 'The wife became the first domestic servant, pushed out of participation in social production'.[43] It is because the labour she is forced into is only domestic, that the woman lacks a historical mission or route to independence. Her unpaid work only reproduces her reliance on her husband: the 'predominance of the man in marriage is simply a consequence of his economic predominance'.[44] The unmarried woman is frequently obliged to sell her body into slavery to support herself and her children: prostitution differs from marriage only in degree.

These forces continue to structure women's subordination but the remainder of Engels's account is curiously ahistorical. For he does not describe different configurations over time despite shifts in production across ancient, feudal and capitalist modes. He offers no account of all those periods when women's social production did make a vital contribution to the economy (it is Marx who recognizes in *Capital* that women's work is essential to the eighteenth-century peasant family, although he still speaks of a natural division of labour there).[45] Consequently, there is no explanation as to why the ideology of the idle wife emerged only in the seventeenth century, or of the ways in which capitalism specifically benefits from women's exploitation both inside and outside the home. Although Engels's earlier studies of *The Condition of the Working Class in England* had shown him to be well aware that working women receive lower wages than men,[46] there is no explanation for this aspect of female dependence, in the *Origin*. In fact, the 1884 work does very little to analyse the specific patterns of female exploitation under capitalism. It does acknowledge that proletarian women suffer special hardships since they must perform family duties as well as work, and this is offered as a reason for abolishing the family. But under current conditions, Engels seems to perceive this as largely a natural misfortune; certainly, he had previously spoken of unemployed men doing housework while their wives toiled in the factory, as degrading and shameful (for the former!).[47]

This omission probably occurs because Engels is eager to conclude that proletarians of both sexes share an interest in overthrowing capitalism and have no quarrel among themselves. But by confining himself to his original, and rather limited, observation that women's exclusion from social production underlies their subjugation, he allows himself only an equally simplistic solution: 'the first premise for the emancipation of women is the reintroduction of the entire female sex into public industry'.[48] At this point they regain a power base, re-enter history and inherit the interests of the working class. In other words, it is bourgeois women who are oppressed as women under capitalism (because of their husbands' relationship to private property), while proletarian women are oppressed only as workers. The realization that women's oppression varies across class is a significant advance over liberal analyses, but it goes little further in describing working women's problems.

Engels says very little about sexual relations under socialism, but three related changes he envisages are the socialization of domestic labour, the abolition of the family and the evolution of authentic 'sex-love'. The former solution was of course already on the agenda of Utopian Socialism, and Engels adds no details, merely writing that private housekeeping will become a social industry and the care and education of children a public matter, thereby reducing domestic activities to a 'minor degree'.[49] Without private property, the rationale for monogamy will disappear, as will concern for legitimacy. This, Engels concludes, will have a salutary effect on public opinion regarding 'virginal honour and feminine shame'.[50] In sum, once economic conditions change, so will the sexual ideology that rests upon them; without private property, all the trappings of female debasement will atrophy. This is especially important regarding 'sex-love'.

Under conditions of private property, the relationship between the sexes is an economic one. Like all class relations, it spawns contradictions: prostitution and adultery are manifestations of the forces of desire which cannot be contained within this mode of reproduction. With the demise of private property, sentiment and passion will be released and sex-love is the form which Engels believes they will take. This is emancipatory because it betokens reciprocity, predicated on amorous rather than material considerations. In other words, socialist sex-love must represent the true humanization of that most natural relation between sexes of which the young Marx had spoken. In a sense, the unity Engels anticipates is tantamount to Hegel's ethical life and although Hegel would doubtless have relegated the 'mutual affection' on which Engels founds it to the realm of caprice, Engels himself seems to believe that lovers who fulfil his standards will tend to a voluntary monogamy. The legal trappings of marriage and divorce will be simply superfluous and the free association of producers which sees the withering away of the state will similarly find a free association between the sexes accompanied by a withering away of the family. Despite this nice symmetry, however, the solution is undoubtedly less imaginative than that of Fourier, leading one critic to complain that, in the end,

Engels 'admitted no other model acceptable to future lovers than the conjugal union stripped of its capitalist impediments'.[51]

The demise of the family is presented by Marx and Engels as both inevitable and already underway even within capitalism. For they suspect that while private property continues to sustain the bourgeois family, the proletarian variety both lacks the conditions that uphold monogamy and faces elimination due to the workings of capitalism itself. In its insatiable appetite for surplus value, capitalism must continually introduce new groups to wage-labour. The drawing of women into the workforce therefore performs the task which legal juggling or utopian experiment have so far failed to perform: the family disintegrates into individuals who compete for wages and lack the time or energy for domestic life. Although this development is viewed as 'terrible and disgusting', it also creates 'a new economic foundation for a higher form of the family and of the relation between the sexes'.[52]

In the *Origin,* Engels is more optimistic about such developments, perceiving the proletarian family's decay as more benign. Lacking property, the proletarian has no investment in legitimacy; lacking money, he has no access to the legal means of control over his wife available to the bourgeois. Most decisively, however, the fact that the wife works gives her the independence brought by social production. Thus 'the last remnants of male domination in the proletarian home have lost all foundation—except, perhaps, for some of that brutality towards women which became firmly rooted with the establishment of monogamy'.[53] Feminists might, of course, argue that 'that brutality' is the whole point, but Engels clearly sees it as a superstructural residue which will disappear once free production and free love are established—nothing to worry about. As Vogel points out, this romantic picture fails to appreciate the extent to which the working-class family exists to reproduce labour power, rather than to transmit property.[54] It does not therefore lack function under capitalism as long as women continue to bear children while working, and so it is likely to endure, albeit in impoverished form.

Finally, this sketch puts bourgeois women in a strange position, since they have a class interest in sustaining capitalism (whose benefits they reap via their husbands) and a gender interest in overthrowing it (since private property is the *raison d'être* for the monogamy that oppresses them). This conflict is never satisfactorily resolved, although Marxists favoured the first alternative and viewed bourgeois feminists with distrust.

In conclusion, what are the strengths and weaknesses of a Marxist approach to the woman question? First, it shows that their oppression has material foundations even though it does not locate these very precisely. It opens the door to interrogation of the ongoing causes of oppression rather than presenting it as a legacy of custom and prejudice which rational discourse and goodwill might sweep away. Second, the notion of the family as a 'series in historical development'[55] and women as subject to a changing status which once gave them superiority, is important in dispelling naturalist claims, even if Marx and Engels do not themselves carry through their argument adequately. Again, neither thinker is very adventurous in the type of sexual relationship they envisage for the future, but at least their method opens up possibilities of radical change. Historical materialism is therefore often fertile for feminist thought despite, rather than because of, Marx and Engels's own application of it to women.

Third, the critique of capitalism itself offers an approach that is useful for subsequent analyses of women's role in the economy. For a later generation of feminists concerned to unearth the benefits capitalism reaps from women's oppression and to disclose the differential effects of that mode of production on the two sexes, formulas about the value of labour power, determination of wage levels and the industrial reserve army, have proven invaluable. At the same time, however, Marx and Engels's own analyses here are of limited use. For as Heidi Hartmann says, they 'give no clues about why *women* are subordinate to *men* inside and outside the family and why it is not the other way round. *Marxist categories, like capital itself, are sex blind*'.[56] Alison Jaggar suggests that this methodological flaw nevertheless has its advantages: 'Marxist theorizing seems to have been toward the abolition of gender distinctions in the market and thus towards . . . an androgynous future'.[57] Yet there are places where the beginnings of an explanation for women's differential economic role are offered. In *The Communist Manifesto* it is recognized that industrialization favours women's being drawn into the workforce, because work is reduced to the unskilled variety of which women are capable and for which they are cheaper (though it is not explained why they are cheaper or why they lack the skills that bring higher wages). Women thus become as valuable as men as producers of value, but more valuable, hence more exploited, in so far as greater surplus value can be extracted from them.[58] Ultimately, however, Marx and Engels needed to pay little attention to women's relatively greater exploitation under capitalism since they associated their liberation with a communist society in which wage-labour and economic dependency would have disappeared altogether.

On the debit side, we have already encountered Marxism's main drawback which is its reductionism. Although not all Marxism is reductionist, the treatment of women by Engels and his successors has often presented sexual relations as simply determined by economic ones, implying that women's fight should be within the proletarian fraternity and that socialism will automatically emancipate them. The resulting hostility to bourgeois feminism, as a movement of class traitors who peddle dangerous diversions that threaten proletarian unity, makes impossible any solidarity among women or recognition of a specifically sexual oppression. We will see how future Marxists approached such problems in the two final chapters. But in any case, concentration on the labour–capital conflict eclipsed the broader view of social antagonisms that an earlier socialism had developed. Sexual problems were simply not accorded much interest and the solutions sketched, despite a resemblance to those offered by Utopians, are diluted and unimaginative in comparison.

9 Social Democrats and Bolsheviks: Socialism and the Woman Question

The 'woman question' (as it came to be known) was ardently debated among socialists over the half century 1870–1920. Discussions disclosed the theoretical weaknesses of Marxism in this context and presented a challenge to those who wished to combine socialist commitment with feminist sympathy. While Marx and Engels had not been especially interested in the topic, there were now practical concerns which incited greater preoccupation with it.

During the nineteenth century, a women's movement had developed but had remained of largely bourgeois inspiration: feminism was for it predominantly a rights issue. Socialists recognized the need for female support if they were successfully to defeat capitalism and were especially concerned that proletarian women recognize where their true interests lay. It was therefore necessary to develop a critique of liberal feminism; to show that women's interests resided in socialist transformation, and to offer the analysis of the form of oppression specific to working women, which was missing both from liberal accounts and from Marx and Engels's own analyses. As the century progressed, mass socialist parties and trade unions came into existence, offering a real power base for working-class women in so far as they could be persuaded to champion the women's cause.

Unfortunately, many socialist men, while supporting women in principle, did so in highly traditional ways. In France, Proudhon's vision was popular, with its emphasis on a Utopia founded on the peasant-artisan family, the woman safely ensconced in the home safe from capitalist corruption.[1] In

Germany, socialists were divided between welcoming women into the labour force, as proposed by Bebel and Liebknecht, and Lassalle's demand that they be honoured in the home. In the first case it was hoped that the increased level of exploitation would hasten the demise of capitalism; in the second, that men's current employment prospects and wages would improve with less competition.[2] Marx and Engels's belief that women's emancipation relied on their entry into the workforce thus competed with attempts to re-evaluate domestic labour and motherhood as significant social contributions.

The German Social Democratic Party (SPD) became the largest socialist party in the Second International. It was co-founded by August Bebel, who led the party until 1913. His *Woman in the Past, Present and Future,* also known as *Woman under Socialism,* appeared in 1878, was revised 1883 and 1891, and went through more than fifty editions. It was immensely popular, winning many women to the socialist cause and inspiring female activists like Clara Zetkin (who described it as 'an event, a deed') and Alexandra Kollontai (who referred to it as the 'woman's bible'),[3] as well as provoking Engels into a swift alternative with his *Origin.*

Bebel's work offered a highly readable account of women's oppression, supplementing the rather dry Marxist account of its structural determinants with descriptions of its daily ramifications and a visionary portrait of transformation in a socialist future. The Marxism underlying his account is of the revisionist and confident variety typical of the SPD. Bebel depicts a history advancing relentlessly towards socialism: mounting exploitation will engender successive crises of overproduction culminating in mass proletarianization, class-consciousness and the demise of capitalism. All social and political institutions, he stresses, are but reflections of relations of production. Seeing a new depression under way, Bebel judged capitalism's collapse to be imminent. It was not therefore surprising that the sexual and familial relations it sustained should also be in ferment—a fact Bebel demonstrates by extensive use of statistical data (the advent of such a method being applied to the woman question is itself interesting if we recall how many previous theorists had merely deduced women's status from the logic of their system, with little regard for their empirical role).[4]

Nevertheless, it is a Parliamentary road that Bebel advocates. In backward Germany, where there had been no bourgeois revolution and few liberal reforms, socialists believed that they must perform the tasks for which the indigenous middle class was too weak. Liberal rights must be won before their formal propositions could be made concrete under socialism; historical stages could not be skipped. Accordingly, Bebel has some sympathy for the demands of bourgeois feminism, arguing that suffrage is vital as a means to political education and enlightenment and even that the fight for a few talented middle-class women to enter the professions is valuable in dissolving prejudices about the sex's inferior intellect. Indeed, at times Bebel sounds like a natural rights theorist, as when he claims that 'woman has the same right as man to unfold her faculties and to the free exercise of the same: she is human as well as he'.[5] His language shows the continuing potency of such appeals to justice and Bebel proves himself conversant with the liberal case when he sketches Wollstonecraft's position and quotes from Mill's *Subjection*.[6] In fact, Bebel's criticism of arguments from nature or custom, his condemnation of an education that enhances feeling at the expense of intellect and his claim that women might reach unimaginable heights of perfection with the opportunity for free development, are all reminiscent of Mill. Where he goes beyond Mill, is in demonstrating the economic factors that underlie social and legal inequality and in focusing on the proletarian family to demonstrate that women's emancipation is incompatible with capitalism.

Bebel is graphic in his description of a specifically sexual form of oppression which women suffer. Those who are seduced have little claim to support from seducer or state; many seek back-street abortions while others catch venereal diseases from dissolute males. Restrictions on their sexual experience also lead to its unnatural expression and vice, to prostitution and neurosis. It is, however, bourgeois women who seem to suffer most from explicitly sexual forms of oppression. Their dress injures health and hampers movements; narrow lives and poor education mire them in habit while rendering them unappealing companions; dependence on husbands throws them into competition with one another and into obsession with ridiculous fashions, where success itself can mean only relegation to a piece of property. In sum, the bourgeois wife is 'miserably going to pieces'.[7] Bebel concludes that men 'gladly accept such a state of things: they are its beneficiaries. It flatters their pride, their vanity, their interest to play the *role* of the stronger and the master'. Since such posturing is impervious to reason, 'women should expect as little help from men as workmen do from the capitalist class'.[8] For most men under capitalism 'see in woman only an article of profit and pleasure; to acknowledge her an equal runs against the grain of their prejudices'.[9]

Were Bebel really to blame the above abuses simply on men, this would carry him outside a Marxist analysis, but he avoids this by giving them a materialist explanation. The emphasis on dress, for example, arises from women's need to lure a husband under conditions where they require material support from men who are in short supply. Under socialism, Bebel reasons, vanity and the folly of fashion will disappear alongside their economic *raison d'être:* women will achieve independence, and equality in sexual numbers will be restored since a socialism placing greater value on human lives will minimize industrial accidents and military obligations.[10] The example illustrates how far Bebel went beyond Engels in offering a detailed historical materialist account of the vicissitudes of female oppression rather than the blanket account founded on the requirements of private property.

Bebel's description of the proletarian family also takes him beyond liberalism while eschewing Engels's romanticism. He sees that poverty and insecurity ruin relationships here; that working women perform double toil in productive and domestic labour; that exhaustion destroys love and leaves children uncared for; that overcrowding brutalizes youth while undermining decency; that women are ill-nourished and so bear degenerate offspring. But perhaps more importantly, Bebel also attempts to explain why women workers fare worse than their male counterparts—a significant advance over Marx and Engels's largely asexual workforce.

A woman gets lower wages firstly because 'her material demands are less'. In other words, her labour has less value (it costs less to reproduce) so greater surplus value can be extracted. This is precisely why women are attractive to employers. Moreover, they must sell themselves more cheaply if they are to compete with men, since their sexual functions necessitate periodic stoppages from work. Concerned about their children's needs, married women are also more submissive; they rarely join other workers' struggles and so earn less under worse conditions. Bebel recognizes that industries dominated by female employees are generally the worst employers. As capitalism continues its quest for surplus value, however, it uses more machines and child labour, and these then present even cheaper forces, further reducing women's wages as women once had men's. It follows from Bebel's analysis that competition between women and men is only relative within a general process of increasing exploitation. Finally, however, and in conformity with his belief in increasing proletarianization, he sees that new types of employment are drawing middle-class women into the labour force, where they too are exploited, as saleswomen, clerks and teachers.[11] Bebel argues that such women have been accorded these opportunities not because of the success of their own agitation but because of capitalism's appetite for labour. Thenceforth, they share proletarian women's primary interest, which is the abolition of capitalism.

The conclusion is that despite competition over wage levels, workers of both sexes remain allies. Indeed, Bebel suggests that women need proletarian males to show them the nature of their subjection: it is the man who 'strives to enlighten woman on her position in society, and to *educate her into a fellow combatant in the struggle for the emancipation of the proletariat from capitalism*'.[12] In other words, this is the socialist version of that recurrent claim that women must be wrenched by men from their narrow lives if they are to act responsibly (as citizens; class-conscious proletarians). It is up to enlightened socialist men to show women the fallacies of any sort of autonomous feminism.

Towards the end of *Woman under Socialism,* Bebel offers a beguiling picture of life in the future. The vision relies heavily on Fourier, describing moderate, agreeable and freely chosen work exchanging for vouchers which replace money. The state will wither away to be replaced by elected administrators who compute supply and demand, calculating from the result the amount of socially necessary labour required from each person. Bebel believes that this may well amount to less than two hours daily, leaving time for leisure, arts, science and general creativity. Production will be maximised by eliminating wasteful, poorly made articles and by using machinery. Like the Utopians, Bebel is fascinated by the potential of technology and he speaks fervently of chemically produced, low-cost food; irrigated deserts, air travel and solar, tidal, wind and hydro-electric power. Women are to be equal beneficiaries of this essentially sexually neutral future, but Bebel does cite some advantages which will help them in particular and it becomes evident that socialism cannot, after all, be strictly androgynous.

The key to socialism's specific benefits for women again lies with technology and especially with cheap, abundant power. Impressed by the 1892 exhibition in Chicago, later editions of Bebel's text bristle with eulogies to electrical gadgets from doors, lifts and newspaper deliveries to dishwashers, carpet-cleaners and garbage disposers. The bourgeoisie, he argues, in *Communist Manifesto* style, has fulfilled its historic mission in making available such liberating productive forces. All that remains is to render them common property so that everyone might benefit. Bebel is especially interested in the application of electricity to domestic tasks: 'with the central kitchen may also be connected central heating, warm water along with cold water pipes, whereby a number of bothersome and time-consuming labours is done away with'.[13] One is left with the impression that he is less concerned with the joys of communal eating, the solidarity of sisterly food preparation or the demise of the isolated and selfish, single-unit family, than with efficiency. It is the drudgery of domestic labour, rather than domestic labour *per se,* which oppresses women and like capitalism itself, its end is nigh: '*The small private kitchen is, just like the workshop of the small master mechanic, a transitional stage, an arrangement by which time, power and material are senselessly squandered and wasted*'.[14]

Although this enthusiasm for science-*cum*-socialization owes much to Utopian Socialism, the spirit is rather different. In particular, the concern is more with the requirements of the social whole and with a Marxian faith that collective ownership of massive productive forces will automatically engender new social relations. The emphasis on individual (erotic) energy is missing, as is the commitment to the small community and the belief that sexual relationships are a fundamental precursor of socio-economic change. Instead, the more reductionist elements of Marxism mean that scant attention is paid to the actual transformation of sexual or familial relations and patriarchal attitudes. Although changes in the economic base are supposed to solve such problems, Bebel's references to the role of woman under socialism are not always encouraging here.

Children are to be made a public responsibility since they represent society's future. Public education for all will be provided and supervised by women and men elected to boards of education. Bebel's claim that lighter work will allow parents more time with their children, nevertheless implies that some version of the biological family will endure, and he does say that despite removal of the legal and economic imperatives to marriage, the 'power of natural instincts' will restore the equilibrium of the family.[15] Motherhood is also to be recognized as a public service and supported accordingly, with, the provision of good nutrition, agreeable surroundings and a comfortable home.[16] Bebel seems to believe that women will gravitate to motherhood despite the new options available to them, although he also suggests that as women achieve higher positions, some sort of population check will ensue. How this would operate is however unclear given Bebel's distaste both for abstinence (which he correlates with suicide in women) and 'unnatural preventatives'.[17]

Bebel summarizes his vision of woman in the future as follows. She will be socially and economically independent, 'free, the peer of man, mistress of her lot'. She will receive the same education as men, choosing her occupation and work under identical conditions with them. She will freely select her lovers, entering into private contracts with them and leaving them should love end, without public interference. Like Engels, Bebel believes that relationships will nevertheless remain more or less monogamous and entirely heterosexual.

Having said all this, however, Bebel clearly does not envisage an identity of roles. A woman's children—'where she has any'—will no longer hamper her freedom, we are told, but this is because 'nurses, teachers, female friends, the rising female generations' will be on hand to help the mother in need (as examples of work that women might choose, educator, teacher or nurse have already been suggested).[18] It is evident, then, that although everyone is to be a productive worker under socialism, this is partly facilitated by redesignating domestic and childbearing tasks as public work, for some sort of 'natural' division of labour will survive. While individual women may not reproduce, women collectively will still be responsible for the reproductive realm. Similarly, they will not be freed from domestic labour, but it will be re-evaluated and lightened. Calculations of necessary labour time will include women only 'in so far as these are not otherwise engaged in the education of children, the preparation of food, etc'.[19] Perhaps this failure truly to redistribute function is not surprising: despite a belief that sexual identities are constructed by education, Bebel does occasionally lapse into naturalistic claims. He finds women more impulsive, naïve and passionate; less reflective than man 'by nature'; more inclined to melancholy and derangement due to physical differences in the brain, and unfit for hard labour, which strips them of 'womanliness'.[20]

History will finally come full circle, Bebel concludes. His book has opened with an account of the origin of woman's oppression which draws on Morgan, Bachofen and (in the later editions) Engels. It ends with women resuming the active role they undertook in the matrilineal gens.[21] But their status there was, of course, quite sexually specific, and it is apparently to remain so under socialism, at least to an unspecified degree. Although Bebel's account of women's oppression in the present goes far beyond Engels's, it too fails to come to terms with the sexual division of labour. The idea of male involvement in domesticity seems simply to have been too monstrous to contemplate. At times perceptive of ideological aspects of women's oppression, Bebel's conviction that these are all reducible to distortions imposed by a capitalist economy, which will be automatically eliminated when it is, allows no room to consider that patriarchy might have its own history and interests or that women's continued association with domesticity might prove an enduring factor in their future subordination.

The purpose of Bebel's book was to mobilize women in the fight against capitalism, but the case that capitalism was alone responsible for their oppression ultimately remained unconvincing. Vogel concludes that *Woman under Socialism* retained an impoverished theoretical apparatus which was a mix of utopian vision and mechanical, though reformist, Marxism.[22] I would add that there was also a great deal of liberal inspiration, but the point remains that no compelling synthesis between Marxism and feminism had yet been offered. Rendered conservative through years of domesticity, women were still to see their own problems through men's eyes, to be tutored into their world and to fight for their hi-tech vision. 'To woman also in general, and as a female proletarian in particular, the summons goes out not to remain behind in this struggle in which her redemption and emancipation are at stake'. She must prove that she understands her place in the movement by joining it, but it is up to men to help her understand.[23] There is to be, in short, no autonomous women's movement nor independent assessment of their needs.

At times Bebel's descriptions had lifted him above the reductionist implications of his theoretical framework, but the underlying problem of reduction continued to haunt Marxist analyses of the woman question, as testified by his successors. When Bebel's book appeared in English in 1886, it inspired an article by Marx's daughter Eleanor Marx Aveling and her husband Edward Aveling. This appeared in the *Westminster Review,* that organ of progressive liberalism once patronized by the Utilitarians.[24]

The Avelings shared Bebel's optimism regarding capitalism's imminent collapse and also his claim that the woman question 'is one of economics' and thus 'one of the organization of society as a whole'.[25] The disjunction between the description of women's oppression and the analysis of capitalism is, however, preserved, embodied in the very structure of the article, which is merely divided into accounts of each. The first part offers a recognizably liberal attack on bourgeois marriage (the woman's 'moral' dependence on men; the sexual double standard etc.), supplemented by a tirade against the evils of sexual repression (homosexuality and lesbianism, both 'unnatural' and 'diseased forms'; lunacy; suicide) and frequent reminders that economics underlies these horrors.[26] Socialism is again presented as the definitive solution: equality in all spheres, minimal hours of social labour, personal relationships that are satisfying because they are unmediated by financial considerations, will be an outcome of collective ownership. The piece ends with a sentimental picture of the future couple: 'For ourselves we believe that the cleaving of one man to one woman will be best for all, and that these will find each in the heart of the other, that which is in the eyes, their own image'.[27]

Sexual relations are now on the socialist agenda, then, but they have not yet been accepted as problematic beyond their economic elements. There remains an ideal of monogamous mutual transparency, nature rendered rational, the Hegelian image of two-merged-as-one. It is an extraordinarily rationalist ideal, given the authors' appreciation of the irrational effects of repression.

At one point, the Avelings' article does suggest that women's interests are specifically gendered and that women must therefore liberate themselves. The model for understanding their oppression is still that of class and is not therefore entirely appropriate, but at least women are seen as analogous to the proletariat rather than being reduced to it:

Women are the creatures of an organized tyranny of men, as the workers are the creatures of an organized tyranny of idlers. . . . Both the oppressed classes, women and the immediate producers, must understand that their emancipation will come from themselves. Women will find allies in the better sort of men, as the labourers are finding allies among the philosophers, artists, and poets. But the one has nothing to hope from man as a whole, and the other has nothing to hope from the middle class as a whole.[28]

And later, 'women, once more like the labourers, have been expropriated as to their rights as human beings, just as the labourers were expropriated as to their rights as producers'. In each case, a loss of rights is blamed on force.[29]

Nevertheless, the recognition of an independent sexual oppression cannot be followed up for obvious reasons. Had socialists collapsed working women's problems completely into those of the proletariat, then they would have denied that there was a woman question to be addressed, and they could not have challenged bourgeois feminism. Yet almost all of the analysis of a specifically female subjugation continued to draw on hardships suffered by bourgeois women, whose plight could then be attributed to the economic foundations of monogamy. In this situation, cultural, moral and psychological elements of patriarchy were glimpsed and yielded conclusions exhorting women to independent struggle. As soon as the proletarian wife was discussed, however, such dimensions of oppression were ignored lest dissension harm working-class unity. If women's lot was still perceived as relatively worse than men's, this was blamed not on men themselves but on natural disadvantages rooted in reproduction and exploited by capitalists in the form of lower wages. The attitudes of working men, the advantages that they might gain from wives' subordination, in short the possibility of relatively autonomous dimensions of patriarchy, were either ignored or dismissed (as they had been by Engels) as legacies of bourgeois behaviour. Such an outcome was inevitable, partly because of the theoretical premises of a scientific socialism which wanted to blame women's plight solely on property relations and partly because of the practical requirement of eliminating the attractions of bourgeois feminism for proletarian women. Class had to be shown to take priority over gender—and the recognition that female subjugation varied across class was one of the advances over liberalism—and this left no grounds for anticipating continued sexual inequality under socialism.

The internal tension provoked by this position, which both conflated all proletarian problems and recognized a woman question, was reflected in the practical difficulties of socialist parties. They attempted to mobilize women behind the cause while recognizing a need for separate women's organizations because roles and scope were denied them in the parent movement. In this context, Clara Zetkin is an important figure.

By the 1890s, the SPD was committed to full support for female equality, yet in its own ranks there was neither much enthusiasm for the issue nor much respect accorded its female exponents. Despite the political and theoretical impetus to integration, a quasi-autonomous socialist women's movement was thus deemed necessary, and organized in 1890. The following year, Clara Zetkin co-founded *Die Gleichheit* (*Equality*), the journal which would provide the theoretical link between the movement's various workers. The latter were limited in what they could do because female party membership was illegal in Germany until 1908, but Zetkin laid theoretical foundations for the movement in her 1896 Gotha speech: 'Only with the proletarian woman will socialism be victorious!'[30]

Zetkin's speech is notable because it offers a materialist account of the rise of the women's movement itself as well as explaining why it finds different expressions according to class. Although women have been subjected as long as private property has existed, she argues, recognition of lack of rights emerged only when capitalism destroyed the traditional household economy and the narrow but meaningful life it afforded. Once material and emotional sustenance had to be found outside the home, women realized that they fared worse than the men of their class, and this gave rise to the different facets of their struggle.

For a wealthy minority, this meant fighting for control over their own property: possession of wealth must be blind to sexual identity, and the obstacle to this was men of the same class. Similarly among bourgeois women, it is men who are the competitors. Zetkin argues that capitalism's crises impoverish such men, causing them to delay or decline marriage, which leads to intense hardship for the women who depend on that institution. The latter are obliged to fight for equal education and occupational openings in order to support themselves, but this places the sexes in direct economic conflict. All the various arguments used by men against female equality are but attempts to legitimize women's exclusion from the workforce, and this in turn impels women to pursue political rights as a means to fight for access. Zetkin acknowledges, nevertheless, that the struggle for a satisfying moral and intellectual life is an important and 'entirely justified' aspect of liberal feminism which cannot be reduced to merely economic exigencies.[31]

For the proletarian woman, as we might expect, the movement has rather different causes and goals. Her problems stem from her economic exploitation. Motivated by a desire to supplement the family income, she is unwittingly transformed by the system into one who undercuts her husband's wage and destroys the family. She thus gains economic equality and independence but at the cost of sacrificing her satisfaction as woman or wife. Instead of competing with men for the economic equality which the logic of capitalism in any case yields her, she needs to fight alongside them for 'her rights as wife and mother' and for barriers against her special exploitation, such as the legal working day to ease her double toil. Thus she must, paradoxically, demand greater recognition as a sexual being whose needs are *irreducible* to her status as worker. While bourgeois rights like the vote are to be sought, they can be only instrumental in the more important pursuit of socialism.

Zetkin's analysis is significant for a number of reasons. First, she offers a more historical account of women's oppression than Engels had managed, explaining how it alters over time as well as class. Second, in order to promote proletarian solidarity while recognizing particularly female dilemmas within that class, Zetkin breaks with the Marxian goal of androgyny: when women are equal as workers, they are unequal unless their reproductive functions grant them special consideration. And third, she clarifies what had remained implicit and ambiguous in Bebel and the Avelings: for bourgeois women, men are the immediate enemy; for proletarian women, it is capital. Any uniform, trans-class theory is thus ruled out beyond the overall materialist method Zetkin offers. As far as working-class women are concerned:

We have no special women's agitation to carry on but rather socialist agitation among women. It is not women's petty interests of the moment that we should put in the foreground; our task must be to enrol the modern proletarian woman in the class struggle. We have no separate tasks for agitation among women.[32]

But Zetkin does go on to acknowledge the special difficulties of socialist agitation among women and of engaging them in trade-union activity, due to their frequent isolation as homeworkers or their belief that work is but a temporary expedient prior to marriage. Moreover, 'it is out of the question that the task of socialist women's activity should be to alienate proletarian women from their duties as wives and mothers'.[33] Her claim that mothers imbuing husbands and children with class-consciousness perform as valuable a task as those who are politically active, is after all only the socialist version of Wollstonecraft's plea that women be educated into their familial role as socializers of virtuous citizens. Under socialism, she believes, the family will be a moral rather than an economic unit, and then women will be able to 'fulfill their functions as wife and mother to the highest degree'.[34] Thus there is no sense in 1896, that the family's abolition is either imminent or necessary. This is at odds with her earlier position, more inspired by the Utopians, which had found the family imprisoning women.[35]

The greater sexual distinctions which the mature Zetkin was willing to allow within the working class only exacerbated tensions between feminism and Marxism. Hostility to bourgeois feminism was combined with recognition of the importance of the rights it demanded; a commitment to an integrated socialist movement sat uneasily with the increased recognition of working women's special interests and the need for an independent organization to pursue them. These tensions were exacerbated as the SPD became increasingly revisionist at a time when Zetkin, moving closer to Rosa Luxemburg, was determined to commit the women's movement to a revolutionary—and hence more separatist—position.[36]

The debate about women, led in the case of German Social Democracy by Bebel and Zetkin, shows that conflicts within the Marxian account remained unresolved even if they had become more refined. The nature of women's oppression had been shown to be fractured, contingent on the class of the victim. Among middle-class women, the syndrome described by liberals was largely accepted but given a deeper economic explanation. Their struggle for rights was generally recognised as important though insufficient. Here the debate mirrored that within the Second International as a whole, between revisionist and revolutionary factions. Greater recognition of working women's distinct problems had emerged, but to some extent this was at the price of a less radical vision of their emancipation: greater honour and support for motherhood was supplemented by images of happy families and monogamous couples, the woman performing light domestic tasks alongside her sisters and productive labour alongside her comrades. Between couples, no model was developed other than that devised for the economy: free association between the sexes was to mirror that between producers and to follow from it. The conflicts and naïveties underlying all these rather precarious beliefs would be sorely tested when socialists did come to power, as happened in Russia in 1917.

In Czarist Russia, women had been subjected to suppression as elsewhere in Europe and a small group of feminists emerged out of the intelligentsia in the 1860s. Their main demand was for education but most of them had to be satisfied with foreign study. Abroad, they were radicalized by Russian exiles like Bakunin. At home there was a dearth of both civil rights and bourgeoisie, thus feminism lacked the institutional support it relied on elsewhere. Many women joined the revolutionaries, inspired by Fourier's vision, exhilarated by a Nihilist tradition of sexual freedom and supported by revolutionary heroes like Chernyshevsky. The Socialist Revolutionaries attracted many women to their ranks, Vera Zasulich among them. Until 1905, both sexes were equal in a shared lack of rights. A modest feminist movement emerged following male enfranchisement, but it remained tiny, squeezed between the more powerful revolutionary and reactionary forces. However, industrialization finally produced an embryonic proletariat and as the twentieth century appeared, so did a social democratic party. It was inspired by Bebel and Zetkin and found a leading spokesperson in Alexandra Kollontai. During her travels abroad, Kollontai met Zetkin, Luxemburg and Lenin; she corresponded with Bebel and contributed to *Die Gleichheit*.

It was women who helped initiate the Revolution in February 1917, when they took to the streets in search of bread and in celebration of International Women's day. The resulting Provisional Government granted them full civil rights, but it was the Bolsheviks who wooed female supporters most successfully, agitating in factories and speaking to women via the journal *Rabotnitsa*. Only after October, however, did Kollontai persuade the Bolsheviks that a woman's organization was necessary.[37]

From October 1917 until 1923, a select group of women held prominent positions in the Party; Kollontai was the most active of them. Already a member of the Central Committee when the Bolsheviks seized power, she was Commissar of Public

Welfare from October 1917 to March 1918,[38] then director of *Zhenotdel* (1920–1), the women's section established in 1919 as part of the Central Committee with responsibility for women's liberation and their revolution from below. As Commissar, Kollontai introduced immediate measures to simplify marriage and divorce and to provide for pregnant women and new mothers, In *Zhenotdel* she confronted the overwhelming problems of women's situation and the patriarchal attitudes governing it. Field-workers, who suffered immense hardships in their journeys to far-flung parts of the Union, found extremely reactionary practices and attitudes towards women in peasant and Muslim households. A massive task of consciousness-raising had to be faced, along with extensive practical help that *Zhenotdel* gave from child-care, food distribution and housing provision to public health and anti-prostitution and propaganda campaigns.

In the early 1920s, Clara Zetkin herself inspected *Zhenotdel* campaigns in the Caucasus. Emma Goldman was personally invited to participate by Kollontai but refused, suspicious of the powerful role being played by the state.[39] In 1921 Kollontai joined the Workers' Opposition, herself disillusioned by the Party's bureaucratic tendencies. Her subsequent jobs were foreign postings unconnected with the women's cause. *Zhenotdel* was dismantled in 1929 and policies of family integrity, sexual puritanism and traditional sex roles were reimposed by Stalin. Real radicalism on the woman question had in any case ended with War Communism. In 1919, the Party had pledged support to replace separate households with communal child-care, laundry and dining facilities. After the introduction of the New Economic Policy in 1921, these were gradually withdrawn and more conventional marriage laws reinstated. Although further analysis of the brief Soviet experiment is outside our scope here, it is important because its early aim was for precisely that integration of previously private activities into the public sphere, that socialists from Fourier to Engels and Bebel had advocated. What we do need to do, is to look at Lenin's and Kollontai's writings to see whether they had any new theoretical insights to contribute to the woman question in the light of Soviet experience.

Lenin wrote little about women although he was fully aware of the importance of their support. A speech that he made to non-party working women in 1919 is representative of his views and discloses a number of interesting points.[40] Here, he outlines a twofold task facing the new republic as far as women are concerned. First, full legal equality is required. He distances this move from that of the bourgeois democracies by denying the possibility of real sexual equality under conditions of private property. Under capitalism, (bourgeois) 'men retain their privileges' while workers are kept in poverty and wage-slavery, with women 'in a state of double slavery'. They experience humiliation in 'day-to-day family life', but socialism rectifies this by passing new laws on divorce, legitimacy and maintenance. However, these are insufficient reforms and so a second and more difficult task opens up. To begin with, there is the classic Marxist requirement: woman must participate equally in common productive labour. But Lenin stresses that this means less identical conditions of labour, than liberation from domestic drudgery:

Here we are not, of course, speaking of making women the equal of men as far as the productivity of labour, the quantity of labour, the length of the working day, labour conditions, etc., are concerned; we mean that the woman should not, unlike the man, be oppressed because of her position in the family. You all know that even where women have full rights, they still remain factually downtrodden because all housework is left to them. In most cases housework is the most unproductive, the most barbarous and the most arduous work a woman can do. It is exceptionally petty and does not include anything that would in any way promote the development of woman.[41]

The first part of this passage shows the extent to which participation in productive labour was already being subtly turned from an opportunity and a right, to a duty. Lenin predicts that it will in any case take 'many, many years' before the transition takes place.

In 1919 Lenin is looking less to reliance on the state to bring change and support, than to the work of millions of women who will develop the sort of institutions they want and who will grow through their acts of public reconstruction. Unfortunately, when he goes on to describe the sort of tasks for which women are valuable during civil war, he places a rather strong emphasis on their work in food production and distribution and on public catering, suggesting that even where they enter social production, they are to remain in those areas associated with women's work. The text thus suggests an early faith that the revolution has swept away traditional institutions sufficiently for women to choose and work towards an alternative; the subtext shows that traditional assumptions remained more deeply rooted. In a speech given on International Women's Day the following year, Lenin again promised women liberation from 'their stultifying and humiliating subjugation to the eternal drudgery of the kitchen and the nursery' and called for a 'reconstruction both of social technique and of morals'.[42]

The utopian panacea of collectivized and socialized domestic labour is thus retained; there is no suggestion that such work is to be merely lightened by technology or revalorized, as some socialists (Bebel, Lassalle) had implied. It was becoming clear, nevertheless, that such structural changes would be neither practicable nor sufficient without painstaking changes in attitudes. It was Kollontai who devoted herself to consideration of this superstructural dimension, and while she did not contribute a great deal to social democratic views on women in other capacities, her writings are highly significant in opening up the whole complex question of personal relations and feelings under socialism.

Kollontai's thoughts on the woman question can be usefully divided into two interrelated sections. In the first, she attempts to integrate the problems of sexuality and morality into a Marxist framework. In the second, she deals more specifically, and often practically, with the particular relations between men and women, women and children, family and state.

The first phase is more evident after 1908 but before 1917, when Kollontai left Russia and became active in the SPD. Her writings of this period reveal the influence of Bebel and Zetkin. She wrote extensively on the dangers of bourgeois feminism, taking the now familiar line that the woman question could be neither discussed nor resolved without challenging the economic conditions that kept women in submission. She is adamant, however, that women of all classes are oppressed by the family and goes further than her colleagues in arguing that to 'become really free woman has to throw off the heavy chains of the current forms of the family, which are outmoded and oppressive'.[43] Unlike them, she never doubts that the family must wither away, although she is equally vehement in her attack on those bourgeois libertines who simply abandon the traditional morality to practise 'free love', seeing that this can offer no solution as long as woman remains economically dependent, since it merely leaves her 'the task of caring, alone and unaided, for her children'.[44] If the old morality is to be abandoned, a collective effort is required to build a new one.

Kollontai is nevertheless unwilling to accept that personal relationships will be resolved once the economy has been collectivized; she recognizes something of their opacity and inertia. Because the Marxism of the SPD made difficult any consideration of social relations in their own right, Kollontai was obliged to develop a more dialectical framework for herself, which recognized exchanges between economy and superstructure. Accordingly, she writes that 'the new morality is created by a new economy, but we will not build a new communist economy without the support of a new morality'.[45] While she agrees that the family is, along with morality, culture, religion and interpersonal relations generally, a part of the ideological superstructure,[46] she contends that change here can have an influence on the socio-economic base: 'the way personal relationships are organized in a certain social group has had a vital influence on the outcome of the struggle between hostile social classes'.[47] Thus a breakdown of the monogamous family destabilizes the bourgeoisie while the quiet moral revolution towards more co-operative relations yields the workers a 'new weapon' in their struggle. She denies that a new proletarian morality need wait until the economy is socialized; history shows that new moralities are worked out in the process of class struggle.[48]

This line of analysis draws Kollontai into serious consideration of ideological questions. She accepts the Marxist tenet that morality corresponds with class interests, but instead of reducing bourgeois marriage to its material preconditions, she shows how bourgeois marriage is itself riven by internal contradictions at the level of personal relations. The individualism it embodies leads to great loneliness and a search for the love that will assuage it. It thereby reveals the search for togetherness which only communism can actually bring. Meanwhile, the bourgeois solution of a soul-mate (the companionate marriage, the passionate affair) remains chimerical. For the egoism, individualism and possessiveness of bourgeois society make real love impossible, while the double standard of morality betokens a sexual inequality which yet presents woman as the appendage of man, constrained by domestic virtues and obligations.[49] Joyful relations cannot transpire until mutual consideration, freedom and comradeship are accepted. In other words, there must be a 'radical re-education of our psyche'. The question of sexual relations cannot be seen in isolation.

Like Mill and Owen, then, Kollontai recognizes that free association and solidarity between workers is incompatible with either relations of subordination between the sexes, or the selfishness inspired by the nuclear family. A new proletarian morality—that is, a revolution in the superstructure—is first essential. It follows that the woman question must be central to the class struggle because it raises vital questions pertaining to the values and attitudes that will structure the new collectivity. While continuing to acknowledge the economic foundations of women's oppression, Kollontai thus began to move towards a more dialectical position which overcame the usual problems of reductionism. The danger of her position, and one which we will come across shortly, was that once morality was given an active role in deciding the outcome of socio-economic change, it could be viewed in a utilitarian and functionalist manner, suggesting that the workers' state, like that of its bourgeois predecessor, had an interest in dictating sexual relations in a manner which Engels and Bebel had renounced.

After Kollontai had taken up her position as Commissar in 1917, she was obliged to think about these rather abstract questions in a much more practical and detailed way. Thus we come to the second aspect of her thought. As far as women's liberation was concerned, she followed Marxist orthodoxy in associating it with entry into productive labour. This correlated well with the interests of the new Soviet state in a large labour force, but it conflicted with its equal need for new generations of workers in the light of huge losses in war and civil war. Women's roles as producers and reproducers had thus to be reconciled with each other as well as with women's own demands for independence. Fortunately, a solution was at hand. Kollontai takes the important theoretical step of separating domestic labour from mothering (thus she speaks not of women's double burden under capitalism but of triple toil involved in wage-labour, housekeeping and mothering[50]) and mothering from sexual relations. This broke with the naturalistic bonds that Engels *et al*, had assumed between the different facets of domesticity while allowing Kollontai to deal with each one separately. The result was a greater scope for imaginative solutions.

As far as domestic labour is concerned, Kollontai accepts the Utopian solution of communal households: communism 'liberates woman from domestic slavery'.[51] Here she is less concerned with the technological paraphernalia that had excited Bebel—hardly surprising given the state of the economy—than with the emancipatory effects of making housework part of a national productive effort. Her descriptions sound like Fourier (with whose work Kollontai was quite familiar): 'Instead of the working woman cleaning her flat, the communist society can arrange for men and women whose job it is to go round in the morning cleaning rooms'. Central laundries, mending centres etc., will free such women for evenings of reading, meetings or concert-going.[52] It is also to Kollontai's credit that having challenged the sexual division of labour on the domestic front, she vows to tackle it in the workforce. Women labourers must be given practical help via vocational training, the raising of political consciousness, sex education and the provision of housing communes for young or mobile women.[53]

If domestic labour becomes a public concern, Kollontai deals with motherhood in a similar manner in so far as this is practicable. Woman is, she contends, first a labourer; motherhood is important but supplementary. It remains nevertheless no 'private matter but a *social* matter'. 'Soviet power views maternity as a social task'.[54] Because the pregnant woman is carrying a future member of the socialist collective, she has a social duty to look after her health: at such times her body is not just her own. On the other hand, this duty entails a reciprocal social obligation to care for her welfare. The only functions the woman must perform for herself are those of gestating and nursing and to facilitate these, the state will grant maternity leave and benefit, rest homes etc. Subsequently the mother returns to her primary status as worker. While Kollontai insisted that the state would not force parent and child apart, she clearly preferred that the collective should take over childrearing at this point. Crèches, kindergartens, children's colonies, health resorts and hospitals, restaurants, free education, books, clothes and food, were all to be provided in order to render the family obsolete. 'Just as housework withers away, so the obligations of parents to their children wither away gradually until finally society assumes full responsibility'.[55] The arrangement benefits women by giving them independence from a husband and by allowing them to return swiftly to work, where they are men's equals (men themselves are permitted to choose whether to accept the role of fatherhood).[56] Society also benefits since women's capacity for productive labour is quickly restored while the new socialist morality is also encouraged by the communalization of the whole process. The qualified educators at work in the new system can raise each child a 'conscious communist', teaching the necessity of solidarity, mutual aid and loyalty to the collective. Kollontai believes that while the maternal instinct is strong, it can flow to all children. There will be no need to abolish the family because it will simply atrophy as it loses its functions.

Finally, we come to the question of sexual relations themselves. Lacking a socio-economic function, Kollontai holds that these alone will remain an entirely private matter.[57] With all dependency gone, she envisages a rather more erotic outcome than the usual Marxist eulogy to monogamous sex love, motivated by 'a healthy instinct for reproduction, prompted by the abandon of young love, or by fervent passion, or by a blaze of physical attraction or by a soft light of intellectual and emotional harmony'.[58] However, the accusation of a crude stimulus-response theory of sexuality, with which her critics tormented her, is simply wrong. Kollontai's views on ideal relationships remained very much a part of her concern for the new proletarian morality. She simply believed—and here again there are echoes of Fourier—intense love between two people to be antisocial, because it isolates the individual from the collective. She also saw that love makes women, in particular, highly vulnerable and dependent, regardless of economic circumstances. Love must therefore be kept in its place and additional sustenance drawn from work and comradely bonds. Jealousy or possessiveness were anathema to the new morality.

This leads Kollontai to deconstruct the sex-love dyad itself. Love means more than physical attraction ('Wingless Eros'): it also implies compassion, sensitivity and sympathy. This means that it can flow out beyond one's partner. Kollontai's description of sublimated, winged Eros is in fact close to the Freudian notion of Eros (and it is unlikely that her sojourn in Germany would have spared her some acquaintance with Freud's early work), that great unifier of mankind whose libidinal bonds are so much stronger than are those of necessity.[59] For the proletariat, emotions need a 'wider and richer range' than the exclusive bonds of bourgeois marriage. While erotic love between two people may last a longer or shorter time, it must remain subordinate to the 'love-duty' to the collective, where its expressions will be 'firmer, more complex and organic'.[60]

Kollontai's treatment of the woman question is, in conclusion, much broader than that of other social democrats. She both eschews reductionism to seek a more dialectical relationship between economy and morality and she breaks women's oppression down into its constituent elements in order to deal with each separately. She sees that childrearing can be as oppressive as domestic drudgery although once it is supported, she tends to glorify motherhood; she does not suggest that inequality is anchored in the reproductive function itself.

Such ideals are engagingly portrayed in Kollontai's novels. In *The Love of Worker Bees* (1923), Vasilisa Malygina is their vehicle. Vasya lives in a communal house during War Communism. She falls in love with Vladimir and is deliriously happy. Subsequently, however, her husband falls in with NEPmen, supports a lavish private home and has an affair with the beautiful but idle Nina. Vasya is consumed with jealousy and only manages to regain her autonomy with the help of comrades at work. Returning to her village and to political work at the local textile factory, she discovers that she is pregnant. The doctor asks how she will manage and in the ensuing discussion of crèches, subsidies and salaries, she quite forgets the news of her pregnancy. With collective support, single motherhood can be both a joy in itself and, Kollontai makes clear, a way of raising good communists:

A baby! How wonderful! She'd be a model mother! After all it should be possible to bring up a child in true communist fashion. There was no reason for women to set up with their husbands, in families, if it merely tied them to the cooking and domestic chores. They'd get a crèche going and re-purchase a children's hostel. It would be a demonstration of childrearing to everyone. And as she began to think about it, Vladimir vanished from her thoughts as though he had no connection with the baby . . .[61]

I suggested earlier that despite the theoretical advances made by Kollontai, these did embody a danger of functionalism. It is not perhaps merely fortuitous that the policies she recommends above are conducive to the needs of the new Soviet regime. For if the economy does not simply determine social relations, then the latter must be designed to help the economy. This line of thought is strongest during the early, hazardous days of the new order but even in her early work, Kollontai had often implied that a scientific approach might be possible in ascertaining the most propitious morality for the proletariat.

In her speech 'Prostitution and ways of fighting it' (1921), Kollontai condemns prostitution. It had been supposed, of course, to disappear along with its economic supports, but she acknowledges the continuing hardships which drive women onto the streets. Her attack on the institution is however almost a moral one: it is antisocial because it harms the Soviet economy. It realises an unearned wage (sic), it is 'labour desertion'. It threatens the nation's health (thus productivity) as well as proletarian solidarity, since it is predicated on relations of subordination and of buying and selling. It thus falls into the same category as the kept wife.[62]

Such concerns also leak into the ostensible privacy of sexual relations. The collective is interested in questions of health (especially regarding sexually transmitted diseases and the health of pregnant women) and this allows it to condemn both excess and restraint in sexual activity. Wingless Eros exhausts the body and leaves insufficient energy for labour; it impoverishes the soul and hinders more positive emotions.[63] Believing that the psychological state of the parents at the time of conception is significant for the wellbeing of the infant,

Kollontai counsels interference here, too: communists must be dissuaded from pursuing merely physical pleasure.[64] The state has a further interest, as Plato, Aristotle, Smith, Mill and Thompson had all recognised, in controlling population, and this gives a public edge to conception itself. When abortion was legalised in 1920, Kollontai made it clear that the reason was the state's inablity to support more foundlings and the burden that women became on workers, if illicit terminations injured their health. Much of the work in 1921 similarly suggested that maternity benefits etc. reflected a desire to hasten women back to work rather than to give them control over their own fertility.[65] Although Kollontai was undoubtedly deeply concerned about women's plight, then, once the socialist experiment got underway, she emphasised the extent to which sexual and reproductive relations might be subordinated to the tasks of economic reconstruction. Of course, it was difficult to supply the necessary material supports until recovery was underway, but as Stalin would eventually demonstrate, the concession was a dangerous one.

Kollontai herself did not usually speak of the state but of the collective. Here something of the Hegelian-Marxian notion of an organic community was retained, suggesting that women's interests could not be separated from those of the public body of which they were members. As power crystallized into a bureaucracy that made decisions on behalf of the masses, however, it became evident that women could not rely on the state to promote their interests. Many of the welfare policies that Kollontai had promoted as Commissar, were measures which liberal democracies with a social democratic element would themselves enact later in the century, yet here, too, it would become evident that such advances were always under threat when economic conditions became unpropitious. This point is a significant one because of the faith placed in state action by liberal and early socialist feminists alike. The former, of course, looked to the franchise as their most important means for gaining rights and they saw legally-guaranteed rights themselves as the apogee of their emancipation. While Marxists were generally dismissive of this panacea, their solutions, too, tended to focus on welfare measures enacted by a central administration. There were, however, two alternatives. The first was found in the more anarchistic bent of Utopian

Socialists (and even early Bolsheviks), who looked to self-organisation within small, fairly autonomous communities. The second appeared in the more self-conscious anarchism of feminists like Emma Goldman. Although Goldman failed to develop any ideal of sisterhood but relied on a rather liberal vision of self-liberation and refusal, she warned, even before the state had fully embarked on the path of rights and welfare for women, that it could never be a reliable instrument for feminists.[66] Many women would agree with her when a second wave of feminism swelled later in the century but this time, the elusive conception of sisterhood would be developed.

Over the last three chapters, we have seen how socialists responded to women's subjection. Although there were significant methodological differences between Utopians and Marxists, the Marxist feminism which had developed by the early twentieth century was in large measure a synthesis: the Marxist account of women's oppression culminated in Utopian solutions to it.

The more rigorous and scientific Marxist method allowed a materialist explanation of those symptoms of inequality which liberals and Utopians had done little more than describe. Its later practitioners were able to use this approach to refine Marx and Engels's rather general location of female subordination in private property. They explained manifestations of oppression that were specific to capitalism and refined the class differences that structured it. The framework within which all of this took place nevertheless remained problematic because the suggestion that private property caused sexual oppression still implied that the latter would automatically disappear once collective ownership was won. Only in Kollontai's work did a more dialectical model begin to appear. Nevertheless, it should be pointed out that Marxism is by no means necessarily as determinist or reductionist a philosophy as might be believed from its application to the woman question thus far. It was perhaps unfortunate that such application was undertaken primarily by Engels and by members of the Second International, all of whom tended toward such interpretations of Marx and who were schooled on Marx's later writings, which tended more in such directions. Marxism itself, however, has been able to accommodate some rather different readings which are more favourable to feminism, as we will see in the next chapter.

It was because the Utopians had paid more attention to the practical aspects of women's emancipation that their solutions were generally appended to the Marxist analysis, although of course the latter generally looked to a workers' collective rather than to the self-sufficient communities envisaged by the Utopians. The overall Marxist solution, that women would be men's equals when they entered social production on the same terms, inevitably opened discussion about women's traditional domestic role and how, given their continuing responsibility for reproduction, this was to be organized. Utopians had offered fertile suggestions here but although these were eagerly seized upon, it soon became obvious that they could imply two significantly different scenarios.

The first alternative acknowledged a continued, if narrower, differentiation of sex roles which ultimately hinged on biological function. Some form of natural family was expected to endure and where women worked, their identity as wives and mothers was to be taken into account. The other alternative anticipated a more androgynous future, virtually eliminating any private realm—especially the family—or distinction between sex roles. Rather than identifying women, reproduction now became a public activity and those small parts of it which remained specific to the individual female, shrank into virtual insignificance. It is this position which best takes a socialist solution to sexual inequality, to its logical conclusion. It could hardly be more different from those natural but antithetical roles which an Aristotle, Rousseau or Hegel had described. Yet it is not an unproblematic solution. Where the collective becomes redefined as the bureaucratic state, women are again in danger of losing power over their own lives and fertility.[67] While decentralized communities offered a theoretical alternative, they seemed to be rapidly disappearing from the historical menu as the twentieth century progressed. The idea of sisterhood would offer a somewhat equivalent, though more feasible, solution in looking to networks of sympathetic women. But this was a phenomenon which Marxists were unable to conceptualize as long as they gave priority to class solidarity. And when a new wave of feminists did evolve the idea, they would come to criticize Marxism precisely for its androgynous images which, like the Western tradition as a whole, equated emancipation with transcendence of things female. Finally, capitalism did not collapse as expected and this made even more crucial the analysis of women's specific oppression there as well as the question of whether women were to struggle for their own emancipation, in a situation where real socialism no longer appeared imminent.

10 Contemporary Feminism and Political Thought

Following a resurgence of anti-feminist ideas and practices during the decades spanning the Second World War, an explosion of literature has burst forth since the late 1960s to constitute what has come to be known as feminism's 'second wave'. It has been complemented by an influential women's movement, which has fought to transform those phenomena which feminist analysis located at the heart of women's oppression. Analyses of that oppression have been considerably deepened since the early liberal and Marxist accounts, and the aim of this chapter will be to show how they have built upon, and gone beyond, previous formulations.

Liberal feminism requires little further discussion here, since despite a broader programme than formerly, it has not made substantial changes in its theoretical position. Liberal feminists have always accepted the importance to women of equal rights and opportunities; demands for their realization, in areas such as pay or tax laws, persist. Recognizing that women must compete with men in the job market, contemporary liberal feminists have often been drawn towards the more radical end of the liberal spectrum in demanding the welfare provisions—nurseries and so on—that would allow more genuine equality of opportunity. Their commitment to ideals of personal responsibility and radical autonomy has also drawn them into political support for legal abortion, in order that women might control their own fertility and hence life-choices. Liberal values and analyses can accommodate a range of positions, from libertarian to social democratic, within the spectrum of conventional parliamentary politics. Their exponents' goal has essentially been for a competitive society, with the sexual division of labour now largely rejected in favour of access to jobs on the basis of merit. Domestic necessities may be fulfilled through the market; supplemented via the welfare state; shared between partners and minimized by technology (washing machines, microwave ovens, etc).

Unfortunately, the structural reforms needed to bring the liberal vision to fruition have remained patchy and vulnerable. While a minority have succeeded in the job market and paid other women to perform domestic tasks, for many the opportunity to work has meant simply combining industrial and domestic drudgery since private services have been expensive; public provision inadequate; husbands recalcitrant and technology expensive and time-consuming. In other words, and despite its undoubted victories and advances, liberal feminism has remained susceptible to objections levelled at it by nineteenth-century critics.[1]

It is Marxist and radical feminism, often locked into debates which resemble those between the Marxist and bourgeois varieties of the previous century, which have contributed most to a second wave of theory. Unlike liberal feminists, contemporary Marxists have had to continue their theoretical labour, since the framework which they inherited was so inadequate to their specific needs. But it is radical feminism which has been most theoretically innovative, rejecting traditional definitions of both politics and theory while condemning all previous political theory as patriarchal. Unlike the Marxist approach, it has not struggled to incorporate women into a pre-existing political framework, but instead attempts to shift our whole perception of society, to restructure it in terms of a radically new set of woman-centred meanings. Its aim has been to recast personal identities; to reclaim language and culture from their masculine forms; to relocate significant political power; to reassess human nature and to challenge traditional values.

It is on these two aspects of contemporary feminist thought that this chapter will concentrate. I shall look first at developments within the Marxist account of woman's oppression and then at Marxist and radical attitudes towards the state. It is radical feminism which fostered the claim that the personal is political, and I shall next discuss the ways in which this phrase signifies a departure from conventional politics, before moving on to a discussion of patriarchy—that set of power relations which encapsulates the specific oppression of women. Finally, radical analyses of the gendered personality will be examined in so far as they yield a critique of conventional modes of theorizing.

Contemporary Marxist feminism is by no means a homogeneous theory, but some basic differences between second- and first-wave approaches can be located. Most generally, of course, the very notion of a hybrid called Marxist feminism marks a departure from an earlier Marxism, which considered the woman question while rejecting feminism as irremediably bourgeois. Although a satisfactory synthesis remains elusive, this for many women has been the goal. There has been less emphasis on the more apocalyptic elements of the doctrine, since communism has remained even more elusive than a theoretical synthesis and since Marx's definition of the proletariat as a privileged and universal class with a historical mission, inevitably marginalizes an interest in women. Engels's broad approach in explaining their oppression as a world-historical effect of private property has also been considerably refined. Clearly, female subordination is not limited to propertied males' need for legitimate heirs; women's oppression has remained endemic within the working-class family while jobs have brought neither equality in the productive realm nor release from economic dependence on husbands. In this sense, sexual inequality must have a more extensive foundation than Engels saw. On the other hand, a more specific account of women's oppression over time has been sought. Feminists have been especially interested in the analysis of capitalism and the more general elements of Marxist analysis, such as the theory of value, have often proven more useful here than the specific accounts of female subordination. Rather than comparing a defeated female sex with a hypothetical primitive matriarchy, twentieth-century Marxists have made much of distinctions between the feudal household, where women's work was economically essential, and capitalism, where the material bases of oppression have been more evident. The division between home and work, with its accompanying ideology of private and public realms, is seen as especially pernicious since through it the sexual division of labour has become more distinct and rigid. Even Engels succumbed to its influence, feminists argue, when he accepted as natural those sexual roles that are largely social constructs. Much recent Marxist analysis has indeed studied such roles in terms of their function for capitalism. Both the family, and women's tasks within it, have been analysed in this light.

Contemporary Marxist feminism thus offers both a more detailed account of women's oppression as it is specific to a capitalist mode of production and an account of its operation in the family. It finds women oppressed in work as well as in their exclusion from it, and here it blames a familial ideology which accompanies women into the public world. This undoubtedly marks the biggest departure from the first-wave analysis: ideological as well as material factors have been deemed responsible for sexual inequality.

A major reason for this development is that the treatment of women has followed the vicissitudes of Marxist scholarship in general. Thus in the nineteenth century it was a scientific and deterministic orientation which gave shape to discussions of the woman question. When Simone de Beauvoir produced her path-breaking *The Second Sex* shortly after the Second World War, it was under the influence of searches for a more humanistic form of Marxism, inspired in France by a Hegel revival, the recent publication of Marx's youthful writings and disillusionment with the Stalinist rigidities of the Communist Party. Second-wave feminism itself emerged out of the New Left and the student movements of the 1960s. It shared that decade's enthusiasm for a counter-culture and its fascination with questions of sexuality. The interest in cultural revolution has been reinforced by intellectual developments. First, there was a revival of interest in Gramsci's work, with its emphasis on the cultural hegemony of the ruling class and the consequent need for ideological struggle within civil society. And second, there was the popularity of structuralist Marxism, exemplified by the work of Louis Althusser. The stress which Althusser laid on ideology, now designated as relatively autonomous and determined only in 'the last instance' by the economic, encouraged feminist interest in such aspects of oppression.[2]

At the same time, the Marxist approach to feminism has

been vulnerable to the fortunes of Marxism itself. If the second wave's birth coincided with a surge in the popularity of the Left, the 1980s have so far witnessed a general decline in the doctrine's influence. Feminism has of late inclined more towards radical varieties which emphasize symbolic rather than material factors of sexual oppression and which present the cultural generation of gendered (feminine/masculine) personalities as absolutely autonomous examples of patriarchy. Such an approach has been especially popular in the United States, where Marxism has never been widely embraced. The structuralism which animated many Marxist accounts has also inspired psychoanalytic approaches, under the influence of Jacques Lacan. Although these are sometimes brought together, as in the work of Juliet Mitchell, the combination has not been an especially felicitous one and emphases on the unconscious have again tended to stress symbolic and linguistic, rather than material, factors. Finally, the emergence of post-structuralism has meant the abandonment of beliefs in grand theories of global oppression. This has in turn underwritten Marxists' continuing inability to establish a unified theory to account for sex, class, and more recently race, oppression. In order to illustrate some of the Marxist approaches to women's oppression, I shall look briefly at de Beauvoir's existentialism, Mitchell's structuralism and finally, at the Domestic Labour Debate.

The Second Sex departed significantly from previous forms of Marxism. Like Sartre, de Beauvoir was committed to an existentialism which stressed the radical freedom of consciousness to define and change its situation. This involved a rejection of all determinism, and it is from this perspective that the book opens with a critique of biological, psychoanalytic and historical materialist accounts of women's oppression. Regarding the latter, de Beauvoir takes issue with Engels's explanation in the *Origin*. The significance of Bronze Age tools to women's defeat was not, she argues, that they yielded men new sources of wealth, but that they excluded the weaker women from using these new means of changing the world. They allowed men a means of transforming the earth, thereby reinforcing their status as historical subjects and their designation of women as 'other'. Subsequently, technological advances have made men's greater muscle an irrelevance and women might join them in production. But de Beauvoir is adamant that this cannot in itself liberate them: woman 'was not created by the bronze age tool alone; and the machine will not abolish her'.[3] For a history in which woman has been 'other' results in certain meanings which cling to her sexuality, ensuring that even where her objective situation is identical to a man's, its significance for the two sexes will differ.

The woman who is economically emancipated from man is not for all that in a moral, social, and psychological situation identical with that of man. The way she carries on her profession and her devotion to it depend on the context supplied by the total pattern of her life. For when she begins her adult life she does not have behind her the same past as does a boy; she is not viewed by society in the same way; the universe presents itself to her in a different perspective.[4]

The source of this difference is ultimately located by de Beauvoir in the female body. The pregnant woman finds herself subordinated to the imperatives of species continuity. Following ejaculation during the sexual act, the male recovers his individuality and uses the species' energy for his own activities. The female on the other hand is enslaved by it; her body is the site of an alien drama in which she is both self and other. Even when she is not pregnant, the reproductive function dominates her body, 'the theatre of a play that unfolds within her and in which she is not personally concerned'.[5] While women are consigned to the repetitive domestic tasks which combine readily with motherhood, men embark on a cultural adventure; they use their freedom to define the world. De Beauvoir insists, nevertheless, that woman's body yields a situation rather than a destiny. With the availability of abortion, contraception, artifical insemination and anaesthetized childbirth, she might gain control of her anatomy and join men in the transcending projects of cultural creation to become a historical subject.

Writing only some thirty years after Kollontai, de Beauvoir still subscribed to the Second International's distrust of feminism.[6] She looked back on the early Soviet experiment as a necessary, if insufficient, basis for women's liberation. Yet again, she valued the control over fertility and the opportunity for productive labour which it promised, primarily in terms of women's greater freedom to engender meaning; to participate in the definition of the species rather than being defined by it.

From a Marxist perspective, the work undoubtedly had flaws. De Beauvoir herself recognized that most women would fail to achieve the liberation she anticipated, since they would 'not escape from the traditional feminine world; they get from neither society nor their husbands the asssistance they would need to become in concrete fact the equals of men'.[7] There was no real analysis of the economic obstacles that confronted them; even trade-union activity is presented as primarily a route towards redefinition of the self as an efficacious being. De Beauvoir herself subsequently asserted that the analysis should have been more materialist.[8] From the perspective of later feminists the book has also been problematic, since it seems to espouse precisely that androcentrism which we have so often encountered among exponents of sexual equality. Women will be free, de Beauvoir suggested, only when they abandon their traditional identities and roles to adopt male practices; when they use medical technology plus more egalitarian socialization, to surmount the anonymous rhythms of their bodies and enter the ethereal realms of transcendence. As Carol Ascher complains, 'in reading *The Second Sex,* one is often left with the unhappy question: why can't a woman be more like a man'?[9] Subsequent feminists would be unhappy with both the graphic descriptions of the horrors of the female body and the conclusion that women had contributed nothing of significance to human culture. Yet in one sense de Beauvoir's book marked the logical culmination of the Marxian solution to the woman question, by further shrinking the realm of reproduction that distinguished the sexes. Only Firestone would go further, in suggesting that gestation itself be transferred from womb to test tube.[10]

For all its shortcomings, *The Second Sex* represented a brilliant and unprecedented account of woman's subordination, detailing the myths and practices of history and the minutiae of everyday life in which woman was made, constructed via a network of meanings into an alien and artificial being. It thus showed how profound a cultural transformation was required before sexual equality could be realized. In this context, de Beauvoir offers some fascinating and prescient concluding remarks. Anticipating a future 'new woman', she quotes the poet Rimbaud: 'Woman will find the unknown! Will her ideational worlds be different from ours? She will come upon strange, unfathomable, repellent, delightful things'. But she draws back from the answer that would excite later feminists, in their pursuit of a new ethic, epistemology and aesthetic: 'It is not sure that her "ideational worlds" will be different from those of men, since it will be through attaining the same situation as theirs that she will find emancipation'.[11] It would be on precisely this issue that much debate would focus, for if attaining the same situation as men meant initiation into an identical world of (man-made) values and meanings, the victory began to appear a rather Pyrrhic one. The question was whether human culture represented some neutral undertaking into which women might be assimilated without loss, or whether it existed as a particularly masculine project which, masquerading as a human norm, had suppressed an alternative feminine culture.

When Mitchell presented *Woman's Estate* early in the 1970s, she accepted that no adequate theory of women's oppression yet existed. She was fully cognizant of the weaknesses of traditional Marxism's treatment of women and blamed this on a tendency to impose abstract theory on events. She argued that theory must rather emerge out of experiences of oppression and therefore valued the attempt by radical feminists to articulate the previously mute lines of women's subjection, by encouraging them to speak for themselves in women-only groups. Here, as Dale Spender would write, 'women came together to *participate* in the process of generating some of the new feminist knowledge. This was a very active form of knowledge-making, with a collective dimension'.[12] For Marxist feminists, there could of course be no guarantees that the dimensions of oppression which emerged from such discussions would fit with the basic tenets of Marxism. But Mitchell contended that once data was available, it would require a theory to bring out its significance in a systematic way, and this theory was scientific socialism.[13] In other words, radical feminism was to yield the content, and Marxism its form. That form was to be of the structuralist variety and would allow Mitchell to criticize the two central panaceas which earlier Marxists had offered—women's entry into social production and the abolition of the family—as both abstract and inadequate.

The problem with traditional Marxism, as Mitchell saw it, was that it had simply deduced sexual oppression from its analysis of capitalism. It was necessary to recognize that women were in fact oppressed on a number of levels, their subjection being overdetermined and irreducible to the requirements of production. Together, a variety of structures would lend to their subordination a specific form at any one time. It was therefore impossible to offer an evolutionary account of their history as a single narrative; instead, a complex analysis must be undertaken to discern how structures articulated with one another during different periods. One of its aims would be to locate contradictions within each structure. If these coalesced, a revolutionary situation would be imminent, but even without it, the system might be attacked at its weakest link.

The key structures which Mitchell identified as responsible for women's situation were those of production, reproduction, sexuality and the socialization of children. The latter three had been traditionally conflated within a single unit, the family. When Marxists called for the abolition of that institution, they therefore took this abstraction at face value. Instead, it was necessary to deconstruct it into its constituent parts, to see how each sustains woman's oppression as well as its potential for change.

By arguing that each structure within the family has a certain autonomy in its capacity to subject women and that these structures themselves rebound on the economy, Mitchell was able to show that women's entry into the workforce would be insufficient to emancipate them since gains (e.g. in entry to occupations or control over fertility) are compensated by losses elsewhere (e.g. a renewed emphasis on mothers' socializing role).[14] Some feminist demands might then be fulfilled without effacing the overall reality of oppression. Productive work, for example, could not itself bring equality, because it was suffused with a familial ideology. Both sexes, she found, tend to perceive women's labour as an extension of their family (they gravitate into caring, serving jobs which are accorded low status); as dispensable (women only supplement the family budget, and when unemployment is high, they should relinquish jobs to male breadwinners); as not serious (performed for the social life rather than the work or the wage). Raised to think of themselves as first wives and mothers, women thus find themselves—as de Beauvoir had noted—circumscribed by a familial ideology even at work. 'Their exploitation is invisible behind an ideology that masks the fact that they work at all—their work appears inessential'.[15] It is no accident that their labour is accordingly poorly paid, insecure and unrewarding. It is not entry into production *per se,* but entry on the same terms as men, which is required, and this means sorting out other structures of oppression, whose vulnerability lies in their own internal contradictions.[16]

Mitchell's solution to this type of multi-faceted analysis is, appropriately, a pluralist one. It is crucial that women should enter production and struggle for equality there.[17] But at the same time, change must be wrought within the family since it is here that 'the psychology of men and women is founded. Here is the source of their definition'.[18] The nub of this change must be precisely that disaggregation of family structure in practice, which Mitchell's deconstruction had carried out in theory: 'It is the poverty and simplicity of the institutions in this area which are such an oppression'.[19] Thus sexuality, reproduction and socialization might all be carried out and combined in a number of ways; in particular, biological and social parenting need not coincide. The family will not then be abolished, but relegated to one choice among others, which include couples, singles and groups of varying sexual orientation, all with or without children.

The strength of Mitchell's approach was that she refused to reduce the family to a superstructural institution merely reflecting capital's needs. Certainly, it was functional in fulfilling these needs, but she also granted to its patriarchal ideology a relative autonomy: although 'ultimately' determined by the economy, there is 'nothing less "real" or "true" or important about the ideological than there is about the economic. Both determine our lives'.[20] Struggle must therefore take place on both fronts, since the demise of capitalism would promise no automatic termination of patriarchy. A cultural revolution was also required.

Although the family played a part in sustaining capital for

Mitchell, she was criticized for presenting its internal dynamics in purely ideological terms. Its triple constitution made no reference to domestic labour; instead, patriarchy operated on the level of ideas, identities and values while production alone related to the material processes of capitalism.[21] Subsequent Marxist feminists felt unhappy with this dualism and sought a material base for patriarchy which would explain its relationship with the economy via the medium of domestic labour.

For Marx, women's labour had been theoretically significant only in so far as it realized a wage and in this capacity it simply fell into the general category of proletarian labour power, whose importance to capitalism lay in the generation of surplus value. Accordingly, working women were perceived as exploited rather than oppressed, and as we saw earlier, Marx and Engels themselves made little attempt to analyse the structural causes of women's inferior position in the labour market.[22] While contemporary feminists have attempted to rectify this, they have also concerned themselves with that other category of women's work which falls outside of social production, namely domestic labour. Earlier generations had condemned the activity as inefficient and unpleasant, but it is only recently that a political economy of women has emerged and, with it, what has become known as the Domestic Labour Debate.

One of the main aims of protagonists in this debate was to avoid the dualism implied by Mitchell. The family itself was now analysed as a site of production, although this expedient by no means automatically provided a coherent thesis. One major question which remained was whether such production benefited capitalism or men. The relationship between domestic and commodity production also remained problematic, as did the connection within the family itself, between production and reproduction. Reproduction, finally, raised further questions since its product might cover a range of things including children, the daily workforce and the conditions of capitalism.[23]

A materialist account of the family did not necessarily yield Marxist conclusions, even if the terms of the debate were largely those of Marxist discourse. Christine Delphy concluded in *The Main Enemy,* for example, that there were two modes of production, the capitalist and the domestic, which were practically and theoretically distinct and with the latter exhibiting a specifically patriarchal mode of production. Although women's work at home realizes no exchange value and therefore has no value in the technical Marxist sense, she argued, it is valuable to the men who benefit from it. In farms and family businesses, women actually produce goods which their husbands take to the market. In a purely domestic capacity, they perform services which their wage-earning partners would have otherwise to purchase and which in any other context would realise a wage. Men therefore benefit directly from the labour of women, such that the latter constitute a class in their own right. Their situation is, however, almost feudal, since lacking a labour contract, women are dependent upon the generosity of individual husbands.[24]

Most contributors to the Domestic Labour Debate nevertheless concluded that women's unpaid work in the home was to the advantage of capitalism. Indeed, the discussion here often illustrated the objections which feminists made regarding the reductionist and functionalist nature of Marxist analysis. For if patriarchy was collapsed into those familial arrangements that were functional for capital, then the whole sexual dimension once again disappeared. Moreover, the implications of this position were chilling for feminism itself, since if patriarchy could be subsumed beneath the logic of capital, it was equally possible that feminism had itself appeared only to fulfil capitalism's needs (e.g. to hasten more women into the labour force when labour was scarce).[25] The existence of patriarchy prior to capitalism also remained unexplained. Despite such difficulties, the Domestic Labour Debate nevertheless offered a serious analysis of women's work in the home, for the first time.

Wally Seccombe, one of the main protagonists in the Debate, adopted a classic Marxian definition of value and used it to show how domestic labour and commodity production related. By tracing the flow of value through the reproduction cycle of labour power, he completed a system which Marx had only partially analysed, thereby integrating the household into the broader economy. 'Without this value connection', he contended, 'the chasm which looms between the family unit and the economy at large becomes insurmountable. Inevitably, then, analysis will tend to fall back into a dualist conception, where the household appears outside of the economy, completely impervious to its laws of motion'.[26] In 'The Housewife and her Labour under Capitalism',[27] Seccombe argued that the labour process was split into domestic and industrial units with the appearance of Industrial Capitalism. The function of the former unit lay in its reproducing labour power, now identified as women's sphere. Unpaid, it was not considered to be part of the economy. Women depended on men for their subsistence via the marriage contract and since capital could realize no surplus value here, it had no interest in making domestic labour more efficient or productive: it operated outside the law of value.[28] Nevertheless, Seccombe found it indirectly affected by this law as it is mediated through the husband's wage. Like Delphy, he sees that domestic labour is a crucial stage in rendering material fit for consumption (via cooking, etc.) but unlike her, he includes this additional labour as a necessary stage in the reproduction of labour power on which capitalism depends. When wages fall, women must provide more of the labour which makes the incomplete commodity fit for consumption, since less of these processes can now be purchased on the market. More careful shopping, more basic cooking, mending more clothes, all make reproduction possible where labour power falls below its value. Women's domestic labour may, then, indirectly allow for the increase of surplus value.[29]

While Seccombe acknowledges that it might make more sense for the housewife to take a job and herself pay for the materials of reproduction, this does not challenge his conclusion that it is the law of value which indirectly underlies women's domestic labour, either intensifying or abolishing it as conditions change and satisfying the original contention that the 'family is ultimately dependent upon the dominant mode of production for its existence and form'.[30] He acknowledges that the family also plays an ideological role, especially in socializing the next generation of workers into appropriate attitudes, but his conclusion that the family is 'both a part of the base and superstructure',[31] carrying out economic as well as ideological tasks, sustains his overall theoretical claim that ultimately women's oppression is rooted in the impersonal logic of capitalism rather than in the interests of individual men.

Although Seccombe succeeded in integrating family and economy through the category of labour, neither the consciousness of individual female participants, nor the state of their struggle with men, were accorded significance—resulting in an 'unhappy marriage' of Marxism and feminism as far as many exponents of the latter were concerned.[32] And Seccombe himself acknowledges in a later article that his categories had replicated Marxism's own sex-blindness: 'While the overall labour burden of the household was amenable to Marxist explanation, its unequal allocation between spouses was not'.[33] In other words, Marxism was still weak when it came to sexual relations and to the experiences of the women who performed the labour it discussed; nothing of de Beauvoir's vivid description remained. The very power of Marxism to explain the proliferation of anonymous structures according to their own inner logic, seemed to fly in the face of feminists' concern with personal experience.

There were additional problems with the domestic labour approach. For one thing, it ignored women's particular plight in production, as well as the fact that many performed both social and domestic labour. Yet it was in precisely the contradictions created by this dual role, critics argued, that the particular nature of women's oppression lay.[34] In fact, as Maxine Molyneux points out, participants in the Debate generally ignored many critical dimensions of women's oppression. They overemphasized the more trivial aspects of housework while virtually ignoring the vastly more arduous experience of childrearing, thus centring women's subjection in wifehood rather than motherhood. They also ignored the ideological and psychological dimensions of the family-household complex.[35] Looking at the Debate overall, then, it seemed to imply that women's oppression could be reduced to their performance of housework.[36] Within the parameters of the Debate, it might still be asked why men and women sharing housework, or single males performing their own, might not be equally functional for capitalism.[37]

If traditional family arrangements were only contingently functional for capitalism, it followed that there was no necessity in their co-existence and that capitalist structures could not therefore be used to explain patriarchal ones. Capitalism might have done no more than collude with a pre-existing system of sexual oppression, such that each transformed the other as they converged.

Writing in 1980, Michele Barrett was still able to contend that in regard to a synthesis of Marxism and feminism, 'no such reconciliation has yet occurred'.[38] Like Mitchell, Molyneux and Hartmann, she recognizes that women's subordination is reinforced on many fronts which are irreducible to a single cause. Aspiring to tread a precarious path between dualism and reductionism, she sees capitalism and patriarchy interacting differently over time, depending upon the state of struggle between the sexes and with capitalism using patriarchy where it already exists. While a patriarchal ideology and rudimentary sexual division of labour preceded capitalism (and we saw both in Chapter 3 earlier), she sees the continuation of that division as critically constituted by competition for jobs during the 1830s and 1840s, when men in their better-organized craft unions won a decisive victory in having protective legislation passed which would limit women's work opportunities.[39] In establishing a material base in capitalism, a patriarchy anchored in the family-household system became difficult to overthrow or isolate without challenging the whole edifice of the modern economy. This account has the advantage of accommodating functional contingency and a dialectic between ideological and material factors, which avoids separating patriarchy and capitalism into independent spheres.

The theoretical implication of Barrett's claim was that specific historical analyses needed to be undertaken, as well as empirical studies of particular aspects of contemporary women's experience, since the articulation of capitalism and patriarchy could not be pronounced on in the abstract. It follows, as Barrett herself recognized, that 'there is no programmatic answer to the question of whether women's liberation might be achieved within capitalism'.[40]

In conclusion, then, the overriding problem for Marxist feminists has been the relationship between two types of oppression: class and sex/gender. The search for a unitary theory has tended in two directions: to collapse one into the other or to posit two separate systems. Barrett's middle position, which perceives a dialectic that is always changing, is useful, yet it points away from the kind of grand and all-embracing theory that Marxist feminists had traditionally sought. Indeed, many on the Left have come to abandon the idea of history as a relentless logic working itself out and have accepted, instead, that it constitutes itself out of the debris of the past, incorporating new themes in a meaningful, yet unpredictable, manner. Such a position is not necessarily at odds with Marxism. It has engendered a greater emphasis on detailed historical and empirical studies, such as Marx himself undertook in relation to capitalism, in order to locate the changing mix over time, of a variety of modes of oppression.[41]

While Marxist feminists were hastened in such a direction by difficulties in reconciling sexual and class oppression, radical feminists, contending that patriarchy is the most fundamental and universal form of oppression, apparently suffered no such theoretical anguish. Both approaches have, however, found themselves accused of ethnocentrism and racism and have therefore been obliged to try to incorporate a further level of oppression into their analyses.

Black feminists have accused both positions of a false universalism. This has been partly a problem of ethnocentric sociology: the family which is attacked is atypical of many non-European cultures; the issues which have been emphasized have not necessarily been those which concern black women or women of colour; the solidarity which men and women experience in fighting racism is ignored by feminists when they present sexual oppression as fundamental. In this sense, the emphasis on personal experience has been a damaging and myopic one. There is also a political problem in that many feminist groups have unwittingly operated in a racist way, while gains made by white women, especially in the labour force, have often been at the expense of ethnic minorities. But there is also a more general theoretical problem. The tradition of political thought which has been discussed in this book, and out of which feminism has been seen to emerge, is very much a Western one. Its postulates are essentially predicated upon European experience, which has in turn been associated with a white culture, whose historical and geographical specificity has been portrayed as universal. In reality it is both perspectival and imperialist. Amos and Parmar point out that in accepting much of this conceptual framework, feminists inherit its assumptions. Thus pre-capitalist economies are associated with ideological and cultural backwardness: either women's liberation is equated with the arrival of capitalist relations or white feminists assume that they must educate politically immature sisters according to their own more 'advanced' theories: 'Because they are not acquainted with traditions outside of their cultures and histories, the ideological and the theoretical legacies that they write from inevitably deny as valid any modes of struggle and organization which have their origins in non-European philosophical traditions'.[42] The symbols associated with women which exclude and subjugate them, are also shown to be racially specific (American black women, for example, were never saddled with the stereotype of the weak, idle, dependent, gentlewoman) and their collusion in the system is suggested.[43]

Simply to integrate a broader cultural perspective has not been an adequate solution to such accusations. As Amos and Parmar have argued, black women's absence from previous theories cannot be resolved by making them merely more visible: 'the process of accounting for their historical and contemporary position does, in itself, challenge the use of some of the central categories and assumptions of recent mainstream feminist thought'.[44] Barrett and McIntosh claim that socialists are in a better position to deal with this since they have always been more aware than radical feminists, of the diversity of patriarchy and of its mediation by other structures of oppression. But they also acknowledge that a difficult and familiar problem arises once we try to apply Marxist concepts to a content for which they were not originally intended:

From this point of view the question of race as an independent social division is an extremely pressing one. Do we take the view that the introduction of a third system must necessarily fragment the analysis that was already creaking at the seams over feminism? Or should we regard race as easier to incorporate into a classic Marxist analysis than feminism proved to be? Or should we concentrate on the relations between race and gender and ignore for the moment the consequences of this for a class analysis? Or should we apparently back down from these academic debates and adopt a more pragmatic political approach by identifying areas of common and progressive struggle? Can we argue that racism, like women's oppression, has independent origins but is now irretrievably embedded in capitalist social relations?[45]

While the questions raised here are central, there are no obvious solutions to them. As Bonnie Thornton Dill argues, 'we must look carefully at the lives of Black women throughout history in order to define the peculiar interactions of race, class and gender at particular historical moments'.[46] Such a programme of empirical research accords well with the recent conclusions of Marxist feminists; whether it can eventually yield a more complex but integrated theory remains to be seen.

It is now time to focus more explicitly on feminism as a theory of politics and here the emphasis will be predominantly on radical feminist innovations. I shall begin with a discussion of attitudes towards the state before going on to assess first the contention that the personal is political and second, the related concept of patriarchy.

Traditionally, the state has been viewed as the privileged institution of the political sphere. The modern state in particular has been portrayed as a body which mediates the power relations that criss-cross civil society, at the same time representing some higher consensus which is manifested in its authoritative provision of law and in its monopoly of coercive power. As we have seen, women were excluded from this political arena until modern times; they began to undertake political activity only during the nineteenth century, when they campaigned for citizenship. For liberal feminists, the state has remained the primary vehicle for change since it is here that rights become inscribed as law. Other second-wave feminisms have, however, inclined more towards a sort of romantic anarchism.

Among radical feminists, the state is perceived as a patriarchal institution from which women have nothing to gain. On the Left this position has been reinforced by Marxism's traditional presentation of the state as a class instrument reflecting more fundamental economic forces: again, women are perceived to have little to hope for here, in so far as they seek material changes which are incompatible with capitalism. Similar problems arise regarding the significance of rights. For radical feminists, the language of rights seems oddly inappropriate. It implies a society of antagonistic individuals who make claims against each other, and this is anathema to their vision of reciprocity and mutuality. Legislation also appears a blunt and clumsy instrument when it comes to massive social regeneration; to a transformation of values, attitudes, the ways people love and relate in their daily lives. The means to such transformation must be consonant with these ends. Marxists have also been generally sceptical of rights, perceiving them as formalities which bring no material change and which are worth little unless protected groups have the power to demand their enforcement. In so far as a framework of civil rights may benefit women in their struggles within bourgeois society, this is in any case perceived as the product of a battle essentially won during the first wave. Rights pertaining to economic or socio-cultural equality seem to demand such massive upheaval in those areas, that struggle seems better aimed at direct change there. For rights appear to reflect, rather than initiate, the balance of power at any particular time. For all these reasons, radical and Marxist feminists have inclined towards a communitarian vision of collective acts which would aim at transforming civil society from within; there has been little expectation of *emancipation* via central government.

Nevertheless, the state's contribution to women's *oppression* cannot be ignored. As Lynne Segal writes,

from the very beginning socialist feminists argued that male power over women *is* centralised through state policies which make women caring for others in the home financially dependent upon men, as well as its being embedded in other structures of the workplace and the home which cannot be best understood as operating primarily at an individual level.[47]

For such feminists, there has been little *theoretical* difficulty in identifying this contribution. To put the matter rather crudely: if the state functions to sustain capitalism, and if capitalism benefits from patriarchy (whether intrinsically or via a historical collusion that is entirely contingent), then it follows that one purpose of the state will be to support patriarchy.

It is this position which is broadly argued, for example, by Mary McIntosh in 'The State and the Oppression of Women'.[48] She points out two major ways in which the state contributes to women's oppression to the benefit of capital: it sustains the family-household and it manipulates the supply of wage labour.[49] McIntosh acknowledges the functionalist foundations of her argument[50] and suggests that the state steps in precisely because of the family's inadequacy in performing the tasks capitalism requires of it, due to its inflexibility. The state bolsters the position of the dependent wife by controlling fertility (its laws control abortion, legitimacy, contraception, etc.) and by tax and benefit systems which support women only where no man is able to do so, although levels will be finely tuned so that the attractiveness of work varies with demands for labour.

Michele Barrett adds a number of ways in which the state both promotes women's oppression and itself operates in a sexist way. Thus women are excluded from certain sorts of work by protective legislation; state regulation of education structures expectations and opportunities along gender lines; the state exercises control over the way that sexuality is represented (pornography laws, etc.); its legal, judicial and penal systems operate according to massive assumptions about gender; its housing policy is resistant to the needs of non-nuclear families.[51]

Despite such incursions by the state into the personal and working lives of women, both McIntosh and Barrett point out that the very public–private split which the state vaunts, has meant its less conspicuous intrusion in women's lives. Where this does occur, they argue, it is often via husbands (tax/benefit systems); via pressures which do not appear to be overtly political (e.g. psychiatry has been a popular alternative to prison in correcting female 'deviance') or by a simple refusal to act at all (domestic violence is inadequately policed; welfare needs are not met, etc.).[52] Thus either the political is mediated through the personal or the personal is denied to be political at all: despite its contribution to women's oppression, the modern state tends to exercise this role in a quiet and indirect way. Of course, feminist analysis is able to clarify that role, but state policies have generally been perceived by it as reflections of some deeper (cultural or economic) level of discrimination where change is more essential.

At the same time, many feminists have been wary of contamination by the sort of practices 'high' politics encourages. Simply to engage in conventional politics without first changing its cultural and ideological context has not seemed a particularly promising strategy to non-liberal feminists, and unlike other radical movements, feminism has never envisaged any seizure of state power. For apart from its sheer impracticability, feminists have generally subscribed to more exotic and utopian goals than merely to replace their oppressors in the institution they created. To quote Segal again:

we did want real power, in every sphere. By power we meant not the power to control and dominate others . . . but rather the freedom and space to express our own desires, creativity and potential: to flourish and find 'our place in the sun'. We sought to build the collective power of all women. We wanted power to participate in the making of a new world which would be free from all forms of domination.[53]

For a more specifically feminist politics, local rather than central government has seemed a more conducive area for women since it allows a more personal style of participation and involvement in areas directly affecting their lives: transport, planning, housing, community health-care, education, and so on. This is not to deny, of course, that the women's movement has sometimes organized very efficiently over a single issue—most notably abortion—on which it has successfully affected state policy. But in Britain, at least, it has evinced a real scepticism towards conventional party politics. Radical suspicion of the patriarchal state, coupled with the Marxist dismissal of liberal-democratic institutions, has left little space for theories of feminist participation outside of liberalism. There are, nevertheless, indications of a gradual shift on the Left. Anne Phillips captures the new mood:

Feminism is sometimes said now to have come of age—one of the signs of this supposed maturity being the recent rapprochement with parties and power. Edgily but definitely, feminists have moved into the world of the Labour Party, local government, state funding, social policy, legislation . . . trying to translate visions into practical demands. The shift in emphasis was both urgent and necessary.[54]

This has been facilitated in part by hopes that mainstream practices might be moved in a more feminist direction. When

Beyond the Fragments appeared in 1979, for example, it provoked considerable interest precisely because it suggested that women might participate in the full spectrum of issues in a feminist way.[55] Autonomous political fragments, made up of oppressed groups that were loosely federated for united action, aiming for change across many fronts but modelled on the lessons of the women's movement, seemed to capture the new spirit of multi-faceted analysis and post-modernism. While the rise of the New Right has forced feminists to recognize that the state, despite its liberal and patriarchal ethos, nevertheless provides some rights and benefits worthy of protection, the emergence of new social movements has inspired hope that change might be won within civil society. Tentative engagements in the conventional channels of political power have yet to prove themselves, but in any case they can provide only one avenue for change, to be complemented by the theoretically more innovative category of sexual politics.

The notion that 'the personal is political' has been central to contemporary feminism and has been in danger of becoming something of a cliché. Yet it is the sheer fecundity of the maxim which has allowed it so broad and popular a usage. From it has sprung a new praxis: that of sexual politics.

The claim that the personal is political is intimately related to the idea of consciousness-raising, which yields both a theory (of patriarchy) and a programme for action, drawn from the lives of individual women. Luise Eichenbaum and Susie Orbach illustrate the connections clearly:

Within the consciousness-raising group each person's experience, each woman's life story was a matter of interest. We understood that through listening to an individual's experience we could draw a much richer picture of how society was put together. Sexual politics provided an understanding of how society works both at an ideological level and at a material level and deepened the understanding the left had of human experience. The Women's Liberation Movement built an analysis of society founded on the nuts and bolts of individual life experience. It enlarged and challenged previous understanding of the social, economic and political basis of society.[56]

Rather than imposing a preconceived doctrine on events, a theory was to be constructed out of the fragments of personal histories. Private life was now declared the site of political relationships, not an other dimension governed by an apolitical ethic. Kate Millett justified the fusion by arguing that sexual relations were indeed political ones if politics referred to 'power-structured relationships, arrangements whereby one group of persons is controlled by another'.[57] Throughout history, she argued, sexual relations have taken the form of dominance and subordination. Sex has remained a status category whereby one half of the population dominates the other. Patriarchy thus emerges as the pre-eminent political *system,* but it also decrees that the most *intimate personal interaction* assumes political form.

This last conjunction is an important one, since feminists never argued that personal politics meant private suffering ameliorated by individual action. It is true that the effects of male dominance are daily and intimately experienced because they radiate from the most personal contacts. But patriarchal power is not exercised arbitrarily or gratuitously by specific men. From the data culled from everyday life, a systematic and structured edifice emerged, sustained by a series of interlocking institutions. From the realization that personal experiences were part of a richer fabric, woven from typical and recurrent practices, women were released from their lonely and silent plight. If sexual politics meant that every woman could act to change her life (by negotiating with, or even rejecting, male partners), then, it also meant both support from a network of sisters during such struggle and a platform for collective action within the women's movement. Unlike state activities, politics was no longer a specialized and circumscribed engagement. It could take place even in the intimacy of one's bedroom. Sexual politics gave to many women a new sense of efficacy and power. Yet some reasoned that if every sexual encounter meant engaging, beside the individual male, the whole edifice of patriarchy which sustained him, any reform of heterosexual relationships was hopeless. Lesbianism became a political act and not merely a civil rights issue, although there remained unease as to whether separatism could really offer an effective politics.[58]

Over time, definitions of what the personal connotes have deepened. Referring originally to sexual relationships, it has come to be associated with even more intimate parts of oneself. Adrienne Rich has argued that heterosexuality and motherhood are to be recognized as political institutions and points to 'the full complexity and political significance of the woman's body, the full spectrum of power and powerlessness it represents'.[59] Psychoanalysis has shown that the unconscious, one's very self-identity and personality, are structured by patriarchy and are thus sites for political struggle. The language and concepts in which we express ourselves are similarly suffused with masculinity. No crevice of female existence seems to remain free from the tentacles of male power, and so every dimension is politicized. Yet again, these intensely personal sites of oppression/repression are not unsystematized: they are all components of a protean system wherein change in one part might be won through change in another.

Claims that the personal is political thus shift traditional notions of politics in fundamental ways. First, they locate the family and the sexual identities constituted there, rather than the state, as the primary site of power relations. They mean that 'politics is about personal life not simply about electoral battles and ambitious individuals: that the way we live in our private lives is as much the stuff of politics as parliamentary debates or theories of state'.[60] Who raises the children and does the housework becomes a political issue. Second, they isolate men, rather than economic classes or self-interested individuals, as the prime power-seekers. Third, they find that power is exercised through a whole range of channels but tend to focus on psycho-cultural ones, since consciousness-raising is needed before victims recognize the full scope of their oppression. Fourth, then, the scope of politics is considerably broadened; it no longer makes sense to locate a circumscribed political arena and juxtapose it to an apolitical private realm. As women's experience testifies, there is no escape from power relations in the world as we know it.

All this means that many of the questions traditionally posed by political theorists are either irrelevant or marginal. Questions of legitimacy and obligation which haunt the state, for example, cannot be raised, or at least not in their usual form. Women are socialized in such a manner that asking for reasoned consent to a power which remains largely invisible, makes little sense. Millett points out that patriarchy always gains (tacit) consent because it appears so natural.[61] The whole idea of rational, self-interested actors who make decisions about the power structures that govern them, has in any case seemed inappropriate to the realm of sexual politics. If love, guilt and desire have conventionally been exiled from the public realm, where sexual power relations are concerned they are the very forces that bind antagonists to one another. To speak of just and impersonal rules of conduct here is highly problematic.

The issues over which political activity has taken place have been, due to the above analysis, quite different from the usual ones. As Hester Eisenstein writes:

the questions addressed by feminists seemed increasingly difficult to place anywhere along the traditional political spectrum from left to right. Precisely because they concerned the erstwhile 'private' domain to which women had been consigned, women's issues began to appear, to some, as finding a place that was entirely off the map of male politics. The analysis of patriarchy, of rape, lesbianism, gender identity, pornography, and the like, seemed to require a different set of axes from those defining the traditional political grid.[62]

While liberal or Marxist feminism are partly defined in terms of the usual right–left spectrum, due to their interests in rights and resources, respectively, feminism in its radical form seems to inscribe a quite novel continuum. Here, the spaces in which power is exercised and the time scale over which it changes, are quite new. It is not at all clear at what point, if at all, the spectra cross; whether they are interwoven, superimposed, parallel or simply unrelated. The answer given largely depends upon one's commitment to the primacy of patriarchy.

Finally, the style of politics which its personalization engenders, is at odds with traditional practices. Feminists' reluctance to engage the liberal-democratic state, due to its rewarding particular types of competitive activity which are considered anathema to the women's movement, has already been noted. They see that impersonal, bureaucratic, conservative, hierarchical organizations are favoured where pressure groups and political parties are the main channels of influence: women have taken to heart the iron law of oligarchy.[63] Even where collective action is required, feminists have still looked to personal networks and loose, egalitarian organizations, for if the personal is political, then politics must also be personal. This does not mean that public life is rejected; instead, it is rescued from its impoverished modern form and expanded in a rather Aristotelian manner. Thus real public existence is anticipated: a space for discussion, self-expression and wide-ranging debate; a radical, participatory, grass-roots democracy; a politics of everyday life which is no longer limited to choices between impotence or occasional and highly ritualized acts. Paradoxically, it is only by engendering such an enriched sense of public life, that personal power relations can be mediated, excized, eliminated. Thus we see that a feminist politics both challenges patriarchal power on a personal level and, through this concern with personal life, anticipates a new *style* of politics in which feminists might safely engage. It is now necessary to look more carefully at the concept of patriarchy which a personal politics has exposed.

It is the concept of patriarchy which marks the most distinctive and innovative contribution by feminism to political thought. It is a term associated most explicitly with radical feminism (the most theoretically 'pure' form taken by feminist theory), although it has also gained currency on the Left. Only with the contemporary notion of patriarchy has the male sex been explicitly singled out as the key agency of (women's) oppression. By using patriarchy as a descriptive term, all the interlocking structures which had been previously identified as constituents of sexual domination could be integrated, even if the explanatory properties of the concept have remained rather less compelling.

We already came across the notion of patriarchy in the seventeenth century (see Ch. 4), when it denoted the power of the father over his household and when it was also used to legitimize monarchical claims to an absolute rule grounded in nature. Revived by feminists in the early 1970s, the term has been substantially amended, although it resists any single definition. While some writers have continued to associate it with the rule of the father, patriarchy today frequently denotes simply men's power over women.

Juliet Mitchell's *Psychoanalysis and Feminism* offers a good example of the former definition. Here she explained patriarchy as the law of the father.[64] She claimed that patriarchy is inherited intergenerationally via the unconscious and that prior to captalism, it was synonymous with civilization itself. For at the heart of the law of the father lay the incest taboo, prescribing an exogamy which has always in fact been achieved by the exchange of women. This exchange, she argued, broke up the deadend of biological relations by introducing difference. The women functioned as signs such that their systematic exchange facilitated the communication between families which allowed culture to proliferate. Embodied in kinship systems, the patriarchal law is learnt by each infant during the Oedipus Complex. It is the phallus which symbolizes the difference and the authority that force the bisexual child from unity with its mother and into (patriarchal) culture, where it becomes a gendered, differentiated being who will one day be exchanged or will inherit the father's symbolic power.

Mitchell thus establishes that kinship rules are differentially etched into the unconscious, to produce the gendered characteristics that equip the sexes for their transhistorical roles. However, under capitalism the exchange of commodities renders the exchange of women redundant, by offering an alternative structure for meaning. Women might now overthrow patriarchy by a cultural revolution without endangering civilization, since it is only the ideology of capitalism which sustains this outmoded form of kinship relation. Unfortunately, Mitchell's prescription for a cultural revolution is the least compelling part of her analysis. Others who have shared her Lacanian framework have identified the law of the father as discourse: the child who learns to speak during the Oedipal phase is introduced into a Symbolic Order which structures its subjectivity in a way that is always masculine, since language is inherently phallocentric.

The alternative definition of patriarchy, as the rule of women by men generally, was given classic formulation by Kate Millett: 'male shall dominate female, elder male shall dominate younger'.[65] For Millett, patriarchy meant a set of attitudes learnt afresh by each child as it was socialized first by the family and later by a range of other patriarchal institutions. Sex roles are allocated to males and females and the requisite gendered traits internalized. Although there is no inner necessity to this and the cultural processes of learning seem more open than Mitchell's unconscious structures without agents, the universality and resourcefulness of patriarchy as Millett described it, renders it scarcely more vulnerable. Across every culture, every historical period, every mode of production, the subjugation of women by men is identified by her as the primary political relationship. It is reinforced by myth, religion, psychology and education; sustained by family, state, economy and naked force. It cuts across all distinctions of race and class.[66] The ubiquity and universality of male power is similarly conveyed by Adrienne Rich, for whom it covers

a familial-social, ideological, political system in which men—by force, direct pressure, or through ritual, tradition, law, and language, customs, etiquette, education, and the division of labour—determine what part woman shall or shall not play, and in which the female is everywhere subsumed under the male.[67]

Despite such impressive descriptions, they have been criticized for failing to explain why patriarchy occurs: 'it is never made clear what it is about men which makes them into sexual oppressors'.[68] This has been especially valid for acounts which, like Millett's, present patriarchy as a primarily psycho-cultural phenomenon. At best, some sort of universal male will to power seems to be assumed. There is also the problem of how it occurs. Segal has pointed out some of the difficulties in the sort of role theory approach used by Millett, arguing that it tends to find society static and monolithic; the individual passive and infinitely malleable in conforming with social expectations of gender that are in fact adopted only painfully and imperfectly.[69]

Feminist theory has subsequently become greatly preoccupied with precisely the question of how the biological male or female is transformed into a being with masculine and feminine traits that conform to the traditional active/passive dichotomies. Cultural learning in the family and poor education; psychological adaptation by the powerless to their role; the more or less wilful imposition of a sexual ideology to the benefit of capitalism; unconscious processes embedded in kinship structures; the asymmetry of mother-centred childrearing practices and the patriarchal structuration of all available systems of meaning, have all been invoked to explain the sexes' general tendency to exhibit those psychological qualities ascribed to them, where there is no 'natural' foundation for it. They have helped to explain why women collude in their gendered identification where it is against their interests and may even conflict with conscious desires. Patriarchy has thus become popularly anchored in that process by which sex is transformed into gender, but the manner in which this is achieved is now commonly held to be more complex than socialization and the emulation of role models suggest. This is one reason why psychoanalysis has proven such such an important theoretical tool. If at one end of the spectrum we have the confident liberal belief that equal education will produce the rational androgyn, at the other there is a contention that such beliefs and models are themselves part of an all-pervasive patriarchal culture.

Others who have theorized about patriarchy have given it a material foundation. Their contributions fall into two camps: the biological and the economic. One of the problems encountered with the psycho-cultural approach had been its difficulty in accounting for patriarchy's variability over time and place.[70] It is a difficulty shared by biologistic accounts. While ahistoricity has been avoided by economistic explanations, they have in turn tended to succumb to reductionism.

Offering a biological foundation for patriarchy, Firestone has located sexual inequality in that division of labour which finds women reproducing the species. The physical dependency it engendered is reinforced, she argues, by socio-political structures and manifested in a series of psychological dislocations, although the precise causal relations are hard to pin down. On one level the technological means to liberate women from biological reproduction would seem sufficient to emancipate them, but Firestone also recognizes a need for cultural and economic revolutions if that technology is to be used wisely. The relationship between the three revolutions, however, remains unclear.[71]

Susan Brownmiller, Susan Griffin and Andrea Dworkin, on the other hand, have located the biological roots of patriarchy in men's capacity to rape. Accordingly, their power is perceived ultimately to rest on physical coercion. All such

forms of biologism have, however, been criticized for
reductionism and determinism; for a fatalistic overemphasis
on irremediable sexual differences; for exaggerating the role of
biological factors whose expression is overdetermined by
cultural elements which still need explaining.[72]

On an economic level, we have already seen how Christine
Delphy placed the material roots of patriarchy in a domestic
mode of production. Heidi Hartmann has also associated
men's power ultimately with their control over women's
labour power, although in a broader capacity:

The material base of patriarchy is men's control over women's labor power.
That control is maintained by denying women access to necessary
economically productive resources and by restricting women's sexuality.
Men exercise their control in receiving personal service work from women, in
not having to do housework or rear children, in having access to women's
bodies for sex, and in feeling powerful and being powerful. The crucial
elements of patriarchy as we *currently* experience them are: heterosexual
marriage (and consequent homophobia), female childrearing and
housework, women's economic dependence on men (enforced by
arrangements in the labor market), the state and numerous institutions based
on social relations among men—clubs, sports, unions, professions,
universities, churches, corporations, and armies.[73]

Here Hartmann tries to show that patriarchy does take a
particular form under capitalism—to yield 'patriarchal
capitalist society'.[74] But she presents her article as part of an
ongoing struggle to develop an adequate account of relations
between the two, admitting that as she uses the term
patriarchy, it still 'remains more a descriptive term than an
analytical one'.[75] She also writes as a socialist feminist and her
investigations therefore place her outside that position which
has maintained the absolute pre-eminence of patriarchal
power.

In conclusion, it is evident that the concept of patriarchy,
along with the notion that the personal is political, has offered
a fundamental challenge to traditional definitions of politics,
even if a precise definition and location of the term has
remained elusive. Together, these two conceptions have
relocated significant political power as well as anticipating a
new style of politics. In the final section, I shall discuss the
feminist critique of theory itself, suggesting that the very
manner of theorizing has gained political significance for

feminism and therefore become a political issue. In order for this to be asserted, however, arguments have often had to be made for precisely the sort of definitive sexual differences that feminists usually challenge, and this is profoundly problematic.

In the preceding nine chapters, a basic dichotomy has frequently reappeared. On the one hand, conservative thinkers have spoken of natural and unassailable differences between women and men. Aristotle, Aquinas, Rousseau and Hegel all asserted that biological differences yield the sexes fixed and differential roles and that the female mind is endowed with the appropriate innate traits: intuition, passivity, love, and so on. Radicals, on the other hand, have argued that natural differences become significant only where they are socially reinforced. In particular, they have seen in the feminine personality a social construction, superimposed upon a psychology which is in essence ungendered. Plato, Augustine, Hobbes and Locke, Wollstonecraft, J.S. Mill, Marx and Engels had all to a greater or lesser extent endorsed this view.

While conservatives have advised social divisions reflecting irremediable sexual differences, radicals have demanded changed arrangements in order to permit greater flexibility of function and an opportunity for women to develop their rational potential. Nevertheless, it became clear that this radical position was generally less egalitarian than it at first appeared. Rather than anticipating an elimination of the sexual division of labour and the flourishing of an androgynous personality, it too often expected women to carry out their reproductive and servicing functions in a more masculine (hence more responsible) manner. Passion, irrationality, immorality, were still associated with the female, but individual women were credited with a capacity to transcend their (inferior) sexed nature in order to scale the lofty peaks of human (male) achievement: abstract reason and impartial judgement might after all be theirs with sufficient will on their part and the provision of an adequate education by their mentors.

This androcentric view found its way into de Beauvoir's work, but when feminism blossomed in the early 1970s, one of its aims was to replace such aspirations with a commitment to genuine androgyny. Many of the political projects encountered in the last section had this goal: to abolish the sexual division of labour at home and work and to eliminate the ideology which both encouraged and reflected it in the form of feminine and masculine personalities. The disaggregation of feminine and masculine traits from their respective female and male bodies, promised a future race of bisexual androgyns, each possessing their own unique capacities and mix of assertive and nurturing orientations. In other words, masculinity as well as femininity was to be transcended in a true synthesis. The apogee of the species was no longer anchored in fidelity to a rational ideal (a male norm), but identified with a healing of the schism between mind and body and between its male—female referents.

This ideal, which was eventually to surmount all significant sexual difference, has nevertheless lost favour among some recent feminists. Mary Daly, for example, has argued that 'attempts to combine masculinity and femininity, which are patriarchal constructs, will result only in pseudointegrity'.[76] Masculine qualities like competitiveness and aggression have also seemed questionable virtues for women to emulate. Just as women were struggling to escape the identities imposed upon them, then, some feminists began to wonder whether those identities might not be worth preserving after all. This did not *necessarily* mean falling back on assertions of innate sexual difference. It might well be, as Utopian Socialists had earlier argued, that women's experiences equipped them with capacities ideally suited to a more co-operative and humanist future and that men must change into their image if the conflicts and violence of previous history were to be left behind. But the line between acquired characteristics of femininity and essential differences between masculine and feminine minds, anchored in women's unique corporeal experiences, has become increasingly fine and indistinct. Several recent accounts which recall two decades of second-wave feminism, have found cause to lament a return to those very differences which conservatives once proclaimed, with only an inversion of the evaluation passed upon them.[77]

The popularity of attempts to revalorize women's lives and characteristics, following the years when feminists agreed that they were ultimately inferior and wretched, is perhaps unsurprising. The idea of the woman-identified woman, who refuses to perceive herself, or be judged, according to male criteria, is undoubtedly exhilarating. Yet the dualities which reappear in this new feminism, whether they are cited as innate or praised as the outcome of specifically female practices, are virtually identical to those which the pre-Socratics had first formulated. Their mere revalorization, in a world where the images and power relations that they have spawned remain intact, seems to be a fragile and dangerous foundation on which to base women's liberation.

One direction which feminist theory has taken in exploring such womanly qualities, is that of epistemology. It has asked how we gain knowledge of the world, what sort of knowledge in thereby attained, by what process it becomes expressed in language and theory, and whether the two sexes might not engage in it in different ways. As we have seen, most previous feminisms had been eager to describe ideals of rationality as gender-neutral and had aspired to emulate them. But of late, some critics have again begun to wonder whether the whole process of rational and scientific discourse might not be somehow inherently masculine. It has already become apparent that feminism seeks a new understanding of the political. It is now necessary, then, to see how the debate over sexual identity and difference has led to a reconceptualization of theory as well.

Over the course of the preceding chapters, it has become evident that feminist scholars have been highly critical of the Western political tradition because it treats the public world as a male concern while offering legitimacy to women's exclusion from it in practice. Nevertheless, critics prior to the emergence of radical feminism had been willing to accept the conceptual frameworks on offer and attempted to incorporate women into them. This is still largely true of liberal and Marxist feminists, and there has been general sympathy for Mary O'Brien's suggestion that the task for feminists studying the political tradition is 'to winkle out those aspects which may be called idelogical', to work in a dialectical manner which separates out justifications for male supremacy from neutral conceptualizations which might be useful to feminist analysis.[78] What some feminists are now, however, contending, is that the sort of theory developed so far (of which political thought would be one example) is inherently masculine in some deeper sense. A reconstructed version might therefore be used to describe women's oppression and even to articulate plans for its transcendence, but as long as a patriarchal mode of expression is used, there can be no escape from a world where women remain 'other' to a masculine norm.

First of all, theory has been attacked as obscure and therefore élitist. This has especially affected women, who have not usually received as good an education as men. Also, as we found in works as varied as those of Plato and nineteenth-century Social Democrats, it has often licensed a minority of men to speak on women's behalf. A typical lament is the following:

We believe in the necessity of an in-depth analysis of women's oppression, but at the same time 'theoretical' too often refers to inaccessible texts that are destined for a privileged élite. Theoretical is then synonymous with hermetic, as if the obscure nature of a text established its 'scientific value', its 'seriousness'.[79]

One solution to such criticisms seemed to be precisely the sort of practice by which a theory of patriarchy arose out of women's discussions. The consequent creation of a new set of meanings and referents which differ from, and circumscribe, men's knowledge, was also seen as intrinsically valuable. As Dale Spender wrote: 'For women to speak for themselves, to dispute the meanings of males, and to validate the meanings of females, was a political act, and a very significant one'.[80]

More radically, however, the process of theorizing has itself been questioned. This is primarily due to its equation with traditional dualisms: it severs knower from known, culture from nature, subject from object (a modern form of the mind–body split). Theorizing is then described as a form of domination, whereby the theorist conceptually appropriates the objects of knowledge at the same time imposing his own laws upon them. Nature is thus mastered and manipulated.

The knowledge which results is further criticized for its impoverished and fragmented content. The knower extricates/imposes discrete pieces of information, but lacking any interaction with the world, he fails to discern the significant relationships which underlie it to yield its inner structure and vibrance. Thus, for example, Mary Daly refers to 'the contrived combinations, the inorganic sticking together of things which is the "genius" af androcratic art, technology, and academic/professional-ologies'.[81] Such criticism is, however, levelled most appropriately at scientific-deductive forms of knowledge. There is a resemblance here to Hegel's critique of the Understanding in his *Phenomenology of Mind*, where it is branded an inferior way of knowing since it grasps only appearances and fails to penetrate the underlying relations that breath life into them. Yet the rationality that Hegel praises, whereby the world finally appears fully transparent before the omniscient and self-conscious Subject, who recognizes there only its own alienated self, must be equally rejected by feminists. For Hegel's Absolute Knowledge is another form of conceptual domination as well as a chimerical goal, since no knowledge severed from nature, from the body and from the unconscious, could be so definitive.

Masculine subjects are indeed acknowledged to be just as Hegel described them in *The Philosophy of Right:* members of that sex which is 'self-diremptive', divided selves who turn back upon their experience to reflect upon and rationalize it. But now such beings, portrayed by Hegel as the bearers of historical reason, are identified as damaged, destructive, limited and deluded egos. They are cut off from themselves and from the truth. To quote Daly again, 'Consciousness split against itself suffers from an inability to reach beyond externals. Thus patriarchally controlled consciousness is broken-hearted. Its impotence to reach beyond appearances expresses itself in reduction and fragmentation of be-ing'.[82] What such thinkers discover in the world is only their own (male) image, endlessly reflected back to them. Knowledge is narcissism. A similar conclusion is reached by those structuralist and post-structuralist feminists who have attacked humanism as both subject-centred and male-centred: it is the male who constructs a mirror of himself which he mistakes for knowledge. Thus:

man confronts himself constantly. He pits himself against and stumbles over his erected self. . . . He is constantly double, he and his phallus. He has established, from the farthest of ages and without giving birth, the binary relation. He has set up the mirror, projected the phantasm. He has become his own representative, his own reference point.[83]

For such feminists, masculine codes structure all language. For others, like Firestone, they refer to a particular, scientific practice. She makes the equation between a technological mode and a masculinity to which it 'corresponds'. Although the nature of this correspondence is not very clear, she is adamant that it 'is' the masculine response: objective, logical, extroverted, realistic, mechanical, pragmatic. The scientist who engages in such empiricism finds himself damaged since in order to be value-free, he must split his personality; he becomes authoritarian, emotionally sterile.[84] Adrienne Rich and Evelyn Fox Keller develop the theme further: objectivity requires distance and separation which correlate well with the male proclivity for autonomy.[85]

In order to establish such claims, two types of explanation have been drawn upon. The first is symbolic, the second psychoanalytic. Regarding the former, both Fox and Genevieve Lloyd refer back to the Baconian origins of modern science, which heralded a new relationship between knower and known. Lloyd shows how Bacon associated knowledge with the control of nature. What was to be known (nature) was associated metaphorically with the female: Bacon used quite explicit sexual metaphors to demonstrate the requisite relations of domination and seduction that were to replace an earlier attitude of wonder and contemplation. To be a good knower now had a specifically male content: 'in Bacon's metaphors the control of the feminine became explicitly associated with the very nature of knowledge'.[86] In other words, we find the misogynous associations of the ancients reappearing even in the transition to rationalism and science.

In order to show why men are especially attracted to deductive modes of thought, other feminists have turned to post-Freudian Object Relations Theory. This theory explains how the development of a sense of self is synonymous with that of sexual identity and how both arise through the child's relations with others. Born into a sense of oneness with its environment (primary narcissism), the infant only slowly develops ego boundaries by separating and individuating itself. The key to a satisfactory resolution to the process lies in its relationship with its primary carer: the one who satisfies needs and whom the child hallucinates as its object of gratification.

Theorists like Nancy Chodorow and Dorothy Dinnerstein have gone on to anchor sexual identity in the asymmetry of this pre-Oedipal situation, where it is invariably women who mother.[87] Seeing in her daughter a reflection of herself, the mother treats her differently from the son, who is at once treated as an other. Due to this differential reception, which is reinforced by cultural pressures in relation to gender, the boy child more quickly breaks from psychological union with his first love-object. He has an early sense of separateness and soon strives to establish his masculine identity as one who is not-mother and not-female. Modelling himself on the father who is often absent, he builds his sexual identity through an abstraction rather than via the more personal relationship. The result is a strong sense of autonomy and of ego boundaries but a weak and brittle sexual identity, which is protected by a deprecation of all things feminine since this is the part of himself which he must repress. The result is a psychological propensity for objective thinking; for rigid self–other distinctions; for rational abstraction and impersonal ways of relating. Regarding scientific thought, then, the strict division between knower and known, the project of mastery and the impersonal approach to value-free knowledge, will resonate well with the male psyche (as indeed it did with Bacon's).

Dinnerstein further contends that children will project their anger and frustration onto the mother who can never fully satisfy them. (This is especially true of boys, since girls realize that they will one day inherit maternal power which therefore becomes less threatening to them.) The result is widespread misogyny and fear of women's power by men, who see there something omnipotent yet capricious. Again, this helps to explain their liking for scientific theories which dominate nature (the mother) and replace her caprice with the regularity of law.

Some attempts have been made to apply this sort of analysis to political thought. Christine Di Stefano, for example, examined Hobbes from this perspective.[88] She associates a specifically masculine perspective and identity with rigorously dualistic thinking, such that the world is rigidly structured in terms of polarities; an emphasis on radical individualism and on the hostility of the surrounding world; a repudiation of relatedness with others and of a natural contingency threatening to the self; an obsession with autonomy and a theory sharply distancing subject from object.[89] Although Stefano's reading is richer than can be conveyed here, it should be apparent from the discussion of Hobbes in Chapter 4, why such an analysis fits well with his descriptions of man and the state of nature. By applying such readings to political thinkers, we gain a deeper sense in which their texts and their whole approach are profoundly masculine projects.

Those who accept the Object Relations explanation of sexual difference succeed in avoiding either biological or role-learning accounts. They do describe stable and enduring identities which are etched into the very structure of the psyche to yield a range of typical gendered characteristics, but these are presented as contingent since they rest upon the mother's being the primary love-object while the father is absent. Yet since this situation has always existed, its effects have been so far universal. Both Chodorow and Dinnerstein anticipate immense changes from shared parenting, which would, they believe, encourage assertive, autonomous women and nurturing, empathetic men. The problem with this political project is, however, that it presupposes an easy solution to all the material problems which combine with the psychological orientations they describe, to drive a majority of women into mothering and into doing it essentially alone.

So far, we have seen how psychoanalysis has been used to explain a correspondence between scientific thought and masculinity, with the former embodying an unconscious misogyny and fulfilling certain psychological predispositions of the male. The other side of the coin is, however, the feminine personality, which also has its identity and proclivity for certain types of knowledge and expression. This aspect of the theory in particular has spilled over into an essentialism at odds with the intentions of its original exponents.

In order to mother well, a person must identify closely with the child and its needs, regressing with it to a pre-individuated state. Chodorow sees this occuring more intensely with daughters due to the sharing of sexual identity. The girl develops a strong and affirmative sense of the latter, which receives an early and personal confirmation. But the duration of her early bonding with the mother also gives her a weaker sense of autonomy and a greater fluidity of ego boundaries, than her brother gained. The result is a feminine personality (itself ideally suited to mothering) which is empathetic and able to relate well to others in a highly personal and intimate way. An oceanic sense of oneness with the world replaces the separation and threats that boys perceive there. As a result, girls are more likely to be co-operative and caring; to relate to others directly rather than via the mediation of abstractions (impersonal rules of justice, etc.).

From this a more feminine way of knowing has been derived. More at home in the world, women gain knowledge of it from a reciprocal relationship with the objects of knowledge. They are more dialectical, more in touch with what they know and therefore less inclined to rationalist abstractions and rigorous distinctions between knower and known. Moreover, the woman is claimed to be less prone to suffer mind—body, subject—object duality, owing to the biological rhythms of the female body. Caught up in the density of her environment, she is able to discern its vectors and themes in a corporeal and intuitive manner.

Earlier in the chapter, we found de Beauvoir speculating, with some scepticism, whether a liberated second sex might not forge a quite new culture. The possibility of a uniquely feminine expression has excited many contemporary feminists. Claudine Herrmann, for example, writes that:

It remains to be seen whether women, once conscious of their identity and without trying to imitate what has been done until now, could inaugurate a new culture. Our knowledge has been following a path that is not necessarily the only one possible . . . not only have the discourses of knowledge been arbitrarily chosen, but their objects as well.[90]

Those who have glimpsed such a possibility have proposed not just a new content and perspective for our knowledge, but an epistemological revolution in which women's unique relationship with their bodies, with nature, and with each other, would facilitate a manner of knowing no longer predicated on domination and dualism.

Adrienne Rich is one exponent of such a view. She argues that the female body is less associated with rigid ego boundaries than the male's, due to experiences like penetration and pregnancy. For women, then, the inner—outer distinction is less clear and so their 'skin is alive with signals'.[91] There is a greater connectedness with the world and its messages, which facilitates a more creative and dynamic means of knowing than the sterile repetitions of rationality. 'Thinking is an active, fluid, expanding process; intellection, "knowing" are recapitulations of past processes'.[92] Rich speaks of a capacity to *'think through the body'* and argues that liberating women means 'to change thinking itself: to reintegrate what has been named the unconscious, the subjective, the emotional with the structural, the rational, the intellectual; to 'connect the prose and the passion' in E.M. Forster's phrase; and finally to annihilate those dichotomies'.[93] The feminist project thus becomes one of the most fundamental reconstructions, contingent upon women's first regaining control over their own bodies. Rich concludes *Of Woman Born* with the suggestion that where that control has been achieved, women will produce 'the visions, and the thinking, necessary to sustain, console, and alter human existence—a new relationship to the universe. Sexuality, politics, intelligence, power, motherhood, work, community, intimacy will develop new meanings; thinking itself will be transformed'.[94]

In Object Relations Theory, a feminine identity was associated with feminine expressions that captured women's greater sense of relatedness to the world. As we saw, such expressions were deemed typical though not essential, since they arose from contingent childrearing practices. With Rich's descriptions of a female capacity for corporeal knowing, however, we move further towards a necessary alignment of biological experience with psycho-cultural expression. Her suggestion that women are uniquely attuned to the rhythms and mysteries of the world is echoed by Mary Daly. She argues that 'creativity means seeing the interconnectedness between seemingly discrete phenomena', which is compared with a (masculine) knowing that does 'not see the patterns of the cosmic tapestries' or 'hear the labyrinthine symphony'. Such 'thinking has been crippled and tied to linear tracks'.[95]

The sort of criticisms which feminists make of scientific and rationalist ways of thinking here are not unique to them. Critiques of instrumental reason, with its narrow, calculating orientation; of value-free knowledge with its myth of the disengaged spectator; of Cartesian dualisms which cut the knower off from the living sources of meaning; of a knowledge which dominates rather than participates and wonders, have all been developed as part of an explanation for the crisis of the twentieth century.[96] In a manner not dissimilar to feminists like Rich and Daly, thinkers like Marcuse have looked to more poetic and surreal expressions, motivated by desire and fantasy and structured according to the aesthetic associations of the unconscious, the pleasure principle, rather than the logical progressions of the ego.[97] Phenomenologists like Merleau-Ponty have spoken of a lifeworld, an original and inexhaustible source of significance which is first gleaned via (corporeal) perception and only poorly reproduced in objective theorizations.[98] To cut ourselves off from such unconscious or pre-reflective sources of meaning, under the illusion that we can reduce their openendedness and ambiguity to orderly classifications of truth is, such thinkers argue, to cut ourselves off from creative expression and growth.

What feminists have added to such critiques is the alignment of rationalism with masculinity and of aesthetic-corporeal ways of knowing with femininity. Women are claimed to have an especial affinity with the imaginary and the pleasure principle because they are more attuned to their bodies and to an original unity with the mother's body and its pleasures. None of the earlier critics of rationalism had however suggested that such processes should be abandoned; they only required integration into more fundamental ways of engendering meaning. The danger of some feminist thinking is that it does seem to suggest that reason and logic are intrinsically alien to a feminine epistemology and should therefore be abandoned. Due to their corporeal status, it is claimed, women have access to superior forms of knowledge, to richer 'thought' processes. Such suggestions in fact rely upon precisely those types of equation discussed in Chapter 1, where the female was associated with that which was formless, indeterminate, insane and mysterious. In so far as these are retrieved for Western culture by women's creativity, it is surely enriched. But in so far as they are identified as exclusively feminine expressions, there is a real danger that women's greater opportunities for cultural practice will lead only to a renewed marginalization, from whence they will lack the critical tools needed to redress the balance of power between the sexes.

The difficulties of these developments are reflected in the more theoretically sophisticated work of French feminists such as Hélène Cixous, Luce Irigaray and Julia Kristeva.[99] They, too, rely upon psychoanalysis, but it is that of Jacques Lacan. In Western culture, it is claimed, the male is the central reference point. In order to say 'I', men must define themselves in opposition to women, who thus appear in language only as absence, negativity, other; as mirrors for masculinity. All symbolic expression thus oppresses and silences the feminine since it lacks any voice of its own. This patriarchal discourse is structured in terms of binary oppositions (such as we saw in Chapter 1); it is obsessed with order, unity and lucidity; with classifying, naming, systematizing. It is in disrupting this Symbolic Order that a feminine writing achieves both expression and political significance. In articulating the pleasure of the female body (*jouissance*), with its multi-faceted sexuality, feminine writing remains mobile and decentred. It splits apart stark oppositions, grammatical rigidity and linear structures to reveal a freely meandering openendedness, an endlessly fulminating differentiation. Women's style is fluid and tactile. Chantal Chawaf thus accuses written language of moving 'away from its original sources: the body and the earth'; of being starved by abstraction. She bids us sensitize ourselves to the sensuality of the 'organic life' of the word, which 'has its own way of being granulated, ruffled, wrinkled, gnarled, irridescent, sticky': 'The corporality of language stirs up our sensuality, wakes it up, pulls it away from indifferent inertia. Theories deprive us of whirlpools sparkling and free which should carry us naturally toward our full blossoming, our rebirth'.[100] Feminine writing is defined as one which expresses itself poetically; it escapes and disrupts the phallocentric expressions of the Symbolic Order via fissures, blanks and silences; by ambiguities and broken syntax. It is the voice of primary narcissism; of the pre-Oedipal unity with the mother's body; of a time before desire was repressed. It is profoundly anti-theoretical.

blank pages, gaps, borders, spaces and silence, holes in discourse: these women emphasise the aspect of feminine writing which is the most difficult to verbalize because it becomes compromised, rationalized, masculinized as it explains itself. . . . If the reader feels a bit disoriented in this new space, one which is obscure and silent, it proves, perhaps, that it is women's space.[101]

While some imply that men might also engage in such feminine writing, however, there is again the suggestion for most that women's bodies lend them an essential affinity for such expression. Only here, ultimately, can they escape the androcentrism, the patriarchal law, that ruins the feminist claims to equality which are made in its language.

As a demand for an enriched theory of knowledge, less rigid and manipulative, for which women's historically constructed role has privileged them, these sorts of argument are fascinating and imply a vast political project of regeneration in which women's creativity might play a privileged role. As a description of a merely inward, psycho-metaphysical voyage towards some Truth which women alone can reach, or as a reduction of political action to symbolic disruptions of the most obscure kind, they threaten impotence and reaction.[102] As Toril Moi concludes, 'We must aim for a society in which we have ceased to categorize logic, conceptualization and rationality as "masculine", not for one from which these virtues have been expelled altogether as "unfeminine"'.[103]

Feminists need critical skills if they are to scrutinize and challenge patriarchal arguments, as I hope this book has demonstrated. They need to engage in conventional political discourse and practice if they are to improve women's material situation, which their analyses reveal as a primary area of sexual inequality. They also, however, need to engage in the demystification and deconstruction of patriarchal culture. In so far as this process promotes participation in a more aesthetic, imaginative, erotic and creative laying down of meaning, then feminist theory can make a significant contribution to Western thought. I have suggested already that the emancipation of women is crucially related to the transcendence of those oppositions which have structured such thought and which are associated with a sexual dualism. Non-feminist critics of the tradition and its modern manifestations have also suggested that aspects of expression suppressed by such divisions must be retrieved if rejuvenation is to occur. Modern feminists might therefore play a central role in regenerating that civilization from which women have traditionally been excluded. To the extent that their contribution is defined in terms of an essential female corporeality and psychology, however, the opportunity to emancipate women while redefining the world in which they live, will be lost. For then they will simply come full circle, voluntarily embracing those qualities which the earliest expressions of Western culture imposed upon them, when it structured its thinking in terms of a sexual polarity in which the male principle was superior and central.

Notes

INTRODUCTION

1. See Diana Coole, 'Re-reading Political Theory from a Woman's Perspective', *Political Studies,* vol. XXXIV, no. 1 (March 1986).
2. An interesting contribution to feminist readings of contemporary thought is offered by Georgina Waylen, 'Women and Neo-Liberalism' in Judith Evans (ed.) *Feminism and Political Theory* (London: Sage, 1986).

1. THE ORIGIN OF WESTERN THOUGHT AND THE BIRTH OF MISOGYNY

1. Sarah Pomeroy, *Goddesses, Whores, Wives, and Slaves: Women in Classical Antiquity* (New York: Schocken Books, 1975), p. 30.
2. M.I. Finley, *The World of Odysseus* (Harmondsworth: Penguin, 1962), p. 48.
3. Pomeroy, *Goddesses,* p. 28; Marilyn Arthur, 'Early Greece: The Origin of the Western Attitude Toward Women' in J. Peradotto and J.P. Sullivan (eds) *Women in the Ancient World: The Arethusa Papers* (Albany, NY: State University of New York Press, 1984). Okin rightly points out, however, that in the *Iliad* at least, women are hardly shown in an elevated light. See Susan Moller Okin, *Women in Western Political Thought* (London: Virago, 1980), p. 16.
4. F. Engels, *The Origin of the Family, Private Property, and the State* (New York: Pathfinder Press, 1972), p. 68.
5. Finley, *World of Odysseus,* p. 28; A. MacIntyre, *After Virtue: A Study in Moral Theory* (London: Duckworth, 1982), ch. 10.
6. Finley, *World of Odysseus,* p. 33.
7. MacIntyre, *After Virtue,* p. 116.
8. Homer, *Iliad,* trans. R. Fitzgerald (New York: Anchor Press, 1975), I, lines 1–10.

9. *Ibid.*, lines 310–74.
10. See Finley, *World of Odysseus*, pp. 48–130; Arthur, 'Early Greece'; Mary O'Brien, *The Politics of Reproduction* (London: Routledge & Kegan Paul, 1981); M.I. Finley, *The Ancient Economy* (London: Chatto & Windus, 1973), p. 18; T. Sinclair, *A History of Greek Political Thought* (London. Routledge & Kegan Paul, 1951), ch. 1.
11. A.N. Athanausakis, Introduction to Hesiod, *Theogony, Works and Days, Shield*, trans. A.N. Athanausakis (Baltimore and London: Johns Hopkins University Press, 1983).
12. *Ibid.*, p.7.
13. *Ibid.*, *Theogony*, lines 570–612.
14. *Ibid.*, lines 588–601.
15. *Ibid.*, *Works and Days*, lines 56–105.
16. *Ibid.*, *Theogony*, lines 602–10.
17. *Ibid.*, lines 886–926.
18. *Ibid.*, *Works and Days*, line 375.
19. *Ibid.*, lines 693–9
20. *Ibid.*, lines 702–3.
21. Regarding *Antigone*, see Hegel's account where he speaks of an antagonism between 'female' law, the law of the ancient gods, and public law. 'This is the supreme opposition in ethics and therefore in tragedy; and it is individualised in the same play in the opposing natures of man and woman'. G.W.F. Hegel, *The Phenomenology of Mind*, trans. J.B. Baillie (New York: Harper & Row, 1967). §166, pp. 114f. Also, see Charles Segal, 'The Menace of Dionysus: Sex Roles and Reversals in Euripides' *Bacchae'* in Peradotto and Sullivan, *Women in the Ancient World*.
22. Aeschylus, *The Eumenides*, trans. H. Lloyd-Jones (London: Duckworth, 1979), lines 137–8.
23. *Ibid.*, lines 68–70.
24. *Ibid.*, lines 831.
25. *Ibid.*, lines 835–6.
26. Engels, *Origin* pp. 29f; S. Freud, *Moses and Monotheism* in *The Standard Edition of the Complete Works of Sigmund Freud*, trans. James Strachey (London: Hogarth Press, 1964), vol. 23, pp. 113f. Freud writes that the transition from a matriarchal to a patriarchal culture must have 'involved a revolution in the judicial conditions that had so far prevailed' and 'a victory of intellectuality over sensuality—that is, an advance in civilization, since maternity is proved by the evidence of the senses while paternity is a hypothesis, based on an interference and a premiss'. (p. 114). See additionally Froma Zeitlin, 'The Dynamics of Misogyny in the *Oresteia*' in Peradotto and Sullivan, *Women in the Ancient World*.
27. Aeschylus, *Eumenides*, lines 604–8.
28. *Ibid.*, lines 658–61.
29. *Ibid.*, lines 663–6.
30. Plato, *Symposium*, lines 208–9. All references to Plato's writings are taken, unless otherwise stated, from *The Dialogues of Plato*, B. Jarrett (ed.), 4 vols, 4th edn (Oxford: Clarendon Press, 1953).

31. Aristotle, *De Generatione Animalium*, trans. A.L. Peck (London: Heinemann, 1943), 716a.
32. *Ibid.*, 738b.
33. *Ibid.*, 729a, 729b, 733b, 765b.
34. *Ibid.*, 765b.
35. *Ibid.*, 727b, 765b.
36. *Ibid.*, 728a, 783b, 766a.
37. *Ibid.*, 732a.
38. Plato, *Timaeus*, trans. D. Lee (Harmondsworth: Penguin, 1965), 50, pp. 68f.
39. The later Greeks did move nearer to Aristotle's functionalist view. Xenophon based different sexual functions on differential biological capacities in his fourth century *Oeconomicus*, where he claimed that the gods prepared woman's nature for indoor work while man's body and soul were endowed with the ability to endure extremes of temperature and long journeys. Women were given greater affection because their role was to nourish children. See excerpt in Mary Lefkowitz and Maureen Fant (eds), *Women's Life in Greece and Rome: A Source Book in Translation* (London: Duckworth, 1982), p. 100. The relevant lines are from *Oecomomicus*, lines 7–10.
40. Plato, *Menexenus*, lines 237–8. See also Aristotle, *De Generatione*, 716a, where he relates earth to female and heaven/sun to father.
41. Aeschylus, *Eumenides*, lines 328–32.
42. See Ruth Padel, 'Women: Model for Possession by Greek Daemons' in Averil Cameron and Amelie Kuhrt (eds), *Images of Woman in Antiquity* (London: Croom Helm, 1983).
43. Thus Bachofen, one of Engels' main sources, sees religious change as responsible for the transition to father-right. Both Engels and Freud believed in a prehistoric matriarchy. See also O'Brien, *Politics of Reproduction*, pp. 123–7.
44. Engels, *Origin*, Pt. 2.
45. See, for example, Simone de Beauvoir, *The Second Sex*, trans. H.M. Parshley (Harmondsworth: Penguin, 1972), pp. 106–8.
46. Genevieve Lloyd, *The Man of Reason: 'Male' and 'Female' in Western Philosophy* (London: Methuen, 1984), p. 4.
47. Plato, *Republic*, lines 514–17. All references to the *Republic* are to the F.M. Cornford edition (Oxford: Clarendon Press, 1941).
48. Segal, 'Menace of Dionysus', p. 196.
49. Victor Ehrenberg, *The People of Aristophanes* (Oxford: Blackwell, 1943), pp. 142 f.
50. De Beauvoir, *Second Sex*, p. 123.
51. This function is supported by Aristotle when he criticizes the Spartan constitution for allowing unregulated subdivision of land among the children of large families, reducing many to poverty. Aristotle, *Politics*, trans. Sir Ernest Barker (Oxford: Oxford University Press, 1958), 1270b. For further discussion, see G.E.M. de ste. Croix, *The Class Struggle in the Ancient Greek World: From the Archaic Age to the Arab Conquests* (London: Duckworth, 1981). He argues that Greek wives constituted 'a distinct economic class, in the technical Marxist sense',

although he sees in Athenian inheritance a safeguard against concentrations of wealth since women could not be married into wealthy families in order to amass property there, pp. 98–103.

52. See for example Aristophanes' satire *The Ecclesiazusae*, trans. B. Rogers (London: Heinemann, 1931), lines 118–20.
53. R. Flacière, *Daily Life in Greece at the Time of Pericles*, trans. P. Green (London: Weidenfeld & Nicolson, 1965), p. 69. Also MacIntyre, *After Virtue*, p. 128.
54. Lefkowitz and Fant, *Women's Life in Greece and Rome*, p. 29.
55. De ste. Croix, *Class Struggle*, pp. 100f.
56. Pseudo-Demos in *Against Neaera*.
57. Sir Ernest Barker, *Greek Political Theory, Plato and his Predecessors* (London: Methuen, 1918), p. 218.

2. PLATO AND ARISTOTLE

1. Plato, *Meno*, 71–2.
2. *Ibid.*, 73. Socrates' belief in women's capacities is further attested to in *Protagoras*, 342.
3. See, for example, *Republic*, 395.
4. D. Wender, 'Plato: Misogynist, Paedophile and Feminist' in Peradotto and Sullivan, *Women in The Ancient World*, describes Plato as 'the nearest thing to a systematic feminist produced by the ancient world', p. 213. This view finds general support in Harry Lesser, 'Plato's Feminism', *Philosophy Today*, vol. 54 (1979). It is contested by Julia Annas, 'Plato's *Republic* and Feminism', *Philosophy*, vol. 51 (1976); Linda Lange, 'The Function of Equal Education in Plato's *Republic* and *Laws*' in Lorenne Clark and Lynda Lange (eds) *The Sexism of Social and Political Theory: Women and Reproduction from Plato to Nietzsche* (Toronto: University of Toronto Press, 1979) and Jean Bethke Elshtain, *Public Man, Private Woman* (Oxford: Martin Robertson and Princeton University Press, 1981). Okin remains ambivalent in *Women in Western Political Thought*. Christine Pierce, in 'Equality: *Republic* V', *Monist*, vol. 57, no. 1 (Jan. 1973), gives a useful summary of how Plato's critics have generally dealt with his proposals for women in the *Republic*.
5. In the *Timaeus* (69–70), Plato further equates parts of the soul with parts of the body, such that reason relates to the head, spirit to the chest and appetite to stomach and reproductive organs.
6. *Republic*, 441.
7. *Ibid.*, 431.
8. *Ibid.*, 369.
9. *Ibid.*, 431.
10. *Ibid.*, 374–5.
11. *Ibid.*, 451.
12. *Ibid.*, 454.
13. *Ibid.*, 455.

14. *Ibid.*
15. Julia Annas, 'Plato's *Republic*', pp. 309f.
16. *Republic,* 451, 456.
17. *Ibid.,* 502.
18. *Ibid.,* 540.
19. *Ibid.,* 485.
20. *Ibid.,* 457–8.
21. *Ibid.,* 460.
22. See S. Diamond, 'Plato and the Definition of the Primitive', in S. Diamond (ed.) *Culture in History* (New York: Columbia U.P., 1960), pp. 121f.
23. *Republic,* 464.
24. Plato, *Laws,* 781.
25. *Republic,* 414.
26. *Ibid.,* 387.
27. For an excellent comparison between the *Republic* and the *Laws* on the treatment of women (between 'philosopher queens' and 'private wives'), see Okin, *Women in Western Political Thought,* ch. 2.
28. *Laws,* 739.
29. *Ibid.,* 773.
30. *Ibid.,* 783.
31. *Ibid.,* 802–3.
32. *Ibid.,* 729.
33. *Ibid.,* 738.
34. *Ibid.,* 781.
35. *Ibid.*
36. Jean-Jacques Rousseau, *Emile,* trans. Barbara Foxley (London, Melbourne and Toronto: Everyman, 1911), p. 326.
37. Elshtain develops this further in *Public Man,* ch. 1.
38. Aristotle, *Politics,* 1262b.
39. *Ibid.,* 1263b.
40. *Ibid.,* 1252a.
41. *Ibid.,* 1252b.
42. *Ibid.,* 1278b.
43. *Ibid.,* 'perhaps there is some element of the good even in the simple act of living, so long as the evils of existence do not preponderate too heavily'.
44. *Ibid.,* 1254a.
45. *Ibid.,* 1278b.
46. *Ibid.,* 1254b.
47. *Ibid.,* 1259b.
48. *Ibid.,* 1260a.
49. *Ibid.*
50. *Ibid.* A similar view had been expressed by Pericles in the funeral oration, which had in many ways captured the ideals of Athenian democracy. Speaking of 'womanly virtues', he concluded: 'Great is your glory if you fall not below the *glory* standard which nature has set for your sex, and great also is hers of whom there is least talk among men whether in praise or in blame'. Thucydides, *History of the Peloponnesian War,* trans. C. Forster-Smith (Cambridge, Mass:

Harvard University Press, 1919), 4 vols, vol. 1, sect. xlv.
51. Aristotle, *Politics,* 1277b.
52. *Ibid.,* 1259b.
53. Aristotle, *Nichomachean Ethics* in *The Works of Aristotle,* trans. W.D. Ross (Oxford: Clarendon Press, 1925), vol. IX: VIII, 1158b–61a.
54. Aristotle, *Politics,* 1269b–70a.
55. *Ibid.,* 1355a.
56. *Ibid.,* 1335b.
57. Elshtain, *Public Man,* pp. 52ff.

3. WOMEN IN MEDIEVAL THOUGHT

1. Perry Anderson, *Passages from Antiquity to Feudalism* (London: Verso, 1978), p. 131.
2. Lefkowitz and Fant, *Women's Life in Greece and Rome,* pp. 174, 175, 189.
3. Anderson, *Passages,* pp. 107ff; Engels, *Origin* pp. 77, 130f.
4. Anderson, *Ibid.,* p. 117.
5. Engels, *Origin,* p. 77.
6. Marc Bloch, *Feudal Society,* trans. L.A. Manyon (London: Routledge & Kegan Paul, 1961), vol. 1, pp. 181, 185; Anderson, *Passages* p. 159; Angela Lucas, *Women in the Middle Ages: Religion, Marriage and Letters* (Brighton: Harvester Press, 1984), p. 68; Lawrence Stone, *The Family, Sex and Marriage in England 1500–1800* (London: Weidenfeld & Nicolson, 1977), p. 31.
7. Bloch, *Feudal Society,* p. 135.
8. *Ibid.,* 136; Christopher Middleton 'The Sexual Division of Labour in Feudal England', *New Left Review,* vol. 114 (April 1979), p. 157.
9. Bloch, *Feudal Society,* p. 200.
10. Eileen Power, *Medieval Women,* ed. M.M. Postan (Cambridge: Cambridge University Press, 1975), pp. 38f.
11. Lucas, *Women in the Middle Ages,* p. 85.
12. Power, *Medieval Women,* p. 24.
13. The history of the Beguines suggests an interesting attempt to combine a religious life with economic self-sufficiency. See Gracia Clark, 'The Beguines: A Medieval Women's Community', *Quest. A Feminist Quarterly,* vol. 1, no. 4 (1975).
14. Power, *Medieval Women,* p. 71; Middleton, 'Sexual Division of Labour', p. 154.
15. Stone, *Family,* p. 81; Ann Oakley, *Housewife* (Harmondsworth: Penguin, 1976) ch.2. See also Philippe Ariès, *Centuries of Childhood,* trans. R. Baldwick (London: Jonathan Cape, 1962).
16. Middleton, 'Sexual Division of Labour', p. 155.
17. Power, *Medieval Women,* pp. 60f; Middleton, *ibid.,* p. 162.
18. Marina Warner, *Alone of All Her Sex: The Myth and the Cult of the Virgin Mary* (London: Pan Books 1985), p. 177.
19. George Sabine and Thomas Thorson, *A History of Political Thought,* Fourth edition (Hinsdale, Illinois: Dryden Press, 1973), p. 183.

20. All references to the Bible are to the Authorised Version of 1611 and are incorporated into the text.
21. Warner, *Alone,* p. 178.
22. Ian Maclean, *The Renaissance Notion of Woman* (Cambridge: Cambridge University Press, 1980), p. 16; Lucas, *Women in the Middle Ages,* p. 123.
23. See, for example, Leviticas 12:2–5, 15, 19–28. Also Kevin Harris, *Sex, Ideology and Religion: The Representation of Women in the Bible* (Brighton: Harvester Press, 1984), pp. 98–102.
24. Eva Figes, *Patriarchal Attitudes* (London: Virago, 1978), p. 41.
25. John Locke discusses this passage at length. See *The Works of John Locke* (London: C & J Rivington *et al.,* 1824), vol. 7, pp. 150–5.
26. Harris, *Sex, Ideology and Religion,* p. 48.
27. Lucas, *Women in the Middle Ages,* p. 24.
28. In *De Virginibus* (AD 377), quoted in Lucas, *ibid.*
29. St Jerome, *Comm. in Epist. ad Ephes.* III,5. Quoted in Warner, *Alone,* p. 73.
30. Augustine, *City of God,* bk 22, ch. 7. Excerpt reprinted in Martha Lee Osborne (ed.) *Women in Western Thought* (New York: Random House, 1979).
31. Augustine, *De Bono vid.,* xiii, *ibid.*
32. Augustine, *On the Trinity,* bk 12, ch. 7, *ibid.*
33. *Ibid.*
34. *Ibid.*
35. *Ibid.*
36. *Ibid.*
37. Augustine, *Confessions,* ch. 32, *ibid.*
38. Elshtain, *Public Man,* p. 73.
39. Lloyd, *Man of Reason,* p. 31. See also Rosemary Rutherford in Osborne, *Women in Western Thought,* p. 65.
40. Walter Ullman, *A History of Political Thought: The Middle Ages* (Harmondsworth: Penguin, 1965), p. 159.
41. Saint Thomas Aquinas, *Summa Theologica,* trans. Fathers of the English Dominican Province (London: Burns, Oates & Washbourne, 1921), pt 1, Q.92, art. 1, vol. 20.
42. *Ibid.*
43. *Ibid.*
44. *Ibid.,* art. 2.
45. *Ibid.*
46. *Ibid.,* art. 1.
47. *Ibid.,* pt III (supp.), Q.39, art.3; Q.81, art.3.
48. *Ibid.,* pt 1, Q.92, art. 3.
49. *Ibid.,* pt III, (supp.), Q.39, art.1.
50. Lloyd, *Man of Reason,* p. 36.
51. Bede Jarrett, *Social Theories of the Middle Ages 1200–1500* (London: Ernest Benn, 1926), says that literature from the thirteenth to the fifteenth centuries was full of warnings that women were too engrossed in labour and childbearing, to be godly (p. 90).
52. Eleanor Commo McLaughlin, in Osborne, *Women in Western*

Thought, pp. 77f; Lloyd, *Man of Reason,* p. 34.
53. Osborne, *ibid,* p. 50.
54. Ullmann, *History of Political Thought,* pp. 214–18.
55. Maclean, *Renaissance Notion of Woman,* p. 60.
56. Agnes Heller, *Renaissance Man,* trans. Richard Allen (London: Routledge & Kegan Paul, 1978), pp. 274f.
57. For an interesting account of Machiavelli's sexual imagery, see Hannah Pitkin, *Fortune Is a Woman: Gender and Politics in the Thought of Niccolo Machiavelli* (Berkeley and London: University of California Press, 1984).

4. HOBBES AND LOCKE

1. Stone, *Family,* pp. 141ff.
2. Roberta Hamilton, *The Liberation of Women: A Study of Patriarchy and Capitalism* (London: Allen & Unwin, 1978), p. 74. See her Chapter 3 for an account of the effects of Protestantism on women.
3. Stone, *Family,* p. 135. See also Elizabeth Fox-Genovese, 'Property and Patriarchy in Classical Bourgeois Theory', *Radical History Review,* vol. 4, nos 2–3 (1977), p. 37.
4. Peter Laslett (ed.) *Patriarchia and Other Political Works of Sir Robert Filmer* (Oxford: Oxford University Press, 1949). See also John Locke, *Two Treatises on Government,* Peter Laslett (ed.) (Cambridge: Cambridge University Press, 1960), I, ch.1.
5. Laslett, Introduction to *Patriarchia,* p. 26. For a more detailed account of the significance of patriarchalism for women, see Melissa Butler, 'Early Liberal Roots of Feminism: John Locke and the Attack on Patriarchy', *American Political Science Review,* vol. 72 (1978), esp. pp. 135–42.
6. See Mary Lyndon Shanley, 'Marriage Contract and Social Contract in Seventeenth-Century English Political Thought' in Jean Bethke Elshtain (ed.) *The Family in Political Thought* (Brighton: Harvester Press, 1982).
7. Thomas Hobbes, *Leviathan,* ed. John Plamenatz (London: Fontana, 1962), ch. XI, p. 123. All future references to *Leviathan* will appear in the text, giving chapters and page numbers which refer to this edition.
8. For the development of this theme, see Christine Di Stefano, 'Masculinity as Ideology in Political Theory: Hobbesian Man Considered', *Women's Studies International Forum,* vol. 6, (1983). See also Chapter 10, below.
9. Gordon Schochet, *Patriarchalism and Political Thought* (Oxford: Basil Blackwell, 1975), pp. 239ff.
10. Ibid., ch. XII; Richard Allen Chapman, '*Leviathan* Writ Small: Thomas Hobbes on the Family', *American Political Science Review,* vol. 69, no. 1 (1975); R.W.K. Hinton, 'Husbands, Fathers and Conquerors', *Political Studies,* vol. XVI, no. 1 (1968); Theresa Brennan and Carole Pateman, '"Mere Auxiliaries to the Commonwealth":

Women and the Origins of Liberalism', *Political Studies,* vol. XXVII, no. 2 (1979)

11. Brennan and Pateman, *ibid.,* p. 158; Chapman, '*Leviathan* Writ Small'.
12. John Zvesper, 'Hobbes' Individualistic Analysis of the Family, *Politics,* vol. 5, no. 2 (Oct. 1985).
13. Brennan and Pateman, 'Mere Auxiliaries', p. 185.
14. Thomas Hobbes, *De Corpore Politico,* Pt II, ch. 4, §8. In *The English Works of Thomas Hobbes,* ed. Sir William Molesworth, (London: John Bohn, 1840), vol. 4, p. 175. This is very similar to the power which Filmer gives to fathers.
15. Chapman, '*Leviathan* Writ Small', p. 82. Also *Leviathan,* XXX, p. 300.
16. Schochet, *Patriarchalism,* pp. 230, 235.
17. Keith Thomas, 'The Social Origins of Hobbes' Political Thought' in K. Brown (ed.) *Hobbes Studies* (Cambridge: Cambridge University Press, 1965), p. 198.
18. Thomas Hobbes, *De Cive,* IX, 3, in Molesworth, vol. 2, p. 116; *Leviathan,* XX, p. 198.
19. Thomas Hobbes, *Elements of Law,* ed. F. Tonnies (London: Frank Cass, 1969), 2nd edn., Pt 2, IV, 5–6, p. 133; *De Cive,* IX, 5–7, Molesworth, pp. 117–19.
20. Okin, *Women in Western Political Thought,* pp. 197–9; Brennan and Pateman, 'Mere Auxiliaries', p. 191.
21. Brennan and Pateman, *ibid.,* p. 190; Zvesper, 'Hobbes' Individualistic Analysis', does however incline towards such a solution; see p. 31.
22. Chapman, '*Leviathan* Writ Small', pp. 82ff.
23. Brennan and Pateman, 'Mere Auxiliaries', p. 190.
24. *Ibid.* The quotation is from Hobbes' *Elements of Law,* pt. II, IV, 14.
25. *Ibid.,* p. 185.
26. *Leviathan,* Review and Conclusion, quoted in Chapman, '*Leviathan* Writ Small', p. 76.
27. See Laslett's Introduction to Locke's *Two Treatises,* pp. 63–75.
28. Locke, *Two Treatises,* I: 29, 44. All future references to this work appear in the text and are drawn from the Laslett edn.
29. For development of this theme see Lorenne Clark, 'Women and Locke: Who Owns the Apples in the Garden of Eden?' in Clark and Lange, *The Sexism of Social and Political Theory.*
30. When Locke studied at Oxford, classical texts were still the main source of scientific knowledge, and Aristotle's views on generation would have been widely accepted. See Maurice Cranston, *John Locke: A Biography* (Oxford: Oxford University Press, 1985), p. 39.
31. Fox-Genovese, 'Property and Patriarchy', pp. 38, 55.
32. Brennan and Pateman, 'Mere Auxiliaries', p. 194. See also Carole Pateman, *The Problem of Political Obligation: A Critique of Liberal Theory* (Cambridge: Polity Press, 1985), pp. 75f.
33. Schochet, *Patriarchalism,* p. 252.
34. Lorenne Clark offers such an interpretation in 'Women and Locke'. It accords well, of course, with a Marxist account.
35. John Dunn, *The Political Thought of John Locke* (Cambridge:

Cambridge University Press, 1969), p. 140.

36. Dunn, *ibid.,* pp. 138ff, and Parry, *John Locke* (London: Allen & Unwin, 1978), p. 106, agree that Locke probably envisaged other modes of express consent which he failed to specify. Of course, there is no knowing whether women would have qualified for these. But the alternative these critics suggest refers to oaths of allegiance. These were common for seventeenth-century office-holders and something of the sort was demanded of all adult males in 1650. But in neither case would women have been included.

37. Regarding women's labour during Locke's time, see Alice Clark, *Working Life of Women in the Seventeenth Century* (London: Routledge & Kegan Paul, 1982).

38. Fox-Genovese, 'Property and Patriarchy', p. 51.

39. Parry, *John Locke,* p. 50.

40. C.B. Macpherson, *The Theory of Possessive Individualism: Hobbes to Locke* (Oxford: Oxford University Press, 1962), p. 223.

41. John Locke, *The Reasonableness of Christianity,* quoted in Macpherson, pp. 224f.

42. John Locke, *Some Thoughts Concerning Education* in *The Works of John Locke in Nine Volumes* (London: C. & J. Rivington *et al.,* 1824), vol. 8, §216. Locke does not advise an identical education for boys and girls, but he does seem to think that one will be possible apart from obvious differences which he does not bother to mention. (§6). He does explicitly counsel a regimen of fresh air and exercise for the girl (§9) while condemning the incitement of vanity in her (§37).

43. Brennan and Pateman, 'Mere Auxiliaries', p. 195.

44. Okin, *Women in Western Political Thought,* pp. 200f.

45. Butler, 'Early Liberal Roots of Feminism', pp. 146ff.

46. A recent article by Susan Mendus discloses striking similarities between, for example, Kant's and Locke's theories of women: Kant is only more explicit in relegating women to passive (as opposed to active) citizenship on the grounds that their dependence renders them unsuitable for law-making. However he also underwrites the contingencies of the marital situation with a more explicit account of natural psychological differences by drawing on Rousseau's ideas. See 'Kant: "An Honest but Narrow-minded Bourgeois"?' in Ellen Kennedy and Susan Mendus (eds) *Women in Western Political Philosophy* (Brighton: Wheatsheaf Books, 1987). Brennan and Pateman are clearly aware of the parallel when they borrow Kant's reference to women as 'mere auxiliaries to the commonwealth' to entitle their critique of Hobbes and Locke.

47. Christopher Hill, *The World Turned Upside Down* (Harmondsworth: Penguin, 1975), p. 311.

48. Quoted by H.N. Brailsford, *The Levellers and the English Revolution* (Nottingham: Spokesman, 1976), pp. 316f.

49. Joan Kinnaird, 'Mary Astell: Inspired by Ideas (1668–1731)' in Dale Spender (ed.) *Feminist Theorists: Three Centuries of Women's Intellectual Traditions* (London: The Women's Press, 1983), argues that Astell's inspiration was mainly Platonic and Cartesian.

5. ROUSSEAU AND WOLLSTONECRAFT

1. J-J. Rousseau, *A Discourse on the Origin of Inequality* in *The Social Contract and Discourses,* trans. G.D.H. Cole (London: Everyman, 1913), p. 205.
2. *Ibid.,* p. 185.
3. *Ibid.,* p. 192.
4. For further discussion about the relationship between sexuality and sociability in Rousseau, see Joel Schwarz, *The Sexual Politics of Jean-Jacques Rousseau* (Chicago: University of Chicago Press, 1984).
5. Rousseau, *Discourse on Inequality,* p. 195.
6. *Ibid.,* pp. 195f.
7. J-J. Rousseau, *Emile,* trans. Barbara Foxley, (London, Melbourne and Toronto: Everyman, 1911), p. 370. The theme of a disjunction between natural and historical models of woman is also developed by Okin, *Women in Western Political Thought,* ch. 6.
8. Rousseau, *ibid.,* p. 393.
9. Rousseau, *The Social Contract and Discourses,* p. 4.
10. Rousseau, *A Discourse on Political Economy,* in *ibid.,* p. 234.
11. *Ibid.*
12. *Ibid.,* p. 233. See also *The Social Contract,* p. 4
13. Rousseau, *Emile,* p. 326.
14. Rousseau, *Discourse on Inequality,* p. 199.
15. Okin, *Women in Western Political Thought,* p. 150.
16. For an account of the relationship between the two texts as well as a summary of Rousseau's novel, see Victor Wexler, '"Made for Man's Delight": Rousseau as Anti-Feminist', *American Historical Review,* vol. 81, no. 2 (April 1976).
17. Rousseau, *Emile,* p. 321.
18. *Ibid.,* p. 324.
19. *Ibid.,* p. 16.
20. *Ibid.,* pp. 325f.
21. *Ibid.,* p. 345.
22. *Ibid.,* p. 353. On the significance of Rousseau's descriptions of the family for women's oppression, see Susan Moller Okin, 'Women and the Making of the Sentimental Family', *Philosophy and Public Affairs,* vol. 11, no. 1 (Winter 1982).
23. Okin, *Women in Western Political Thought,* p. 99.
24. Rousseau, *Emile,* pp. 325, 328f, 33, 339ff, 401.
25. *Ibid.,* pp. 340, 349.
26. *Ibid.,* p. 350.
27. *Ibid.,* p. 359.
28. See Carole Pateman, 'Women and Consent', *Political Theory* (May 1980).
29. Rousseau, *Emile,* p. 348.
30. For a very different conclusion, see Margaret Canovan, 'Rousseau's Two Concepts of Citizenship' in Kennedy and Mendus, *Women in Western Political Philosophy.* To reach her tentative conclusion that Rousseau's notion of citizenship can be given a feminist form, she has in

essence to reduce Rousseau to Locke while at the same time ignoring the significance that women's domestic role had for male citizenship.

31. O'Brien, *Politics of Reproduction,* p. 95.
32. Rousseau, *Discourse on Inequality,* p. 152.
33. Rousseau, *A Discourse on the Moral Effects of the Arts and Sciences* in *The Social Contract and Discourses,* p. 133n.
34. Rousseau, *Emile.*
35. Rousseau, *Discourse on Inequality,* p. 203.
36. Rousseau, *A Letter from M. Rousseau, of Geneva, to M. D'Alembert of Paris, Concerning the Effects of Theatrical Entertainment on the Manners of Mankind* (London: J. Nourse, 1759), p. 57.
37. Rousseau, *Emile,* p. 13.
38. *Ibid.,* p. 326.
39. O'Brien, *Politics of Reproduction,* p. 95.
40. Carole Pateman, '"The Disorder of Women": Women, Love, and the Sense of Justice', *Ethics,* vol. 91 (Oct. 1980), pp. 29f.
41. Lynda Lange, 'Rousseau: Women and the General Will' in Clarke and Lange, *Sexism of Social and Political Theory,* p. 50. But see also Judith Shklar, *Men and Citizens: A Study of Rousseau's Social Theory* (Cambridge: Cambridge University Press, 1969), for an account of the family as an egalitarian Utopia for Rousseau, pp. 21–8. She points out that in Sparta the family can be safely abolished: here the commitment to duty is so strongly internalized that compassionate ties appear superfluous.
42. Rousseau, *Social Contract,* pp. 55, 35f., although Rousseau does warn against a situation where 'domestic cares are all-absorbing', p. 78.
43. *Ibid.,* p. 79.
44. See Dale Spender, *Women of Ideas (and What Men Have Done to Them)* (London: Ark, 1983) Pt I. Also Barbara Taylor, *Eve and the New Jerusalem* (London: Virago, 1983), pp. 1ff.
45. Claire Tomalin, *The Life and Death of Mary Wollstonecraft* (Harmondsworth: Penguin, 1977), p. 51.
46. *Ibid.,* p. 132.
47. Wollstonecraft, *A Vindication of the Rights of Men* in *A Mary Wollstonecraft Reader,* ed. B. Soloman and P. Berggren (New York: New American Library Press, 1983).
48. Page References to Wollstonecraft's *A Vindication of the Rights of Woman* are integrated into the text. They are all taken from the Everyman edition (London, 1929).
49. See Miriam Brody, 'Mary Wollstonecraft: Sexuality and Women's Rights' in Spender, *Feminist Theorists.*
50. See R.M. Janes, 'On the Reception of Mary Wollstonecraft's *A Vindication of the Rights of Woman'*, *Journal of the History of Ideas,* vol. 39 (April–June 1978).
51. Taylor, *Eve,* p. 5.
52. Carolyn Korsmeyer points out that the struggle against the C18 stereotype was nevertheless important to women of all classes. See her 'Reason and Morals in the Early Feminist Movement: Mary Wollstonecraft', *Philosophical Forum (Boston),* vol. 5, nos 1 & 2

(1973–4), p. 108.

53. Mary Wollstonecraft, *Thoughts on the Education of Daughters* in *A Mary Wollstonecraft Reader,* pp. 36–9. Her solutions here are only, however, those of friendship, religion and genteel education.
54. Ray Strachey, *The Cause* (London: Virago, 1978), p. 12.
55. William Godwin, *Enquiry Concerning Political Justice* (Harmondsworth: Penguin, 1976), Bk 8, ch. 8.
56. See Taylor, *Eve,* p. 5.

6. J.S. MILL

1. Okin, *Women in Political Thought,* p. 197.
2. J.S. Mill, *Autobiography,* ed. Jack Stillinger (Oxford: Oxford University Press, 1971), p. 147n. See also J.S. Mill, *The Subjection of Women* (London: Everyman, 1929), p. 219.
3. See Okin, *Women in Western Political Thought,* Pt 4; Leslie Goldstein, 'Mill, Marx, and Women's Liberation', *Journal of History of Philosophy,* vol. XVIII, no. 3 (July 1980); Julia Annas, 'Mill and the Subjection of Women', *Philosophy* 52 (1977); Richard Krouse, 'Patriarchal Liberalism and Beyond: From John Stuart Mill to Harriet Taylor' in Elshtain, *The Family;* Kate Millett, *Sexual Politics* (London: Virago, 1977), pp.88–108.
4. Adam Smith, *The Wealth of Nations,* ed. A Skinner (Harmondsworth: Penguin, 1970), p. 170. For a broader appreciation of Smith on women, see Jane Rendall, 'Virtue and Commerce: Women in the Making of Adam Smith's Political Economy' in Kennedy and Mendus, *Women in Western Political Philosophy.*
5. Smith, *ibid.,* p. 183.
6. *Ibid.,* p. 184.
7. *Ibid.,* p. 431.
8. Karl Marx, *The Economic and Philosophic Manuscripts of 1844,* ed. Dirk Struik (New York: International Publishers, 1964), p. 72.
9. J.S. Mill, *Principles of Political Economy,* ed. D. Winch (Harmondsworth: Penguin, 1970), p. 125.
10. *Ibid.,* p. 126.
11. J.S. Mill, *On Liberty* in *Utilitarianism,* ed. Mary Warnock (London: Fontana, 1962), p. 135.
12. *Ibid.,* p. 238. See also *Principles,* p. 139.
13. *Ibid.,* p. 242.
14. Lea Campos Boralevi, 'Utilitarianism and Feminism' in Kennedy and Mendus, *Women in Western Political Philosophy,* discusses the formal advances which utilitarianism brought to questions of sexual equality, although she never suggests that its view of human nature might not be a neutral one.
15. J.S. Mill, *On Liberty,* p. 136.
16. J.S. Mill, *Principles,* bk IV, ch. VII, esp. section 6.
17. *Ibid.,* p. 138.

18. *Ibid.,* p. 123.
19. J.S. Mill, *Representation of the People Bill* (May 20 1867), *Hansard,* vol. CLXXXVII, pp. 817–29, p. 325. See also Mill, *Subjection,* p. 313 and regarding the working-class vote, *Representative Government* in J.S. Mill, *Utilitarianism, Liberty, Representative Government* (London: Everyman, 1910), p. 277.
20. J.S. Mill, *Subjection,* p. 259.
21. *Ibid.,* pp. 260f.
22. J.S. Mill, *On Liberty,* p. 238.
23. J.S. Mill, *Subjection,* pp. 253, 296.
24. *Ibid.* p. 298.
25. *Ibid.,* p. 298ff.
26. *Ibid.,* p. 254.
27. *Ibid.,* pp. 255, 303.
28. *Ibid.,* p. 304.
29. *Ibid.,* p. 305.
30. *Ibid.,* p. 307.
31. Strachey, *The Cause,* pp. 160, 201.
32. Annas, 'Mill and Subjection', p. 179.
33. J.S. Mill, *Subjection,* p. 245.
34. *Ibid.,* pp. 296, 247f, 251.
35. *Ibid.,* p. 232.
36. *Ibid.,* pp. 263ff.
37. *Ibid.,* p. 256.
38. *Ibid.,* p. 264.
39. *Ibid.,* p. 252.
40. Harriet Taylor, *Enfranchisement of Women,* ed. Kate Soper (London: Virago, 1983), p. 20.
41. *Ibid.,* p. 21.
42. J.S. Mill, *Subjection,* pp. 273ff.
43. J.S. Mill, *On Liberty,* p. 138.
44. J.S. Mill, *Representation, Hansard,* p. 820.
45. Strachey, *The Cause,* p. 67.
46. J.S. Mill, *Subjection,* p. 237; cf. *Principles,* p. 121.
47. *Ibid.,* p. 223.
48. *Ibid.,* pp. 259f. See also *Principles,* p. 133, where Mill offers similar faith in progress towards association, this time among the working class.
49. *Ibid.,* p. 219.
50. *Ibid.,* p. 223.
51. *Ibid.,* p. 228; cf. Taylor, *Enfranchisement,* p. 23.
52. J.S. Mill, *Subjection,* p. 311.
53. Annas, 'Mill and Subjection', p. 181; Soper, Intro. to Mill and Taylor, p. V; Okin, *Women in Western Political Thought,* p. 208. But see Mill's parliamentary speech, *Hansard* pp. 317f: 'I do not mean that the electoral franchise, or any other public function, is an abstract right, and that to withhold it from anyone, on sufficient grounds of expediency, is a personal wrong; it is a complete misunderstanding of the principle I maintain, to confound this with it; my argument is entirely one of expediency . . . there is an important branch of

expediency called justice; and justice . . . does require that we should not, capriciously and without cause, withhold from one what we give to another'.

54. J.S. Mill, *Subjection*, pp. 219, 237.
55. *Ibid.*, p. 238.
56. J.S. Mill, *Utilitarianism* in *Utilitarianism*, ch. V.
57. *Ibid.*, p. 300.
58. *Ibid.*, p. 320.
59. Alan Ryan, *J.S. Mill* (London: Routledge & Kegan Paul, 1974), p. 121.

7. SOCIALISM

1. William Thompson, *An Inquiry into the Principles of the Distribution of Wealth Most Conducive to Human Happiness* (London: William S. Orr & Co., 1850), p. 289.
2. Taylor, *Eve*, p. 22.
3. R.K.P. Pankhurst, *William Thompson (1775–1833): Britain's Pioneer Socialist, Feminist, and Co-operator* (London: Watts & Co., 1954), p. 73.
4. J.S. Mill, *Autobiography*, p. 75. Mill makes clear in this reference that he is familiar with both the *Inquiry* and the *Appeal*, referring to Thompson himself as 'a very estimable man, with whom I was well acquainted'.
5. James Mill, *Essay on Government* in J. Lively and J. Rees (eds) *Utilitarian Logic and Politics* (Oxford: Clarendon Press, 1978), p. 79. James Mill's position was here at odds with Bentham's as well as his son's. See T. Ball, 'Utilitarianism, Feminism and the Franchise: James Mill and his Critics', *History of Political Thought*, 1 (1980); Miriam Williford, 'Bentham on the Rights of Women', *Journal of the History of Ideas'*, vol. 86 (Jan.–Mar. 1975).
6. William Thompson, *Appeal of One-half of the Human Race, Women, against the Pretensions of the Other Half, Men, to Retain them in Political, and hence in Civil and Domestic, Slavery* (London: Virago, 1983), p. 118.
7. *Ibid.*, pp. 123, 177ff.
8. *Ibid.*, p. xxx.
9. *Ibid.*, p. 149.
10. *Ibid.*, p. xxix.
11. *Ibid.*, p. 65.
12. *Ibid.*, p. 132.
13. *Ibid.*, p. xxx.
14. *Ibid.*, pp. 197ff.
15. *Ibid.*, p. xxvi. Emphasis added.
16. *Ibid.*, p. 201.
17. *Ibid.*, p. 179.
18. *Ibid.*, p. 204. See also Thompson, *Inquiry*, pp. 213ff, 417.
19. Thompson, *Inquiry*, p. 405.

20. *Ibid.,* pp. 414–17.
21. Thompson, *Appeal,* p. 211.
22. Robert Owen, *Lectures on the Marriages of the Priesthood of the Old Immoral World, Delivered in the Year 1835, Before the Passing of the New Marriage Act,* Fourth edition with Appendix (Leeds: J. Hobson, 1840), p. 67; see also pp. 23, 24.
23. *Ibid.,* pp. 8, 11, 54.
24. *Ibid.,* p. 37.
25. *Ibid.,* p. 27.
26. *Ibid.,* p. 17.
27. *Ibid.,* p. 63.
28. *Ibid.,* pp. 49, 65, 76. For a similar view, see Godwin's *Enquiry,* p. 763.
29. *Ibid.,* pp. 54f.
30. *Ibid.,* pp. 8, 12, 15, 75.
31. Taylor, *Eve,* ch. 8.
32. Quoted in George Barnsby, *Robert Owen and the First Socialists in the Black Country* (Wolverhampton: Integrated Publishing Services, 1984), p. 3.
33. See Gail Malmgreen, *Neither Bread nor Roses: Utopian Feminists and the English Working Class, 1800–1850* (Brighton: Brighton Resource Centre, 1978) pp. 20–35.
34. Frank Manuel, *The Prophets of Paris* (Cambridge, Mass: Harvard University Press, 1962), p. 226.
35. *Ibid.,* p. 157.
36. Elizabeth Altman, 'The Philosophical Bases of Feminism: The Feminist Doctrines of the Saint-Simonians and Charles Fourier', *Philosophical Forum (Boston),* vol. 7 (spring–summer 1976), p. 280.
37. *Ibid.,* pp. 278–80. See also Leslie Goldstein, 'Early Feminist Themes in French Utopian Socialism: The St-Simonians and Fourier', *Journal of the History of Ideas,* vol. 43, no. 1 (1982).
38. Juliet Mitchell decribes Fourier as 'the most ardent and voluminous advocate of women's liberation and of sexual freedom among the early socialists', *Woman's Estate,* p. 77.
39. Jonathan Beecher and Richard Bienvenu (eds) *The Utopian Vision of Charles Fourier: Selected Texts on Work, Love and Passionate Attraction* (London: Jonathan Cape, 1972), p. 371.
40. *Ibid.,* p. 747.
41. Malmgreen, *Neither Bread nor Roses,* p. 8.
42. Beecher and Bienvenu, *Utopian Vision,* p. 311.
43. *Ibid.,* p. 312.
44. *Ibid.,* p. 245.
45. M.C. Spencer, *Charles Fourier* (Boston: Twayne Publishers, 1981), p. 70. Spencer argues that behind this obsession with food, there lies a matriarchal society: 'the image of the Mother who dispenses *oral* satisfaction'.
46. Beecher and Bienvenu, *Utopian Vision,* p. 308.
47. *Ibid.,* p. 261.
48. *Ibid.,* p. 317.
49. *Ibid.*

8. HEGEL, MARX AND ENGELS

1. For recent discussion of Hegel's treatment of women, see Susan Easton, 'Hegel and Feminism', *Radical Philosophy*, vol. 38 (1984); Susan Easton, 'Slavery and Freedom: A Feminist Reading of Hegel', *Politics*, vol. 5, no. 2 (Oct. 1985); Carol Gould in Osborne, *Women in Western Thought*, ch. 11; Joanna Landes, 'Hegel's Conception of the Family' in Elshtain, *The Family*; Peter Steinberger, 'Hegel on Marriage and Politics', *Political Studies*, vol. XXXIV, no. 4 (Dec. 1986); Joanna Hodge, 'Women and the Hegelian State' in Kennedy and Mendus, *Women in Western Political Philosophy*. Interesting discussions also occur in Lloyd, *Man of Reason*, pp. 80–5; O'Brien, *Politics of Reproduction*; Okin, *Women in Western Political Thought*; Elshtain, *Public Man*.
2. G.W.F. Hegel, *The Phenomenology of Mind*, trans. J. Baillie (New York: Harper & Row, 1967), p. 468; *Philosophy of Right*, trans. T.M. Knox (Oxford: Oxford University Press, 1967), §157, p. 110.
3. O'Brien, *Politics of Reproduction*, p. 25.
4. *Philosophy of Right*, §161, p. 111; *Phenomenology* pp. 474ff.
5. *Phenomenology*, pp. 470f.
6. *Philosophy of Right*, §103, Addition, p. 262.
7. *Ibid.*, §162, p. 111.
8. *Ibid.*, §105, Addition, p. 262.
9. Gould, in *Women in Western Thought*, pp. 175ff.
10. Although Hegel does discuss the need for family property (ethical because for collective rather than selfish use), he relates it specifically to the male 'family head' who goes into civil society to acquire it. Hegel writes, 'it is his prerogative to go out and work for its living; to attend to its needs, and to cover and administer its capital'. *Philosophy of Right*, §171, p. 116.
11. *Ibid.*, §166, Addition, p. 264.
12. *Ibid.*, §166, p. 114; §107, Addition, p. 263.
13. *Ibid.*, §106, Addition, p. 263.
14. *Ibid.*, §107, pp. 263f.
15. *Phenomenology*, p. 496.
16. *Philosophy of Right*, §177, pp. 118f; *Phenomenology*, p. 478.
17. Mitchell, *Woman's Estate*, p. 80.
18. Marx, *1844 Manuscripts*, p. 135.
19. *Ibid.*, p. 134.
20. *Ibid.*
21. Karl Marx, *Capital*, vol. 1, trans. S. Moore and E. Aveling (Moscow: Progress Publishers, 1954), pp. 82, 332. See also Marx and Engels, *The German Ideology*, ed. C.J. Arthur (New York: International Publishers, 1970), pp. 44, 51f.
22. Marx and Engels, *German Ideology*, p. 52.
23. Engels, *Origin*, p. 75.
24. Marx, *1844 Manuscripts*, p. 133.
25. *Ibid.*, p. 134.
26. See Alfred Schmidt, *The Concept of Nature in Marx*, trans. Ben Fowkes

(London: New Left Books, 1971), esp. ch. 2.

27. Marx, 'Afterword' to the 2nd German edn of *Capital,* vol. 1, p. 29.

28. Shulamith Firestone, *The Dialectic of Sex* (London: The Women's Press, 1979), p. 12 *et passim.* Among Marxist feminists the method is self-consciously applied, of course.

29. For example, Jane Humphries, 'The Origins of the Family: Born out of Scarcity not Wealth' in Janet Sayers, Mary Evans and Nanneke Redclift (eds) *Engels Revisited: New Feminist Essays* (London and New York: Tavistock, 1987). For the alternative view, closer to my own, see Terrel Carver, 'Engels' Feminism', *History of Political Thought,* vol. vi, no. 3 (Winter 1985).

30. Marx and Engels, *German Ideology,* p. 49.

31. Engels, *Origin,* pp. 25f.

32. *Ibid.,* 26.

33. *Ibid.*

34. *Ibid.,* p. 45.

35. *Ibid.,* p. 26.

36. *Ibid.,* pp. 57f.

37. *Ibid.,* pp. 52, 59.

38. *Ibid.,* pp. 64f.

39. *Ibid.,* p. 152.

40. *Ibid.,* p. 64.

41. *Ibid.,* p. 152.

42. Lise Vogel, *Marxism and the Oppression of Women: Toward a Unitary Theory* (London: Pluto, 1983), p. 62. For other criticisms. most of which focus on the issue of Engels's naturalism, see Diana Leonard, 'The Origin of the Family, Private Property and Marxist Feminism?' *Trouble and Strife,* vol. 3 (summer 1984); Rosalind Coward, *Patriarchal Precedents* (London: Routledge & Kegan Paul, 1983), ch. 5; Rosalyn Delmar, 'Looking Again at Engels' *Origin of the Family, Private Property and the State'* in Juliet Mitchell and Anne Oakley (eds) *The Rights and Wrongs of Women* (Harmondsworth: Penguin, 1976); also the collection of essays edited by Sayers *et al., Engels Revisited.* Raya Dunayevskaya gives an interesting comparison of Engels's *Origin* and Marx's *Ethnological Notebooks* in her 'Marx's "New Humanism" and the Dialectics of Women's Liberation in Primitive and Modern Societies', *Praxis International,* vol. 3, no. 4 (Jan. 1984).

43. Engels, *Origin,* p. 81.

44. *Ibid.,* p. 38.

45 Marx, *Capital,* vol. 1, p. 82.

46. Engels, *The Condition of the Working Class in England* in Marx and Engels, *Collected Works,* vol. 4 (London: Lawrence & Wishart, 1976), p. 435.

47. *Ibid.,* p. 438f.

48. Engels, *Origin,* p. 81.

49. *Ibid.,* p. 83.

50. *Ibid.,* pp. 83, 152.

51. Richard Stites, *The Women's Liberation Movement in Russia: Feminism, Nihilism, and Bolshevism 1860–1930* (Princeton, NJ: Princeton University Press, 1978), p. 262.

52. Marx, *Capital*, vol. 1, p. 460; Engels, *Condition*, pp. 436ff.
53. Engels, *Origin*, p. 80.
54. Vogel, *Marxism and the Oppression of Women*, pp. 84ff.
55. Marx, *Capital*, vol. 1.
56. Heidi Hartmann, 'The Unhappy Marriage of Marxism and Feminism: Towards a More Progressive Union', *Capital and Class*, no. 8 (1979), p. 8.
57. Alison Jaggar, *Feminist Politics and Human Nature* (Brighton: Harvester Press, 1983), p. 67.
58. Marx and Engels, *The Communist Manifesto*, in L. Feuer (ed.) *Marx and Engels: Basic Writings on Politics and Philosophy* (London: Fontana, 1969), p. 56.

9. SOCIAL DEMOCRATS AND BOLSHEVIKS

1. Richard Evans, *The Feminists* (London: Croom Helm, 1977), pp. 155, 158.
2. Coward, *Patriarchal Precedents*, pp. 172f. For a useful discussion of the SPD's early years and its attitude towards feminism, see Hal Draper and Anne Lipow, 'Marxist Women versus Bourgeois Feminism' in Ralph Miliband (ed.) *Socialist Register* (London: Merlin Press, 1976).
3. Philip Foner (ed.) *Clara Zetkin: Selected Writings* (New York: International Publishers, 1984), p. 79; Coward, *Patriarchal Precedents*, pp. 171, 177.
4. August Bebel, *Woman under Socalism*, trans. Daniel de Leon (New York: Schocken Books, 1971). This is a translation of the 33rd edn of the previously titled *Woman in the Past, Present and Future*.
5. *Ibid.*, p. 192.
6. *Ibid.*, pp. 86, 222.
7. *Ibid.*, p. 117.
8. *Ibid.*, p. 121.
9. *Ibid.*, p. 192.
10. *Ibid.*, pp. 126, 135.
11. *Ibid.*, pp. 105, 167ff. Zetkin offers further reasons for women's lower wages: because women are assumed to perform their own domestic work, no family wage is given to them. Also, they have often worked from home using primitive tools and the idea of their lesser productivity thrived, justifying their lower wage. See 'For the Liberation of Women' (1889) in *Selected Writings*, p. 48.
12. Bebel, *Woman*, p. 90.
13. *Ibid.*, p. 185.
14. *Ibid.*, pp. 238f.
15. *Ibid.*, pp. 326, 347.
16. *Ibid.*, p. 324.
17. *Ibid.*, p. 371.
18. *Ibid.*, p. 347.
19. *Ibid.*, p. 282.

20. *Ibid.*, pp. 121, 195, 180.
21. *Ibid.*, p. 348.
22. Vogel, *Marxism and the Oppression of Women*, p. 101. See also Mitchell, *Woman's Estate*, p. 80.
23. Bebel, *Woman*, p. 378.
24. Eleanor Marx Aveling and Edward Aveling, 'The Woman Question: From a Socialist Point of View', *Westminster Review*, vol. 125 (1886).
25. *Ibid.*, p. 209.
26. *Ibid.*, p. 218.
27. *Ibid.*, p. 222.
28. *Ibid.*, p. 211.
29. *Ibid.*, p. 213.
30. Zetkin, 'Only with the Proletarian Woman Will Socialism Be Victorious'! References are to the version published by Draper and Lipow in *The Socialist Register* (1976) but the speech is also printed in *Selected Writings*, pp. 72–83. For further useful commentary on Zetkin's work, see Richard Evans, 'Theory and Practice in German Social Democracy 1880–1914; Clara Zetkin and the Socialist Theory of Women's Emancipation', *History of Political Thought*, vol. III, no. 2 (summer 1982).
31. Zetkin, *ibid.*, p. 195.
32. *Ibid.*, p. 198.
33. *Ibid.*, p. 199.
34. *Ibid.*, p. 201. For a further account of Zetkin's romanticized view of the socialist family, see her article in *Die Gleichheit* (Jan. 1898), quoted in Evans, 'Theory and Practice', p. 296.
35. Evans, *ibid.*, p. 293.
36. For a fuller discussion of this tendency, see Evans, pp. 300–4.
37. For more detailed accounts of Russian feminism and Soviet responses, see Stites, *Women's Liberation Movement in Russia;* Evans, *The Feminists;* Beatrice Brodsky Farnsworth, 'Bolshevism, the Woman Question and Aleksandra Kollontai', *American Historical Review*, vol. 81, no. 2 (1976); Sheila Rowbotham, *Women, Resistance and Revolution* (Harmondsworth: Penguin, 1972), ch. 6.
38. For an account of Kollontai's work here, see Cathy Porter's biography, *Alexandra Kollontai* (London: Virago, 1980), ch. 13.
39. Stites, *Women's Liberation Movement in Russia*, p. 339. Also Zetkin, 'In the Muslim Women's Club' (1926) in *Selected Writings*, pp. 158–65.
40. Lenin, 'The Tasks of the Working Women's Movement in the Soviet Republic', *Collected Works*, vol. 30 (Moscow: Progress Publishers, 1965), pp. 40–6.
41. *Ibid.*, p. 43.
42. *Ibid.*, p. 409.
43. Alexandra Kollontai, 'Social Bases of the Woman Question', in Alix Holt (ed.) *Selected Writings of Alexandra Kollontai* (London: Allison & Busby, 1977), p. 64.
44. *Ibid.*, p. 64.
45. Kollontai, 'Prostitution and Ways of Fighting It', *ibid.*, p. 270.
46. Kollontai, 'Theses on Communist Morality in the Sphere of Marital

Relations', *ibid.*, p. 225.

47. Kollontai, 'Sexual Relations in the Class Struggle', *ibid.*, p. 240.
48. *Ibid.*, p. 249.
49. *Ibid.*, p. 242.
50. Kollontai, 'Communism and the Family', *ibid.*, p. 252.
51. *Ibid.*, p. 256. On Kollontai's utopianism, see Marie Marmo Mullaney, 'Alexandra Kollontai and the Vision of a Socialist Feminist Utopia', *Alternative Futures*, vol. 4, nos 2–3 (1981).
52. Kollontai, *ibid.*, p. 255.
53. Kollontai, 'Prostitution and Ways of Fighting it', *ibid.*, p. 273.
54. Kollontai, 'The Labour of Women in the Revolution of the Economy', *ibid.*, p. 143.
55. Kollontai, 'Communism and the Family', *ibid.*, p. 256.
56. Kollontai, 'Theses on Communist Morality', *ibid.*, p. 228.
57. *Ibid.*, p. 227.
58. Kollontai, 'Prostitution and Ways of Fighting it', *ibid.*, p. 274.
59. Sigmund Freud, *Civilisation and Its Discontents,* trans. Joan Riviere (London: Hogarth Press, 1972), p. 59. Kollontai could not have known this work, written in 1930, but there are striking similarities here.
60. Kollontai, 'Make Way for Winged Eros', *Selected Writings,* pp. 288, 291.
61. Kollontai, *Love of Worker Bees* (London: Virago, 1977), p. 175.
62. *Ibid.*, pp. 266ff.
63. Kollontai, 'Make Way for Winged Eros', *Selected Writings,* p. 289.
64. Kollontai, 'Theses on Communist Morality', *ibid.*, pp. 228f.
65. See especially 'The Labour of Women in the Revolution of the Economy', *ibid.*, p. 142–9. This is the title of a lecture series Kollontai delivered in 1921. Its productivist/utilitarian ethos is explored by Jacqueline Heinen in 'Kollontai and the History of Women's Oppression', *New Left Review*, vol. 110 (July–Aug. 1978).
66. Alix Kates Shulman (ed.) *Red Emma Speaks: The Selected Speeches and Writings of the Anarchist and Feminist Emma Goldman* (London: Wildwood House, 1979).
67. For an interesting fictional account of what this might mean in a democratic welfare state, see Zoë Fairbairns, *Benefits* (London: Virago, 1979).

10. CONTEMPORARY FEMINISM AND POLITICAL THOUGHT

1. Liberal feminism has been far more popular in the United States than in Britain. The first important text of the second wave there was Betty Friedan's liberal *The Feminine Mystique* (Harmondsworth: Penguin, 1965). For fuller theoretical accounts of this approach's contemporary significance and shortcomings, see Alison Jaggar, *Feminist Politics and Human Nature,* and Zillah Eisenstein, *The Radical Future of Liberal Feminism* (New York: Longman, 1981).

2. Louis Althusser, 'Ideology and Ideological State Apparatuses' in *Essays on Ideology* (London: Verso, 1984).
3. de Beauvoir, *The Second Sex*, p. 91.
4. *Ibid.*, p. 691.
5. *Ibid.*, p. 60.
6. Subsequently, de Beauvoir would be able to declare herself a feminist. See Alice Schwartzer (ed.) *Simone de Beauvoir Today: Conversations 1972–82*, trans. Marianne Howarth (London: Hogarth Press, 1984).
7. de Beauvoir, *The Second Sex*, p. 690.
8. de Beauvoir, *Force of Circumstance*, trans. R. Howard (Harmondsworth: Penguin, 1968), p. 202.
9. Carole Ascher, *Simone de Beauvoir: A Life of Freedom* (Brighton: Harvester Press, 1981), p. 150.
10. Firestone, *Dialectic of Sex*, pp. 192ff.
11. de Beauvoir, *The Second Sex*, pp. 723f.
12. Dale Spender, *For the Record: The Making and Meaning of Feminist Knowledge* (London: The Women's Press, 1985), p. 129.
13. Mitchell, *Woman's Estate*, pp. 90ff. Some of this book had appeared as early as 1966, as 'Women: The Longest Revolution', *New Left Review*, vol. 40 (1966), subsequently reprinted in Mitchell, *Women: The Longest Revolution* (London: Virago, 1984). The emergence of theory out of the experiences of the oppressed and the insistence that the latter must identify with it was not alien to Marxism. See, for example, Georg Lukacs, *History and Class Consciousness*, trans. R. Livingstone (Cambridge, Mass: MIT Press, 1971).
14. For development of this theme see Nancy Chodorow, 'Mothering, Male Dominance, and Capitalism' in Zillah Eisenstein (ed.) *Capitalist Patriarchy and the Case for Socialist Feminism* (New York and London: Monthly Review Press, 1979), pp. 92ff.
15. Mitchell, *Woman's Estate*, p. 139.
16. *Ibid.*, p. 149.
17. *Ibid.*, pp. 149, 180.
18. *Ibid.*, p. 151.
19. *Ibid.*
20. *Ibid.*, pp. 155, 101, 148.
21. See, for example, Hartmann, 'Unhappy Marriage', pp. 8f.
22. A. Kuhn and A. Wolpe (eds) *Feminism and Materialism* (London: Routledge and Kegan Paul, 1978), esp. chs. 1 and 2. Also Veronica Beechey, 'Some Notes on Female Labour in Capitalist Production', *Capital and Class*, vol. 3 (autumn 1977).
23. Michele Barrett, *Women's Oppression Today* (London: Verso, 1980), pp. 19–29.
24. Christine Delphy, *The Main Enemy* (London: Women's Research and Resources Centre, 1977). See also Maxine Molyneux's excellent critique, 'Beyond the Domestic Labour Debate', *New Left Review*, vol. 116 (July/Aug. 1979); M. Barrett and M. McIntosh, 'Christine Delphy: Towards a Marxist Feminism? *Feminist Review*, vol. 1 (1978).
25. This was in fact what Mitchell would eventually assert. See her

'Reflections on Twenty Years of Feminism' in J. Mitchell and A, Oakley (eds) *What is Feminism?* (Oxford: Basil Blackwell, 1986), pp. 42ff.

26. Wally Seccombe, 'Domestic Labour: Reply to Critics', *New Left Review,* vol. 94, (Nov./Dec. 1975), p. 87.

27. Wally Seccombe, 'The Housewife and Her Labour under Capitalism', *New Left Review,* vol. 83 (Jan./Feb. 1974).

28. *Ibid.,* p. 6.

29. See Jean Gardiner, 'Women's Domestic Labour', *New Left Review* (Jan./Feb. 1975), p. 54.

30. Seccombe, 'Housewife', p. 5.

31. *Ibid.,* p. 15.

32. See. for example, Roberta Hamilton's criticism of this and similar positions in her 'Working at Home' in R. Hamilton and M. Barrett (eds) *The Politics of Diversity* (London: Verso, 1986) as well as other articles in the volume which discuss the Domestic Labour Debate.

33. Seccombe, 'Reflections on the Domestic Labour Debate', in *ibid.,* p. 191.

34. See Margaret Coulson, Branka Magas and Hilary Wainwright, 'The Housewife and Her Labour under Capitalism: A Critique', *New Left Review,* vol. 89 (Jan./Feb. 1975), p. 65. Also Sheila Rowbotham, *Woman's Consciousness, Man's World* (Harmondsworth: Penguin, 1973).

35. Molyneux, Beyond the Domestic Labour Debate'. The criticism is specifically levelled at Delphy, but it applies more generally.

36. Hamilton and Barrett (eds) *Politics of Diversity,* p. 42.

37. Molyneux, 'Beyond the Domestic Labour Debate', p. 21.

38. Barrett, *Women's Oppression Today,* p. 1.

39. *Ibid.,* pp. 176–86. For a critique of her emphasis here, see J. Brenner and M. Ramas, 'Rethinking Women's Oppression', *New Left Review,* vol. 144 (Mar./Apr. 1984).

40. Barrett, *Women's Oppression Today,* p. 254.

41. For an excellent example of such a study, see Sally Alexander, 'Women's Work in Nineteenth Century London: A Study of the Years 1820–50' in Mitchell and Oakley, *Rights and Wrongs of Women.*

42. Valerie Amos and Pratibha Pamar, 'Challenging Imperial Feminism', *Feminist Review,* vol. 17, (Autumn 1984), p. 8.

43. Phyllis Marynick Palmer, 'White Women/Black Women: The Dualism of Female Identity and Experience in the United States', *Feminist Studies,* vol. 9, no. 1 (spring 1983).

44. Amos and Pamar, Challenging Imperial Feminism', p. 4.

45. M. Barrett and M. McIntosh, 'Ethnocentrism and Socialist-Feminist Theory', *Feminist Review,* vol. 20 (summer 1985), p. 41.

46. Bonnie Thornton Dill, 'Race, Class, and Gender: Prospects for an All-Inclusive Sisterhood', *Feminist Studies,* vol. 9, no. 1 (spring 1983), p. 137.

47. Lynne Segal, *Is the Future Female? Troubled Thoughts on Contemporary Feminism* (London: Virago, 1987), p. 211.

48. Mary McIntosh, 'The State and the Oppression of Women', in Mary

Evans (ed.) *The Woman Question* (London: Fontana 1982) and in Kuhn and Wolpe, *Feminism and Materialism.* All page references are to the latter.

49. *Ibid.,* p. 259.
50. *Ibid.,* pp. 260, 281ff.
51. Barrett, *Women's Oppression Today,* pp. 231–7.
52. McIntosh, 'The State', pp. 257f; Barrett, *ibid.,* pp. 239f.
53. Segal, *Is the Future Female?,* p. 2.
54. Anne Phillips, 'Divided Loyalties', *New Socialist,* no. 46 (Feb. 1987), p. 34. See also her *Divided Loyalties: Dilemmas of Sex and Class* (London: Virago, 1987).
55. Sheila Rowbotham, Lynne Segal and Hilary Wainwright, *Beyond the Fragments: Feminism and the Making of Socialism* (London: Merlin Press, 1979).
56. L. Eichenbaum and S. Orbach, *Outside In. Inside Out. Women's Psychology: A Feminist Psychanalytic Account* (Harmondsworth: Penguin, 1982), p. 12.
57. Millett, *Sexual Politics,* p. 23.
58. See Campbell, 'A Feminist Sexual Politics: Now You See It, Now You Don't' in Evans, *The Woman Question.*
59. Adrienne Rich, 'Compulsory Heterosexuality and Lesbian Existence' (London: Only Women Press, 1981), p. 9. Also printed in *Signs,* vol. 5, no. 4 (1980); Rich, *Of Woman Born* (London: Virago, 1977), p. 283.
60. Claire Duchen, *Feminism in France from May '68 to Mitterand* (London and Boston: Routledge and Kegan Paul, 1986), p. 44.
61. Millett, *Sexual Politics,* p. 26.
62. Hester Eisenstein, *Contemporary Feminist Thought* (London: Unwin, 1984), p. 127.
63. The Iron Law of Oligarchy suggests that no matter what a party's democratic intentions, the exigencies of organizing for power will inevitably bring an oligarchical and conservative leadership. Robert Michels, *Political Parties,* trans. E. and C. Paul (New York: The Free Press, 1962).
64. Juliet Mitchell, *Psychoanalysis and Feminism* (Harmondsworth: Penguin, 1974).
65. Millett, *Sexual Politics,* p. 25.
66. *Ibid.,* p. 36–9.
67. Rich, *Of Woman Born,* p. 57.
68. Veronica Beechey, 'On Patriarchy', *Feminist Review,* no. 3 (1979).
69. Segal, *Is the Future Female?,* p. 120.
70. For criticisms from this perspective, see Barrett, *Women's Oppression Today,* pp. 12ff.; Rowbotham, 'The Trouble with "Patriarchy"' in Evans, *The Woman Question,* p. 74; Beechey, 'On Patriarchy', p. 80; Hartmann, 'Unhappy Marriage', p. 10.
71. Firestone, *Dialectic of Sex.*
72. On rape as a form of biological determinism, see Eisenstein, *Contemporary Feminist Thought,* pp. 27–34; Segal, *Is the Future Female?'* pp. 102–5.
73. Hartmann, 'Unhappy Marriage', p. 14.

74. *Ibid.*, p. 22.
75. *Ibid.*
76. Mary Daly, *Gyn/Ecology: The Meta-Ethics of Radical Feminism* (London: The Women's Press, 1979), p. 387. Eisenstein dicusses other recent criticisms of androgyny in *Contemporary Feminist Thought,* pp. 62f.
77. Eisenstein, *ibid.;* Segal, *Is the Future Female?*; also the articles by Delmar and Stacey in Mitchell and Oakley (eds) *What is Feminism?*
78. O'Brien, *Politics of Reproduction,* pp. 4–22.
79. The Editorial Collective of *Questions Feministes,* no. 1 (Nov. 1977), trans. Yvonne Rochette-Ozzello for *New French Feminisms,* ed. Elaine Marks and Isabelle de Courtivron (Brighton: Harvester Press, 1981), pp. 212ff.
80. Spender, *For the Record,* p. 165.
81. Daly, *Gyn/Ecology,* p. 400.
82. *Ibid.*, p. 386.
83. Madelaine Gagnon in *New French Feminisms,* p. 180.
84. Firestone, *Dialectic of Sex,* ch. 9.
85. For summary and discussion, see Eisenstein, *Contemporary Feminist Thought,* pp. 98–101.
86. Lloyd, *Man of Reason,* pp. 11–16.
87. Nancy Chodorow, *The Reproduction of Mothering* (London: University of California Press, 1978); Dorothy Dinnerstein, *The Mermaid and the Minotaur* (New York: Harper and Row, 1976).
88. Stefano, 'Hobbesian Man'.
89. *Ibid.*, p. 636.
90. In *New French Feminisms,* p. 173. See also, for example, Silvia Bovenschen, 'Is There a Feminine Aesthetic?' in Gisela Echer (ed.) *Feminist Aesthetics,* trans. Harriet Anderson (London: The Women's Press, 1985).
91. Rich, *Of Woman Born,* pp. 63f., 284.
92. *Ibid.*, p. 284.
93. *Ibid.*, p. 81.
94. *Ibid.*, pp. 285ff.
95. Daly, *Gyn/Ecology,* p. 412.
96. For example, Edmund Husserl, *The Crisis of European Sciences,* trans. D. Carr (Evanston, Ill.: Northwestern University Press, 1970); Martin Heidegger, *Being and Time,* trans. J. Macquarrie and E. Robinson (New York: Harper & Row, 1962).
97. Herbert Marcuse, *Eros and Civilization* (New York: Vintage Books, 1962).
98. See especially the Preface in Maurice Merleau-Ponty, *Phenomenology of Perception,* trans. Colin Smith (London: Routledge & Kegan Paul, 1962).
99. Developments in French feminism have recently been introduced to Anglo-American readers in Toril Moi, *Sexual/Textual Politics* (London and New York: Methuen, 1985); Gayle Greene and Coppelia Kahn (eds) *Making a Difference: French Literary Criticism* (London: Methuen, 1985); Claire Duchen, *Feminism in France.* The Anthology

translated in *New French Feminisms* is also valuable.
Methuen, 1985); Claire Duchen, *Feminism in France.* The Anthology
translated in *New French Feminisms* is also valuable.
100. *New French Feminisms, ibid.,* p. 177.
101. *Ibid.,* p. 164.
102. Thus see Eistenstein's and Segal's critiques of Daly, as well as Moi's of
French Feminism.
103. Moi, *Sexual/Textual Politics,* p. 160.

Bibliography

Aeschylus, *The Eumenides,* trans. H. Lloyd-Jones (London: Duckworth, 1979)

Alexander, Sally, 'Women's Work in Nineteenth Century London: A Study of the Years 1820–50' in J. Mitchell and A. Oakley (eds) *The Rights and Wrongs of Women* (Harmondsworth: Penguin, 1976)

Althusser, Louis, 'Ideology and Ideological State Apparatuses' in *Essays on Ideology* (London: Verso, 1984)

Altman, Elizabeth, 'The Philosophical Bases of the Saint-Simonians and Charles Fourier', *Philosophical Forum (Boston)* 7 (spring–summer 1976)

Amos, Valerie and Pamar, Pratibha, 'Challenging Imperial Feminism', *Feminist Review* 17, (autumn 1984)

Anderson, Perry, *Passages from Antiquity to Feudalism* (London: Verso, 1978)

Annas, Julia, 'Mill and the Subjection of Women', *Philosophy* 52 (1977)

Annas, Julia, 'Plato's *Republic* and Feminism', *Philosophy* 51, (1976)

Aquinas, Saint Thomas, *Summa Theologica,* trans. Fathers of the English Dominican Province (London: Burns, Oates & Washbourne, 1921)

Philippe Ariès, *Centuries of Childhood,* trans. R. Baldwick (London: Jonathan Cape, 1962)

Aristophanes, *The Ecclesiazusae,* trans. B. Rogers (London: Heinemann, 1931)

Aristotle, *De Generatione Animalium,* trans. A.L. Peck (London: Heinemann, 1943)

Aristotle, *Nichomachean Ethics* in *The Works of Aristotle,* trans. W.D. Ross (Oxford: Clarendon Press, 1925), vol. IX

Aristotle, *Politics,* trans. Sir Ernest Barker (Oxford: Oxford University Press, 1958)

Arthur, Marilyn, 'Early Greece: The Origin of the Western Attitude Toward Women' in J. Perradotto and J.P. Sullivan (eds) *Women in the Ancient World: The Arethusa Paper* (Albany: State University of New York Press, 1984)

Ascher, Carole, *Simone de Beauvoir: A Life of Freedom* (Brighton: Harvester Press, 1981)

Augustine, St, *The City of God,* trans. H. Bettenson (Harmondsworth: Penguin, 1972)

Aveling, Eleanor Marx and Aveling, Edward, 'The Woman Question: From a Socialist Point of View', *Westminster Review* 125 (1886)

Ball, Terence, 'Utilitarianism, Feminism and the Franchise: James Mill and his Critics', *History of Political Thought* 1 (1980)

Barker, Sir Ernest, *Greek Political Theory: Plato and His Predecessors* (London: Methuen, 1918)

Barnsby, George, *Robert Owen and the First Socialists in the Black Country* (Wolverhampton: Integrated Publishing Services, 1984)

Barrett, Michele, *Women's Oppression Today* (London: Verso, 1980)

Barrett, Michele and McIntosh, Mary, 'Christine Delphy: Towards a Marxist Feminism?', *Feminist Review* 1 (1978)

Barrett, Michele and McIntosh, Mary, 'Ethnocentrism and Socialist-Feminist Theory', *Feminist Review* 20 (summer 1985)

de Beauvoir, Simone, *The Second Sex,* trans. H.M. Parshley (Harmondsworth: Penguin, 1972)

Bebel, August, *Woman under Socialism,* trans. Daniel de Leon (New York: Schocken Books, 1971)

Beecher, Jonathan and Bienvenu, Richard (eds) *The Utopian Vision of Charles Fourier: Selected texts on Work, Love, and Passionate Attraction* (London: Jonathan Cape, 1972)

Beechey, Veronica, 'On Patriarchy', *Feminist Review* 3 (1979)

Beechey, Veronica, 'Some Notes on Female Labour in Capitalist Production', *Capital and Class* 3 (autumn 1977)

Bible, Authorized Version (1611)

Bloch, Marc, *Feudal Society,* trans. L.A. Manyon (London: Routledge & Kegan Paul, 1961)

Boralevi, Lea Campos, 'Utilitarianism and Feminism' in Ellen Kennedy and Susan Mendus (eds) *Women in Western Political Philosophy* (Brighton: Wheatsheaf Books, 1987)

Bovenschen, Silvia, 'Is there a Feminine Aesthetic?' in Gisela Echer (ed.) *Feminist Aesthetics,* trans. Harriet Anderson (London: The Women's Press, 1985)

Brailsford, H.N., *The Levellers and the English Revolution* (Nottingham: Spokesman, 1976)

Brennan, Theresa and Pateman, Carole, '"Mere Auxiliaries to the Commonwealth": Women and the Origins of Liberalism', *Political Studies* XXVII 2 (1968)

Brenner, J. and Ramas, M., 'Rethinking Women's Oppression', *New Left Review* 144 (Mar./Apr. 1984)

Brody, Miriam, 'Mary Wollstonecraft: Sexuality and Women's Rights' in Dale Spender (ed.) *Feminist Theorists* (London: The Women's Press, 1983)

Butler, Melissa, 'Early Liberal Roots of Feminism: John Locke and the Attack on Patriarchy', *American Political Science Review* 72 (1978)

Campbell, Beatrix, 'A Feminist Sexual Politics: Now You See It, Now You Don't' in Mary Evans (ed.) *The Woman Question* (London: Fontana, 1982)

Canovan, Margaret, 'Rousseau's Two Concepts of Citizenship' in Ellen Kennedy and Susan Mendus (eds) *Women in Western Political Philosophy* (Brighton: Wheatsheaf Books, 1987)

Carver, Terrel, 'Engels' Feminism', *History of Political Thought* VI/3 (winter 1985)

Chapman, Richard, '*Leviathan* Writ Small: Thomas Hobbes on the Family', *American Political Science Review* 69/1 (1975)

Chodorow, Nancy, *The Reproduction of Mothering* (London: University of California Press, 1978)

Clark, Alice, *Working Life of Women in the Seventeenth Century* (London: Routledge and Kegan Paul, 1982)

Clark, Gracia, 'The Beguines: A Medieval Women's Community', *Quest: A Feminist Quarterly* I/4 (1975)

Clark, Lorenne, 'Women and Locke: Who Owns the Apples in the Garden of Eden?' in L. Clark and L. Lange, *The Sexism of Social and Political Theory* (Toronto: University of Toronto Press, 1979)

Coole, Diana, 'Re-Reading Political Theory from a Woman's Perspective', *Political Studies* XXXIV/1 (March 1986)

Coulson, Margaret, Magas, Branka and Wainwright, Hilary, 'The Housewife and Her Labour under Capitalism: A Critique', *New Left Review* 89 (Jan./Feb. 1979)

Coward, Rosalind, *Patriarchal Precedents* (London: Routledge & Kegan Paul, 1983)

Cranston, Maurice, *John Locke: A Biography* (Oxford: Oxford University Press, 1985)

Croix, G.E.M. de ste., *The Class Struggle in the Ancient Greek World: From the Archaic Age to the Arab Conquests* (London: Duckworth, 1981)

Daly, Mary, *Gyn/Ecology: The Meta-Ethics of Radical Feminism* (London: The Women's Press, 1979)

Delmar, Rosalyn, 'Looking Again at Engels' *The Origin of the Family, Private Property and the State'* in J. Mitchell and A. Oakley (eds) *The Rights and Wrongs of Women* (Harmondsworth: Penguin, 1976)

Delphy, Christine, *The Main Enemy* (London: Women's Research and Resources Centre, 1977)

Diamond, Stanley, 'Plato and the Definition of the Primitive' in S. Diamond (ed.) *Culture in History* (New York: Columbia U.P., 1960)

Dill, Bonnie Thornton, 'Race, Class, and Gender: Prospects for an All-Inclusive Sisterhood', *Feminist Studies* 9/1 (spring 1983)

Dinnerstein, Dorothy, *The Mermaid and the Minotaur* (New York: Harper & Row, 1976)

Draper, Hal and Lipow, Anne, 'Marxist Women Versus Bourgeois Feminism' in *Socialist Register 1976,* ed. Ralph Miliband (London: Merlin, 1976)

Duchen, Claire, *Feminism in France from May '68 to Mitterand* (London and Boston: Routledge & Kegan Paul, 1986)

Dunn, John, *The Political Thought of John Locke* (Cambridge: Cambridge University Press, 1969)

Dunayevskaya, Raya, 'Marx's "New Humanism" and the Dialectics of Women's Liberation in Primitive and Modern Societies', *Praxis International* 3/4 (Jan. 1984)

Easton, Susan, 'Hegel and Feminism', *Radical Philosophy* 38 (1984)

Easton, Susan, 'Slavery and Freedom: A Feminist Reading of Hegel', *Politics* 5/2 (Oct. 1985)

Ehrenberg, Victor, *The People of Aristophanes* (Oxford: Basil Blackwell, 1943)

Eichenbaum, L. and Orbach, S. *Outside In. Inside Out. Women's Psychology: A Feminist Psychoanalytic Account* (Harmondsworth: Penguin, 1982)

Eisenstein, Hester, *Contemporary Feminist Thought* (London: Unwin, 1984)

Eisenstein, Zillah (ed.) *Capitalist Patriarchy and the Case for Socialist Feminism* (New York and London: Monthly Review Press, 1979)

Eisenstein, Zillah, *The Radical Future of Liberal Feminism* (New York: Longman, 1981)

Elshtain, Jean Bethke, *The Family in Political Thought* (Brighton: Harvester Press, 1982)

Elshtain, Jean Bethke, *Public Man, Private Woman* (Oxford: Martin Robertson and Princeton University Press, 1981)

Engels, F., *The Condition of the Working Class in England* in Marx and Engels, *Collected Works,* vol. 4 (London: Lawrence & Wishart, 1976)

Engels, F., *The Origin of the Family, Private Property and the State* (New York: Pathfinder Press, 1972)

Evans, Mary (ed.) *The Woman Question* (London: Fontana, 1983)

Evans, Richard, *The Feminists* (London: Croom Helm, 1977)

Evans, Richard, 'Theory and Practice in German Social Democracy 1880–1914: Clara Zetkin and the Socialist Theory of Women's Emancipation', *History of Political Thought* III/2 (summer 1982)

Fairbairns, Zoe, *Benefits* (London: Virago, 1979)

Farnsworth, Beatrice Brodsky, 'Bolshevism, the Woman Question and Aleksandra Kollontai', *American Historical Review* 81/2 (1976)

Figes, Eva, *Patriarchal Attitudes* (London: Virago, 1978)

Finley, M.I., *The Ancient Economy* (London: Chatto & Windus, 1973)

Finley, M.I., *The World of Odysseus* (Harmondsworth: Penguin, 1962)

Firestone, Shulamith, *The Dialectic of Sex* (London: The Women's Press, 1979)

Flacière, R., *Daily Life in Greece at the Time of Pericles,* trans. P. Green (London: Weidenfeld & Nicolson, 1965)

Foner, Philip (ed.) *Clara Zetkin: Selected Writings* (New York: International Publishers, 1984)

Fox-Genovese, Elizabeth, 'Property and Patriarchy in Classical Bourgeois Theory', *Radical History Review* 4/2–3 (1977)

Friedan, Betty, *The Feminine Mystique* (Harmondsworth: Penguin, 1965)

Freud, Sigmund, *Civilization and Its Discontents,* trans. Joan Riviere (London: Hogarth Press, 1972)

Freud, Sigmund, *Moses and Monotheism* in *The Standard Edition of the Complete Works of Sigmund Freud,* trans. James Strachey (London: Hogarth Press, 1964), vol. 23.

Gardiner, Jean, 'Women's Domestic Labour', *New Left Review* 89 (Jan./Feb. 1975)

Godwin, William, *Enquiry Concerning Political Justice* (Harmondsworth: Penguin, 1976)

Goldstein, Leslie, 'Early Feminist Themes in French Utopian Socialism: The St-Simonians and Fourier', *Journal of the History of Ideas* 43/1 (1982)

Goldstein, Leslie, 'Mill, Marx, and Women's Liberation', *Journal of the History of Philosophy* XVIII/3 (July 1980)

Greene, Gayle and Kahn, Coppelia (eds), *Making a Difference: French Literary Criticism* (London: Methuen, 1985)

Grimshaw, Jean, *Feminist Philosophers: Women's Perspectives on Philosophical Traditions* (Brighton: Wheatsheaf Books, 1986)

Hamilton, Roberta, *The Liberation of Women: A Study of Patriarchy and Capitalism* (London: Allen & Unwin, 1978)

Hamilton, Roberta and Barrett, Michele, *The Politics of Diversity* (London: Verso, 1986)

Harris, Kevin, *Sex, Ideology and Religion: The Representation of Women in the Bible* (Brighton: Harvester Press, 1984)

Hartmann, Heidi, 'The Unhappy Marriage of Marxism and Feminism: Towards a More Progressive Union', *Capital and Class* 8 (1979)

Hegel, G.W.F., *The Phenomenology of Mind,* trans. J.B. Baillie (New York: Harper & Row, 1967)

Hegel, G.W.F., *The Philosophy of Right,* trans. T.M. Knox (Oxford: Oxford University Press, 1967)

Heinen, Jacqueline, 'Kollontai and the History of Women's Oppression', *New Left Review* 110 (July–Aug. 1978)

Heidegger, Martin, *Being and Time,* trans. J. Macquarrie and E. Robinson (New York: Harper & Row, 1962)

Heller, Agnes, *Renaissance Man,* trans. Richard Allen (London: Routledge & Kegan Paul, 1978)

Hesiod, *Theogony, Works and Days, Shield,* trans. A.N. Athanausakis (Baltimore and London: Johns Hopkins University Press, 1983)

Hill, Christopher, *The World Turned Upside Down* (Harmondsworth: Penguin, 1975)

Hinton, R.W.K., 'Husbands, Fathers and Conquerors', *Political Studies* XVI/1 (1968)

Hobbes, Thomas, *Elements of Law,* ed. F. Tonnies (London: Frank Cass, 1969)

Hobbes, Thomas, *The English Works of Thomas Hobbes,* ed. Sir William Molesworth (London: John Bohn, 1840)

Hobbes, Thomas, *Leviathan,* ed. John Plamenatz (London: Fontana, 1982)

Hodge, Joanna, 'Women and the Hegelian State' in E. Kennedy and S. Mendus (eds) *Women in Western Political Philosophy* (Brighton: Wheatsheaf Books, 1987)

Holt, Alix (ed.) *Selected Writings of Alexandra Kollontai* (London: Allison & Busby, 1977)

Homer, *Iliad,* trans. R. Fitzgerald (New York: Anchor

Press, 1975)

Husserl, Edmund, *The Crisis of European Sciences,* trans. D. Carr (Evanston, Ill: Northwestern University Press, 1970)

Jaggar, Alison, *Feminist Politics and Human Nature* (Brighton: Harvester Press, 1983)

Jarrett, Bede, *Social Theories of the Middle Ages 1200–1500* (London: Ernest Benn, 1926)

Janes, R.N. 'On the Reception of Mary Wollstonecraft's *A Vindication of the Rights of Woman', Journal of the History of Ideas* 39 (Apr.–June 1978)

Kennedy, Ellen and Mendus, Susan, *Women in Western Political Philosophy* (Brighton: Wheatsheaf Books, 1987)

Kinnaird, Joan, 'Mary Astell: Inspired by Ideas (1668–1731)' in Dale Spender (ed.) *Feminist Theorists* (London: The Women's Press, 1983)

Kollontai, Alexandra, *Love of Worker Bees* (London: Virago, 1977)

Korsmeyer, Carolyn, 'Reason and Morals in the Early Feminist Movement: Mary Wollstonecraft', *Philosophical Forum (Boston)* 5/1&2 (1973–74)

Krouse, Richard, 'Patriarchal Liberalism and Beyond: From John Stuart Mill to Harriet Taylor' in Elshtain (ed.) *The Family in Political Thought* (Brighton: Harvester Press, 1982)

Kuhn, A. and Wolpe, A., *Feminism and Materialism* (London: Routledge & Kegan Paul, 1978)

Landes, Joanna, 'Hegel's Conception of the Family', in Elshtain (ed.) *The Family in Political Thought* (Brighton: Harvester, 1982)

Lange, Lynda, 'The Function of Equal Education in Plato's Republic and *Laws',* in L. Clark and L. Lange (eds) *The Sexism of Social and Political Theory* (Toronto: University of Toronto Press, 1979)

Lange, Lynda, 'Rousseau: Women and the General Will' in Clark and Lange, *The Sexism of Social and Political Theory* (Toronto: University of Toronto Press, 1979)

Laslett, Peter (ed.) *Patriarchia and Other Political Works of Sir Robert Filmer* (Oxford: Oxford University Press, 1949)

Lefkowitz, Mary and Fant, Maureen, *Women's Life in Greece and Rome: A Source Book in Translation* (London: Duckworth, 1982)

Lenin, V.I., *Collected Works* (Moscow: Progress Publishers, 1965)

Leonard, Diana, 'The Origin of the Family, Private Property and Marxist Feminism?', *Trouble and Strife* 3 (summer 1984)

Lesser, Harry, 'Plato's Feminism', *Philosophy Today* 54

(1979)

Lloyd, Genevieve, *The Man of Reason: "Male" and "Female" in Western Philosophy* (London: Methuen, 1984)

Locke, John, *Two Treatises on Government,* ed. Peter Laslett (Cambridge: Cambridge University Press, 1960)

Locke, John, *The Works of John Locke in Nine Volumes* (London: C. & J. Rivington *et al.,* 1824)

Lucas, Angela, *Women in the Middle Ages: Religion, Marriage and Letters* (Brighton: Harvester Press, 1984)

Lukacs, Georg, *History and Class Consciousness,* trans. R. Livingstone (Cambridge, Mass: MIT Press, 1971)

Malmgreen, Gail, *Neither Bread Nor Roses: Utopian Feminists and the English Working Class, 1800–1850* (Brighton: Brighton Resource Centre, 1978)

Manuel, Frank, *The Prophets of Paris* (Cambridge, Mass: Harvard University Press, 1962)

Marcuse Herbert, *Eros and Civilization* (New York: Vintage Books, 1962)

Marks, Elaine and de Courtivron, Isabelle, *New French Feminisms* (Brighton: Harvester Press, 1981)

Marx, Karl, *The Economic and Philosophic Manuscripts of 1844,* ed. Dirk Struik (New York: International Publishers, 1964)

Marx, Karl, *Capital,* 3 vols, trans. S. Moore, and E. Aveling (Moscow: Progress Publishers, 1954)

Marx, Karl and Engels, Friedrich, *The German Ideology,* ed. C.J. Arthur (New York: International Publishers, 1970)

Marx, Karl and Engels, Friedrich, *Collected Works* (London: Lawrence & Wishart, 1976)

McIntosh, Mary, 'The State and the Oppression of Women', in A. Kuhn and A. Wolpe (eds) *Feminism and Materialism* (London: Routledge & Kegan Paul, 1978)

MacIntyre, A., *After Virtue: A Study in Moral Theory* (London: Duckworth, 1982)

Maclean, Ian, *The Renaissance Notion of Woman* (Cambridge: Cambridge University Press, 1980)

MacPherson, C.B., *The Theory of Possessive Individualism: Hobbes to Locke* (Oxford: Oxford University Press, 1962)

Mendus, Susan, 'Kant: "An Honest but Narrow-minded Bourgeois"?' in E.Kennedy and S. Mendus (eds) *Women in Western Political Philosophy* (Brighton: Wheatsheaf Books, 1987)

Merleau-Ponty, Maurice, *Phenomenology of Perception,* trans. Colin Smith (London: Routledge & Kegan Paul, 1962)

Michels, Robert, *Political Parties,* trans. E. and C. Paul (New York: The Free Press, 1962)

Middleton, Christopher, 'The Sexual Division of Labour in Feudal England', *New Left Review* 114, (April 1979)

Mill, James, *Essay on Government* in J. Lively and J. Rees (eds) *Utilitarian Logic and Politics* (Oxford: Clarendon Press, 1978)

Mill, J.S., *Autobiography*, ed. Jack Stillinger (Oxford: Oxford University Press, 1971)

Mill, J.S., *Principles of Political Economy*, ed. D. Winch (Harmondsworth: Penguin, 1970)

Mill, J.S., *Representation of the People Bill*, 20 May 1867, *Hansard* CLXXXVII, pp. 817–29

Mill, J.S., *The Subjection of Women* (London: Everyman, 1929)

Mill, J.S., *Utilitarianism*, ed. Mary Warnock (London: Fontana, 1962)

Mill, J.S., *Utilitarianism, Liberty, Representative Government* (London: Everyman, 1910)

Millett, Kate, *Sexual Politics* (London: Virago, 1977)

Mitchell, Juliet, *Psychoanalysis and Feminism* (Harmondsworth: Penguin, 1974)

Mitchell, Juliet, *Woman's Estate* (Harmondsworth: Penguin, 1971)

Mitchell, Juliet, *Women: The Longest Revolution* (London: Virago, 1984)

Mitchell, Juliet and Oakley, Ann, *The Rights and Wrongs of Women* (Harmondsworth: Penguin, 1976)

Mitchell, Juliet and Oakley, Ann, *What is Feminism?* (Oxford: Basil Blackwell, 1986)

Moi, Toril, *Sexual/Textual Politics* (London and New York: Methuen, 1985)

Molyneux, Maxine, 'Beyond the Domestic Labour Debate', *New Left Review* 116, (July/Aug. 1979)

Mullaney, Marie Marmo, 'Alexandra Kollontai and the Vision of a Socialist Feminist Utopia', *Alternative Futures* 4 2&3 (1981)

Oakley, Ann, *Housewife,* (Harmondsworth: Penguin, 1976)

O'Brien, Mary, *The Politics of Reproduction* (London: Routledge & Kegan Paul, 1981)

Okin, Susan Moller, *Women in Western Political Thought* (London: Virago, 1980)

Okin, Susan Moller, 'Women and the Making of the Sentimental Family', *Philosophy and Public Affairs* XI/1 (winter 1982)

Osborne, Martha Lee (ed.) *Women in Western Thought* (New York: Random House, 1979)

Owen, Robert, *Lectures on the Marriages of the Priesthood of the Old Immoral World,* 4th edn, with Appendix (Leeds: J. Hobson, 1840)

Padel, Ruth, 'Women: Model for Possession by Greek Daemons' in Averil Cameron and Amelie Kuhrt (eds), *Images of Women in Antiquity* (London: Croom Helm, 1983)

Palmer, Phyllis Marynick, 'White Women/Black Women: The Dualism of Female Identity and Experience in the United States', *Feminist Studies* 9/1 (spring 1983)

Pankhurst, Richard, *William Thompson (1775–1833) Britain's Pioneer Socialist, Feminist and Co-Operator* (London: Watts & Co., 1954)

Parry, Geraint, *John Locke* (London: Allen & Unwin, 1978)

Pateman, Carole, '"The Disorder of Women"': Women, Love, and the Sense of Justice', *Ethics* 91 (Oct. 1980)

Pateman, Carole, *The Problem of Political Obligation: A Critique of Liberal Theory* (Cambridge: Polity Press, 1985)

Pateman, Carole, 'Women and Consent', *Political Theory* (May 1980)

Peradotto, J. and Sullivan, J.P. (eds) *Women in the Ancient World: The Arethusa Papers* (Albany, NJ: State University of New York Press, 1984)

Phillips, Anne, *Divided Loyalties: Dilemmas of Sex and Class* (London: Virago, 1987)

Pierce, Christine, 'Equality: *Republic* V', *Monist* 57/1 (Jan. 1973)

Pitkin, Hannah, *Fortune Is a Woman: Gender and Politics in the Thoughts of Niccolo Machiavelli* (Berkeley: University of California Press, 1984)

Plato, *The Dialogues of Plato,* 4 vols, 4th edn, ed. B. Jarrett (Oxford: Clarendon Press, 1953)

Plato, *Republic,* ed. F.M. Cornford (Oxford: Clarendon Press, 1941)

Plato, *Timaeus,* trans. D. Lee (Harmondsworth: Penguin, 1965)

Pomeroy, Sarah, *Goddesses, Whores, Wives and Slaves: Women in Classical Antiquity* (New York: Schocken Books, 1975)

Porter, Cathy, *Alexandra Kollontai* (London: Virago, 1980)

Power, Eileen, *Medieval Women,* ed. M.M. Postan (Cambridge: Cambridge University Press, 1975)

Rendell, Jane, 'Virtue and Commerce: Women in the Making of Adam Smith's Political Economy' in E. Kennedy and S. Mendus (eds) *Women in Western Political Philosophy* (Brighton: Wheatsheaf Books, 1987)

Rich, Adrienne, 'Compulsory Heterosexuality and Lesbian Existence', *Signs* 5/4 (1980)

Rich, Adrienne, *Of Woman Born* (London: Virago, 1977)

Rousseau, Jean-Jacques, *Emile,* trans. Barbara Foxley (London, Melbourne and Toronto: Everyman, 1911)

Rousseau, Jean-Jacques, *A Letter from M. Rousseau, of Geneva,* to M. D'Alembert of Paris, Concerning the Effects of Theatrical Entertainment on the Manners of Mankind (London: J. Nourse, 1759)

Rousseau, Jean-Jacques, The Social Contract and Discourses, trans. G.D.H. Cole (London: Everyman, 1913)

Rowbotham, Shiela, Woman's Consciousness, Man's World (Harmondsworth: Penguin, 1973)

Rowbotham, Shiela, Women, Resistance and Revolution (Harmondsworth: Penguin, 1972)

Rowbotham, Shiela, Segal, Lynne and Wainwright, Hilary, Beyond the Fragments: Feminism and the Making of Socialism (London: Merlin Press, 1979)

Ryan, Alan, J.S. Mill (London: Routledge & Kegan Paul, 1974)

Sabine, George and Thorson, Thomas, A History of Political Thought, 4th edn, (Hinsdale,Ill: Dryden Press, 1973)

Sayers, Janet, Evans, Mary and Redclift, Nenneke (eds) Engels Revisited: New Feminist Essays (London and New York: Tavistock, 1987)

Schmidt, Alfred, The Concept of Nature in Marx, trans. Ben Fowkes (London: New Left Books, 1971)

Schwartz, Joel, The Sexual Politics of Jean-Jacques Rousseau (Chicago: University of Chicago Press, 1984)

Schwartzer, Alice (ed.) Simone de Beauvoir Today: Conversations 1972–82, trans. Marianne Howarth (London: Hogarth Press, 1984)

Schochet, G. Patriarchalism and Political Thought (Oxford: Basil Blackwell, 1975)

Seccombe, Wally, 'Domestic Labour: Reply to Critics', New Left Review 94 (Nov./Dec. 1975)

Seccombe, Wally, 'The Housewife and Her Labour under Capitalism', New Left Review 83 (Jan./Feb. 1974)

Seccombe, Wally, 'Reflections on the Domestic Labour Debate' in Roberta Hamilton and Michele Barrett (eds) The Politics of Diversity (London: Verso, 1986)

Segal, Charles, 'The Menace of Dionysus: Sex Roles and Reversals in Euripides' Bacchae' in J. Peradotto and J.P. Sullivan (eds) Women in the Ancient World: The Arethusa Papers (Albany, NJ: State University of New York Press, 1984)

Segal, Lynne, Is the Future Female? Troubled Thoughts on Contemporary Feminism (London: Virago, 1987)

Shanley, Mary Lyndon, 'Marriage Contract and Social Contract in Seventeenth-Century English Political Thought' in Jean Bethke Elshtain (ed.) The Family in Political Thought (Brighton: Harvester Press, 1982)

Shklar, Judith, Men and Citizens: A Study of Rousseau's

Social Theory (Cambridge: Cambridge University Press, 1969)

Shulman, Alix Kates (ed.) *Red Emma Speaks: The Selected Speeches and Writings of the Anarchist and Feminist Emma Goldman* (London: Wildwood House, 1979)

Sinclair, T., *A History of Greek Political Thought* (London: Routledge & Kegan Paul, 1951)

Smith, Adam, *The Wealth of Nations,* ed. A Skinner (Harmondsworth: Penguin, 1970)

Spencer, M.C., *Charles Fourier* (Boston: Twayne Publishers, 1981)

Spender, Dale (ed.) *Feminist Theorists: Three Centuries of Women's Intellectual Traditions* (London: The Women's Press, 1983)

Spender, Dale, *For the Record: the Making and Meaning of Feminist Knowledge* (London: The Women's Press, 1985)

Spender, Dale, *Women of Ideas (and What Men Have Done to Them)* (London: Ark, 1983)

Stefano, Christine Di, 'Masculinity as Ideology in Political Theory: Hobbesian Man Considered', *Women's Studies International Forum* 6/6 (1983)

Steinberger, Peter, 'Hegel on Marriage and Politics', *Political Studies* XXXIV/4 (Dec. 1986)

Stites, Richard, *The Women's Liberation Movement in Russia: Feminism, Nihilism, and Bolshevism 1860–1930* (Princeton, NJ: Princeton University Press, 1978)

Strachey, Ray, *The Cause* (London: Virago, 1978)

Stone, Lawrence, *The Family, Sex and Marriage in England 1500–1800* (London: Weidenfeld & Nicolson, 1977)

Taylor, Barbara, *Eve and the New Jerusalem* (London: Virago, 1983)

Taylor, Harriet, *Enfranchisement of Women* in Kate Soper (ed.) *The Subjection of Women and the Enfranchisement of Women* (London: Virago, 1983)

Thomas, Keith, 'The Social Origins of Hobbes' Political Thought in K. Brown (ed.) *Hobbes Studies* (Cambridge: Cambridge University Press, 1965)

Thompson, William, *Appeal of One-half of the Human Race, Women, against the Pretensions of the Other Half, Men, to Retain Them in Political, and hence in Civil and Domestic, Slavery* (London: Virago, 1983)

Thompson, William, *An Inquiry into the Principles of the Distribution of Wealth Most Conducive to Human Happiness* (London: William S. Orr & Co., 1850)

Tomalin, Claire, *The Life and Death of Mary Wollstonecraft* (Harmondsworth: Penguin, 1977)

Thucydides, *History of the Peloponnesian War,* 4 vols, trans.

C. Forster-Smith (Cambridge, Mass: Harvard University Press, 1919)

Ullman, Walter, *A History of Political Thought: The Middle Ages* (Harmondsworth: Penguin, 1965)

Vogel, Lise, *Marxism and the Oppression of Women: Toward a Unitary Theory* (London: Pluto, 1983

Warner, Marina, *Alone of All Her Sex: the Myth and the Cult of the Virgin Mary* (London: Pan Books, 1985)

Waylen, Georgina, 'Women and Neo-Liberalism' in Judith Evans (ed.) *Feminism and Political Theory* (London: Sage, 1986)

Wender, D., 'Plato: Misogynist, Paedophile and Feminist' in J. Peradotto and J.P. Sullivan (eds) *Women in the Ancient World: The Arethusa Papers* (Albany, NJ: State University of New York Press, 1984)

Wexler, Victor, '"Made for Man's Delight": Rousseau as Anti-Feminist', *American Historical Review* 81/2 (April 1976)

Wollstonecraft, Mary, *A Vindication of the Rights of Men* and *Thoughts on the Education of Daughters* in B. Solomon and P. Berggren (eds) *A Mary Wollstonecraft Reader* (New York: New American Library Press, 1983)

Wollstonecraft, Mary, *A Vindication of the Rights of Woman* (London: Everyman, 1929)

Williford, Miriam, 'Bentham and the Rights of Women', *Journal of the History of Ideas* 36 (Jan.–Mar. 1975)

Zeitlin, Froma, 'The Dynamics of Misogyny in the *Oresteia*', in J. Peradotto and J.P. Sullivan (eds) *Women in the Ancient World: The Arethusa Papers* (Albany, NJ: State University of New York Press, 1984)

Zvesper, John, 'Hobbes' Individualistic Analysis of the Family', *Politics* 5/2 (Oct. 1985)

Index

DATE DUE